MAYALOGUE

SUNY SERIES, TRANS-INDIGENOUS DECOLONIAL CRITIQUES ARTURO ARIAS, EDITOR

MAYALOGUE

AN INTERACTIONIST THEORY OF INDIGENOUS CULTURES

VICTOR MONTEJO

Cover: "La montée de L'Agonie," engraved by Émile Maillard after a sketch by Manouel Andre, published in *La Tour de Monde, Nouveau Journal des Voyages* vol. 38, p. 363, 1879. Ed. M. Édouard Charton.

Published by State University of New York Press, Albany

© 2021 State University of New York

All rights reserved

Printed in the United States of America

No part of this book may be used or reproduced in any manner whatsoever without written permission. No part of this book may be stored in a retrieval system or transmitted in any form or by any means including electronic, electrostatic, magnetic tape, mechanical, photocopying, recording, or otherwise without the prior permission in writing of the publisher.

For information, contact State University of New York Press, Albany, NY
www.sunypress.edu

Library of Congress Cataloging-in-Publication Data

Names: Montejo, Victor, 1951- author.
Title: Mayalogue : an interactionist theory of indigenous cultures / Victor Montejo.
Description: Albany : State University of New York Press, [2021] | Series: SUNY series, trans-indigenous decolonial critiques | Includes bibliographical references and index.
Identifiers: LCCN 2021022989 (print) | LCCN 2021022990 (ebook) | ISBN 9781438485751 (hardcover) | ISBN 9781438485775 (ebook) | ISBN 978-1-4384-8576-8 (paperback)
Subjects: LCSH: Maya philosophy. | Mayas—History—Methodology. | Mayas—Intellectual life. | Anthropology and history.
Classification: LCC F1435.3.P5 M66 2021 (print) | LCC F1435.3.P5 (ebook) | DDC 972.81—dc23
LC record available at https://lccn.loc.gov/2021022989
LC ebook record available at https://lccn.loc.gov/2021022990

10 9 8 7 6 5 4 3 2 1

CONTENTS

LIST OF ILLUSTRATIONS vii / ACKNOWLEDGMENTS ix

1. Introduction: An Indigenous Point of View 1
2. Anthropological Theories and Indigenous People 15
3. Decolonizing Maya History and Cultures 29
4. Mayalogue: The Treaty of Maya Ideas: *Q'inal*: Time, Life, and Existence 41
5. Mayalogue: From Oral Histories and Traditions to Written Ethnographies 59
6. Native Methods for Documenting History: *Oxlan B'en*: The Cyclical View of Time and History 79
7. Mayalogue: *Ohtajb'al*: Maya Knowledge and Epistemology 95
8. Mayalogue, the Interactionist Model: Humans, Nature, and the Supernatural World 119
9. The Tonal or Spirit Bearer: Human Nature/Animal Nature or the Theory of the Self 145
10. The "Cargo System" and World Maintenance 163
11. Mayalogue as a Cosmocentric Paradigm 179
12. World Building, World Maintenance, and World Dismantling 195
13. Prophetic Cycles and World Renewal 209

BIBLIOGRAPHY 227 / INDEX 239

ILLUSTRATIONS

FIGURE 2.1 Mapa Lingüístico de Guatemala. 28

FIGURE 4.1 Interrelationship as equals between humans, nature and the supernatural to produce meditated action reciprocity. 45

FIGURE 4.2 Sacred House of the Prayer-maker at *Ch'imb'an*, San Miguel Acatán, Guatemala. 49

FIGURE 4.3 Dog dancer during the Patron Saint's festivity. 56

FIGURE 5.1 The Maya Year Bearer. 62

FIGURE 6.1 The Q'anil Mountain and sanctuary of the Man of Lightning. 86

FIGURE 7.1 The four Maya directions and attached colors. 103

FIGURE 7.2 The Jakaltek Maya universe and directions. 104

FIGURE 7.3 The Rainbow (*kaj ch'elep*). 105

FIGURE 7.4 The Maya Calendar (Madrid Codex). 110

FIGURE 8.1 Harvest Corn. 127

FIGURE 8.2 The Dance of the Deer, Jacaltenango. 129

FIGURE 9.1 Structure of the *yijomal spixan* or spirit bearer in a human person. 151

FIGURE 9.2 Structure of *Nawalism*: human-animal transformation. 158

FIGURE 10.1 Divine Origin of the Jakaltek. 165

FIGURE 10.2 The *Aq'oma'* Mountain (Giver of Water) and *Yula'*, the shire of *B'alunh Q'ana'*, the Jakaltek ancestor. 167

FIGURE 10.3 The Maya cross at the outskirt of Concepcion Huista, Jakaltek region. 169

FIGURE 10.4 Prayer-makers in front of the Catholic Church, Jacaltenango. 171

FIGURE 11.1 In God We Trust. 185

FIGURE 12.1 Communal work. The maintenance of the Catholic Church, Jacaltenango. 201

FIGURE 12.2 The Flood (Dresden Codex). 205

FIGURE 12.3 The Maya Calendar in front of the Catholic Church, San Rafael La Independencia, Huehuetenango. 207

FIGURE 13.1 Rath and Wright's Company yard with buffalo hides, Dodge City, Kansas 1878. 215

FIGURE 13.2 *Komi' Ixim*, Mother Corn. 218

FIGURE 13.3 Imagining our place in the Milky Way. 225

ACKNOWLEDGMENTS

THE YEAR WAS 1987. I was in Graduate School at the State University of New York at Albany, surviving with my wife and three children on a small graduate scholarship from SUNY-Albany and a stipend received from the Friends Meeting Committee from Lewisburg, Pennsylvania. My immediate family had recently joined me in exile from Guatemala, so it was very hard for me to carry out graduate education with a family to sustain. Of course, my wife had to work hard to help with the family, as we barely meet our basic needs. She started cleaning houses, and sometimes I had to help her during the weekends.

My professors were very supportive, among them: Robert M. Carmack, Gary Gossen, and Lyle Campbell, who encouraged me to take the challenge of graduate education with my limited knowledge of the English language. Also, we had the good fortune of meeting a good man and scholar, Dr. Christopher Lutz, an expert on colonial Guatemala. He was interested in higher education for the Mayas, so he decided to help me with a scholarship. In this way, I could dedicate myself full time to graduate school because of his unconditional support. My dreams of achieving a university degree in the United States became a reality. In this way, I graduated with a master's degree in anthropology at the State University of New York at Albany in 1989, and with a PhD in anthropology at the University of Connecticut in 1993.

For this reason, I wish to dedicate this book to Dr. Christopher Lutz, an extraordinary person who has helped many students throughout the years with the Maya Educational Foundation. Chris Lutz has been a great admirer of Maya civilization, past and present, and as a historian he has understood the difficulties in which Maya people have survived under colonial rule and postcolonial repressive governments. His desire was to see modern Mayas achieve higher education, so that they can, one day, rewrite their own histories and express themselves freely with a decolonized mind.

Mayalogue, then, is a tribute to this extraordinary man who has dedicated himself to support modern Mayas to reconnect themselves with their ancestors through their continuous creativity and intellectual productions. In this effort, Dr. Stefano Varese at University of California was also my intellectual mentor in my search for a postmaterialist anthropological science. Finally, I am thankful to my colleagues at the Department of Native American Studies, Inés Hernández *Ávila*, the late Jack Forbes, and other scholars, such as Professor Kay Warren, who were very supportive in my development as a native Maya scholar.

INTRODUCTION

ONE

An Indigenous Point of View

AS A WRITER AND A NATIVE SCHOLAR OF MAYA, I want to present some ideas on how Indigenous People create knowledge as they relate themselves to the natural environment. For Mayas, it is important to build a Native theory as a contribution to the dialogue between anthropologists and Natives, and this is what I propose in *Mayalogue*. This dialogue must include the nonhuman persons as part of the cosmic web of life we call *q'inal*, which means *life, time, and existence*.

It is time to remove ourselves from scientific materialism, which has neglected the subjective dimensions of human experience for the past five centuries among the Mayas. Postmaterialist scientists and writers continue to free themselves from colonialist and materialist ideologies as they widen their views of the natural world, while enriching their human experience. The ways in which Indigenous People see the world and their cosmologies have been considered a distortion of reality; by rejecting these other ways of knowing, colonialist writings dismiss the Native's belief systems and values of respect and compassion that leads to a peaceful relationship with the natural world.

My current task is to write on these Native ideas, hoping to show how the world works for us (Maya cosmology). It has been a while—since graduate school from 1987 to 1992—that I wanted to write on this concept, but my work was always postponed because I had to follow the academic tradition, which only approved as scientific the writings that fit within Western frameworks or paradigms.

In addition, my knowledge of Maya culture was put aside during my training in graduate school, where influential works of Western thinkers were the only required text to be used in the classrooms. No Latin American scholars were read, which made me realize that Native traditions were far removed from being considered as a possible source of knowledge. In academia, Native knowledge was seen as irrelevant or even nonexistent. That is why, as a Native scholar, I had to go back to my Maya tradition and rethink what should be an intellectual contribution of modern Mayas to the social sciences and humanities.

I had to follow the great Lakota scholar Vine Deloria, who has hoped that Native Americans would develop a Native theory based on the philosophy of cosmic unity or connectedness with everything that exists in the living universe. Vine Deloria envisioned that "the next generation of American Indians could radically transform scientific knowledge by grounding themselves in traditional knowledge about the world and demonstrating how everything is connected to everything else" (Deloria 1999:39).

The concept of relativity or interrelatedness is a key issue that has differentiated Native human action and attitudes in relation to the natural world. Fortunately, little by little, non-Indigenous People have come to understand that Indigenous Peoples' worldviews are different and diverse as are the thousands of other cultures that exist on earth. We can argue that there are many worlds "to view," and not just one world that everyone must see and agree on, as we were led to believe by Western philosophy and the Cartesian doctrine of scientific objectivity.

Since the early years of contact, called the "discovery of America" by Europeans, the Creationist (Christian) paradigm enforced incorrect views of Indigenous People as half humans. Effectively, the powerful Christian Creationist paradigm excluded Indigenous People from the Great Chain of Beings (God, archangels, angels, saints, and humans created by God), thus, classifying them as creatures outside of God's creation. The negation of the humanity of Indigenous People had a negative effect throughout time, because Native people were not considered "real" human beings, but beasts or cruel savages. The doubts on the rationality of Indigenous People of the Americas gave rise to the famous debate between Bartolomé de las Casas and Juan Ginés de Sepúlveda at Valladolid, Spain in 1555 (Las Casas 1974).

But then, the Catholic King and Queen wanted to know more about their new domains, so they ordered the *encomenderos* to provide reports on the people and cultures that they have found on these invaded territories. A questionnaire was used to elicit information from the elders of the land, so that they could tell them about their antiquities. Curiously, almost all reports contained the same answer to the question concerning their religious belief—that the ancient Mayas: "*Tenían el conocimiento de solo un Dios que crió el cielo y la tierra y todas las cosas*" (had the knowledge of the Only-One-God [Hunab' K'uh] who created heaven and earth and everything that exists) (*Documentos Inéditos* 1898:78). The Spanish encomenderos and priests learned immediately that the Indians of the Maya region of Yucatan had a common religious belief on the Only One God (Hunab' K'uh), or the power of the universe that created everything that exists. Because of the existence of certain similarities in the spiritual world of Europeans and Mesoamericans, it was possible for Indigenous People to adopt and rework some religious symbols into their belief systems. In this way, a syncretic religion was created for accommodating Indigenous worldviews within the imposing and dominant Western religious traditions, such as Catholicism (Bricker 1981; Farris 1984; Ruz y Navarro 2005).

The sacred literary book of the Maya called *The Popol Vuh* is a good example for discussing Indigenous cosmologies. For example, the myths of origin and creation in the *Popol Vuh* are like the stories in Genesis of the Christian Bible. Although, a major difference is that for Indigenous People "creation" did not occur in a distant or unknown "mythical" place (Eden), but on Indigenous territories. These places of creation are a part of the sacred geography such as the "emergence holes" or *sipapuni* among Navajo and Pueblo Indians of the Southwest, United States. In other words, Indigenous People have strong connections with the land, which is the center of their spirituality. To understand earth is to understand ourselves, since everything is interrelated and dependent on human action, which must be based on the values of respect and reciprocity.

With this open-mindedness, Indigenous People, especially the *ahb'eh* or *ajq'ij* (Maya diviners and guides) achieved wisdom by paying attention to nature, while living and experiencing the gifts of life emanating from nature, earth, and the universe. Thus, the common Native phrase "We all are relatives" is a universal Indigenous truth that is shared and promoted by Indigenous People, then and now, as well as by traditionalists and modern Native scholars everywhere.

Most Indians hear this phrase thousands of times a year as they attend or perform their ceremonies, and for many Indians without an ongoing ritual life or religious belief, the phrase seems to be simply a liturgical blessing that includes all other forms of life in human ceremonial activities. But this phrase is very important as a practical methodological tool for investigating the natural world and drawing conclusions about it that can serve as guide for understanding nature and living comfortably within it. (Deloria 1999:34)

As we can see, the concept of interrelatedness with nature and the cosmos is not new, but it is something ill explained and misunderstood by scholars and missionaries. Ancient pre-Hispanic Maya documents such as the Madrid and Dresden Codex show even with illustrations the ritualized relationships that exist between humans, nature, and the supernatural world.

When human beings are not able to perform or practice this respectful relationship, and instead there is an abuse of nature, even warring with other nations for invading and appropriating the other's resources, that reciprocity and unity is ruptured, thus bringing destruction, epidemics, hunger, and death. Respect for life in all its forms is a way of maintaining balance and harmony with the natural world and the universe.

Similarly, the ethnohistorical and prophetic documents called *Chilam Balam* provide us with abundant stories that explain how human beings have suffered hardships because of their reluctance in following the natural law that enforces balance in the world and the cosmos. The Mayas believe that the candle of life can be turned off because of bad management of resources and human's neglect of other living beings. The ethnohistorical texts mentioned above documented the sacred knowledge of ancient Mayas, and this knowledge was maintained for centuries by the *ahb'eh* (calendar experts and diviners) who passed it down to new generations through stories, prayers, and ceremonies. Among the Jakaltek Maya, the *ninq'omlom* was the person who knew the ancient prayers by memory and could recite these poetic or flowered words in discourses that lasted many hours during the Maya New Year ceremony. These sacred discourses or prayers were pronounced eloquently, utilizing the poetic or literary devices called couplets and parallelism. This was the most appropriate way to ask for the well-being of humans, animals, plants, and Mother Earth, while giving thanks to Hunab'K'uh for the gift of life and the goodness of creation. In other words, human beings were created to fulfill a sacred mission, which is to nourish and sustain God and His helpers. They wanted to be invoked and remembered on earth, so they said: "Let us try to make obedient, respectful beings that will nourish and sustain us" (Goetz and Morley 1950:86).

In our modern world, where children are not in contact with nature but immersed in a virtual fantasy fighting monsters and dragons in computer games, it is hard to understand and value nature as our ancestors did as members of a moral community. That is why some Indigenous People, such as the Haudenosaunee (Iroquois) have insisted on the concept of the "seventh generation"—that, we humans can make our own living from earth and use the resources consciously, making sure that we don't put in jeopardy the ability of future generations to make their own living from the same natural resources that earth provides (Lyons 2008; Barreiro 2011). The concept of the seventh generation is an important doctrine or rule to follow. The reason is that, while Indigenous People insist on a respectful and rational use of nature, the doctrine of science and technology ignores this Indian philosophy of life and cosmic unity.

In the past, the most common argument against Indigenous spiritual beliefs in relation to earth and the cosmos was that Indians lived in a mythological world in which their primitive mind could not distinguish reality from fiction. Others insisted that Indians had a wrong observation of nature (earth), which they believed to be a living being, giving spirits to everything that exists in nature. This wrong explanation and interpretation of Indigenous behavior and spirituality was called "animism" by early-nineteenth-century evolutionist scholars (Tylor 1889). From anthropological and sociological explanations, animism is considered an inferior state of mind of the Natives, who believe that sticks and stones or any material object have souls, and this was a proof of their lower stage in the evolutionary process.

There is, then, confusion in the understanding of what Indigenous People have called "*pixan*," the soul bearer or spirit of creation. In Maya philosophy, the concept of *pixan* or the "spirit of creation" is the essence of that "thing" that exists (humans, plants, animals, mountains, rivers, objects, etc.) as belonging to the universe of earth and the universe of heaven. In other words, the living earth and everything that exist on it shares the same breath of creation and all must reciprocate to maintain balance and harmony for a healthy relationship. For the Mayas then, as for other Indigenous People, earth is a living being (*itzitzal yeyi*), a concept used by the *Jakaltek* Maya referring to the generative power of earth to give and sustain life in all its forms, colors, texture, and shapes.

We will always refer to the malicious actions of destruction by early missionaries such as Diego de Landa, who was a fierce enemy of Maya culture.

He condemned their religion and ways of life as the teachings of the devil. Then, in the twentieth century, Mayanists have continued to condemn Maya people as idolaters, as they are said to adore hundreds of gods (Montejo 1993). This misunderstanding is now being clarified by some modern anthropologists who have been more cautious in asking the opinion of "day-keepers" about Maya spirituality. On this issue, Ted Fisher has said the following:

> Despite having different names, different symbolic associations, and different contexts of activity, these "gods" are described by most *ajq'ijab'* as aspects of a single, unified force that animates the cosmos. Viewing unity in diversity is characteristic of Maya cultural logics in a number of domains, and such unity is conceptually associated with balance and harmony within and between both the physical and the metaphysical worlds. (Fischer 2001:180)

Another front of attacks against Indigenous beliefs and worldviews has been carried out by fundamentalist religions such as Protestantism. Fanatics of Protestantism claim to have taken a millennial mission to convert the Indians before the end of times, which will come soon according to them. In other words, Indigenous People are still considered to be lost in a world of paganism as they keep practicing their ancient traditions and ceremonies. Adding to this misunderstanding are those New Age individuals or pseudo-scholars who are engaged in creating esoteric worlds for the Natives, to the point that some have considered themselves as the personification of ancient Maya rulers. This is the case of Jose Argüelles who claims to be the personification of "Lord Pacal" of Palenque, who was supposed to have come to life in 2012 (Argüelles 1987).

My intention here is to discuss how Native knowledge is produced (Maya epistemology) by referring to the traditional knowledge that I learned as a child and as a Maya man who has lived and struggled between two worlds. The ideas presented here are samples of surviving Native knowledge in Maya communities, which early scholars have referred to, but without deepening into its meanings and methodology. This is an effort to synthesize the knowledge system of Indigenous People based on the tri-dimensional cosmic unity and relationship between humans, nature, and the spiritual world. These teachings are not new, but a way of life preached and promoted by Native prophets and wise men and women in ancient times. This was the case of *Topiltzin-Quetzalcoatl*, the ancient Mesoamerican prophet who was responsible for teaching a philosophy of life while maintaining human virtues and values of peace, harmony, and respect for earth, the sacred, and the universe.

It is difficult to comprehend the many characteristics of Mesoamerican civilization if one does not take into consideration one of its most profound dimensions: the conception of the natural world and human being's place in the cosmos. In this civilization, unlike that of the west, the natural world is not seen as an enemy. Neither is it assumed that greater human self-realization is achieved through greater separation from nature. To the contrary, a person's condition as part of the cosmic order is recognized and the aspiration is toward permanent integration, which can be achieved only through a harmonious relationship with the rest of the natural world. By obeying the principles of the universal order, human beings fulfill themselves and meet their transcendent destiny. (Batalla 2002:27)

Similarly, Deganawidah the prophet and Peace-maker of the Iroquois was also a main figure who established the Great Law of Peace and Unity, which was observed and followed by the Iroquois Confederacy. His philosophy has to do with respect and thankfulness to the Creator, who provides the earth with all that we humans need for our subsistence. In his teachings he specified that humans must give thanks, as follows:

To the forest trees for their usefulness, to the animals that serve as food and give their pelts for clothing, to the great winds and the lesser winds, to the Thunders, to the sun, the mighty warrior, to the Moon, to the messengers of the Creator who reveal his wishes, and to the Great Creator who dwells in the heavens above, who gives all thing useful to man, and who is the source and ruler of health and life. (Peterson 1990:76)

This same philosophy of life was preached by Native American chiefs who fought for their land and territories against early European colonizers. In the United States we have the classic case of Chief Seattle, whose thoughts and teachings have remained today as a quasi-religious approach and prayer to nature. In the same way, the great medicine man, Black Elk, kept alive his vision throughout his life, fulfilling his mission to serve his people and to maintain the unity of tradition and Native spirituality (DeMallie 1984). In modern times, Native American leaders such as Chief Oren Lyons (1994) have insisted on the defense of the rights of all living beings and not only that of humans. This philosophy of unity was taken seriously by the Indigenous working group within the United Nations as they developed the now Universal Declaration on the Rights of Indigenous People (UN 2007).

These ideas of unity, interrelatedness and common origin have been also taken by some Western scholars as a new understanding of life and have reworked them into a new philosophy of relationship called "biophilia" (Wilson 1984), or the natural kinship with all living beings. Others, of course, are engaged in developing policies for the protection of the environment, taking the debate of reciprocity and respect for life and earth, to the concept of land ethics, as developed by Aldo Leopold (Leopold 1949). Still others have extended this original Native American concept of unity and respect for nature, focusing their criticism on the interactive use and abuse of natural resources, while proposing a moral ecology, as they question the following: "How can we appreciate the logic of peasant-based ecologies without giving into essentialism and romanticism? I suggest a notion of 'moral ecology of nature use,' which offers an alternative to the rampant hit-and-run ethic of environmental modernization or its antithesis, the fencing off wilderness from human use" (Parajuli 2001:571).

Fortunately, now, some scientists have taken this issue of cosmic unity and universal kinship more seriously, to the point that more attention is given to these original Native ideas. We need to do more, because it is well known that Native ideas are accepted as rational only if Western scholars or scientist promote them. But when Indigenous People are the one who write and refer to these universal ideas of kinship and cosmic relationships, they are immediately dismissed as nonsense. For this reason, Indigenous scholars must continue to struggle to have their ideas accepted, just as Western thinkers propose their own theories and truths. Of course, not many scholars or scientists write and publish on Indigenous epistemological truths. Some write on these issues of natural relativity with certain fear or caution because Indigenous epistemologies are not totally approved by the scientific community. Those who write and make proposals supporting this philosophy of cosmic unity are writing, as Peter Knudson says, "at the border of scientific heresy" (Knudson 1991).

Of course, there is always the problem of romanticizing the lives and knowledge of Indigenous People, a practice that has become pervasive among New Age people and "wannabe" Indians. For this reason, the writings of scientists and Western scholars supporting Indigenous wisdoms and worldviews are always important because they can show that scientists are not a separate species of beings cultivated in laboratories, but human beings who should be in touch with the natural world. There is hope for scientists to embrace or to pay attention to Native knowledge and recognize it as valid information for complementing their scientific worldviews. On this hopeful future, Peter Knudson has written, "I nurture a growing sense that the West has much to learn from the accumulated ecological wisdom of First People whose lives and cultural traditions have emerged from a daily intimacy with the natural world" (Knudson 1991:90).

As we Mayas witness the continuous destruction of the environment all around the world (e.g., the Lacandon, Petén, and the Amazon rainforests), we ask ourselves, When did humans lose their way and became heartless and mindless people, to the point of forgetting their mission as guardians of the natural world? The *Popol Vuh* mentions different eras or periods of creation, while emphasizing the failure of the first humans made of mud and wood, the metaphor for senseless human beings. These creatures were mindless, and they acted without respect for nature, as they abused their utensils and domestic animals. For their senseless action, they were punished and vanished from earth by a flood. These teachings from the *Popol Vuh* remind us of previous eras and the wrong actions of humanity in ancient times, which invited destruction and the dismantling of the world. These are ecological teachings that constantly remind the Mayas of their mission to nourish their Creator, while making their living out of the natural world—always with respect, so that life is replenished on earth.

Obviously, we can also find distant lessons from other non-Indigenous cultures that can help us to understand the needs for a harmonic coexistence with other living beings. Nevertheless, these teachings may have been already forgotten, while fear has resurfaced in the mind and heart of modern human beings living mostly in the Western world. The Nicaraguan poet Rubén Darío wrote a great poem called "Brother Wolf," which is a parable about human fear and the violent behavior against certain animals that are killed or persecuted in their own habitats. I read this poem when I was in middle school and I have internalized it because of its poetical substance and the message of compassion that it provides for correcting human action.

In the story, the poem tells, Saint Francis of Assisi goes to confront the wolf that has eaten sheep and shepherds in the prairie, trying to stop the bloodshed. The saint made peace with the wolf and invited him to the convent to live peacefully, an invitation that the wolf accepted. There, the wolf lived as a docile pet, living with humility and without harming anyone. A little while later, the people got used to its harmless presence among them. After seeing the wolf as a humble and defenseless animal, the people started to kick and hit him with sticks and stones. One day, when the saint was absent, the wolf was insulted and humiliated by the people, so the wolf returned to the prairie where he started to attack and devour people and animals, as before. Once again, the Saint went to convince him to stop such destruction, but the wolf told Saint Francis that the people maltreated him for no reason, and that humans were worse than beasts. The wolf said, "If I kill and cause fear in humans, it is because that's my nature. I do it to secure my food, unlike humans who kill and destroy not for food, but because they take pleasure by killing and doing damages to others without compassion" (Darío 1985).

This time, the wolf rejected the saint's invitation and did not return to the convent, but stayed in the woods, as it was its natural habitat.

The concerns for life and the understanding of human relationship and collective survival in conjunction with everything that exists on earth was a way of life for Indigenous People in precapitalist societies. Obviously, this respectful relationship with nature changed with the colonial exploitation of resources and the development of capitalist economy among indigenous people in Latin America.

In the present era or millennia, Indigenous People who have maintained their respectful relationship with their environment, have been seen as backward people who want to remain poor while sitting on enormous amounts of wealth without exploiting them. So, as industrialized countries turn their attention to Indigenous protected territories, Indigenous People find themselves in precarious situation in the middle of modern conflicts such as guerrilla warfare, drug-trafficking, mining operations, and forced migration that has dislocated entire communities. In the case of Guatemala, Indigenous communities have been accused of sheltering drug lords, so national police and the army have invaded their communities, terrorizing them in order to get them to abandon their territories. The war on drug has been used as a new excuse for directly attacking Indigenous People, to remove them from those lands waiting to be exploited and "developed" for the benefit of the elite and transnational corporations. Against these state sponsored attacks, Indigenous People have resisted total assimilation and have fought for their rights and self-determination for centuries. This is the case of the Zapatista rebellion in Chiapas, Mexico, or the pan-Maya movement for cultural revitalization and decolonization taking place in Guatemala (Warren 1998; Montejo 2005; Del Valle Escalante 2008).

Many external forces are exercising pressure on Indigenous People's traditional ways of life as they are being assimilated by the attractive commodities offered by modern technology and globalization. This process is seen in the massive migration of Indigenous People from their homelands to the United States, where they come with dreams of making money and having a more decent, if not luxurious, life, such as those who have always enjoyed economic opportunities and have discriminated against them in their countries of origin.

Despite all the suffering and changes occurring around them, most Indigenous People are conscious of the importance of revitalizing their cultures, and not giving up to total assimilation or de-Indianization (Batalla 2002; Varese 2006). Some Native Nations have taken the road of economic self-sufficiency as a tool to strengthen Indigenous cultures such as the case of the Pequot and Oneida Indian Nations, who have become economically successful because of operating casinos and other economic enterprises on their territories. Their ultimate concern is to empower themselves economically and to be self-sufficient by creating and running their own institutions for achieving their self-determination.

We can argue that Indigenous People have become more organized for maintaining their worldviews and religious practices that are being shaken by the waves of economic and technological globalization. For example, Maya elders who integrate the Council of Elders and a*jq'ij* (Maya spiritual leaders) continue with their missions by using the sacred Maya calendar, which guides their spiritual actions and ceremonies. For the Mayas, all human beings are born with a mission to be fulfilled on earth, and it is up to the person to find that mission and to be responsive to the Creator, while serving the community and protecting life on earth. Unfortunately, with the recent wave of massive transnational migration going on now, the early teachings of the ancestors are being forgotten. Young people are abandoning their communities, attracted by the powerful economy of the United States and the technology that compels them as never before.

Chapter 2 provides a brief historical background of some anthropological theories from which our Western understanding of Indigenous cultures was built. From these major contributions, other anthropological theories were developed and chapter 3 focuses on the process of decolonizing Native histories and cultures.

Chapter 4 is dedicated to building a Native theory that I call Mayalogue or the treaty of Maya ideas and contributions to the dialogue between anthropologists and Natives. This dialogue includes nonhuman persons as part of the cosmic web of life. Chapter 5 focuses on Native methodologies and the importance of the oral tradition as a method for documenting history, which for Mayas is cyclical, such as the closing of a major cycle called *Oxlanh B'en* or *B'ak'tun*. Chapter 6 focuses on the process of "telescoping" of time (Bricker 1981), which is a Maya method for integrating past histories into recent ones. This process is completed with the mythification process in which a leader or a hero enters the cannon of history as a supernatural being. Chapter 7 focuses on Maya epistemology and the importance of using

Maya terminology for referring to Maya ideas, rather than replacing them with Greek or Latin terms. To use native concepts such as *ohtajb'al*, the instrument for knowing, or the accumulation of knowledge is part of an effort to decolonize the mind.

Chapter 8 develops the ideas central to Mayalogue: the interconnectedness between humans, nature, and the spiritual world—the three elements of the interactionist model. Chapter 9 refers to the spirit bearer or *yijomal spixan*, which is a Mesoamerican concept of the alter ego, or the animal companion of an individual. This is a spiritual animal that shares its destiny with the individual and is explained here as a proposed theory for the Maya self. Chapter 10 focuses on the "cargo system" or communal service to the community, and God. The service is like a burden to be carried out by an individual for the purpose of maintaining a healthy world and in harmony with nature and the Creator.

Chapter 11 describes the interactionist model. This model explains the relationship between humans and nature, which is always connected to the spiritual world, and makes Mayalogue a cosmo-centric paradigm. Chapter 12 focuses on the cyclical concept of life and existence on earth, and the need for maintaining that world and keeping it alive (Berger 1977). Earth and civilizations have passed through major cataclysmic changes and processes of world building, world maintenance, world dismantling, and world renewal. Finally, chapter 13 returns to the cyclical concept of time and discusses the 13 B'ak'tun as the ending of a major time-cycle. For the Mayas, time is cyclical and there were prophetic times embedded within the Maya calendar, such as the recently ended 13 B'ak'tun (12/21/12).

The basis for Mayalogue comes from an empiricist contribution as well as from the ideological understanding of the world and life (*q'inal*) taking fundamental lessons from the *Popol Vuh: Sacred Book of the Mayas*. The Maya calendar is used as a unifying element of universal categories, which includes in its twenty day names the days for the ancestors, plants, animals, rivers, mountains, wind, sun, moon, earth, universe, and so on. Once again, we insist that Indigenous People do not separate nature from humans, body from mind, religion from human activities, and so forth. "Instead there is an understanding of the holistic connectedness of all that exists. For a people holding such a holistic view of the world, everything would be sacred and imbued with spirit, a part of a greater whole inseparably interwoven" (Kaiser 1991:116).

This is the Native or Indigenous contribution to the study of humanity, which is not human centered, but as an integral part of a universal system known as *q'inal*, or the expression of *Wakan* in Lakota philosophy. This is an effort to document Indigenous wisdom and synthesize it in a body of knowledge that can be useful for Indigenous and non-Indigenous students and scholars. It is then, a response to what Vine Deloria always proposed in terms of developing Native theories and methodologies. "If tribal wisdom is to be seen as a valid intellectual discipline, it will be because it can be articulated in a wide variety of expository forms and not simply in the language and concepts that tribal elders have always used to express themselves" (Deloria 1999:66).

From this juncture, I have developed this Native interpretation and affirmation of Native worldviews within the context of the *Oxlanh B'ak'tun*, or ending of the great Maya cycle 13 *B'ak'tun* or the fifth Maya millennia. The Maya calendar marked the date December 21, 2012 as the ending of this great Maya cycle, which also marked the beginning of a world dismantling, as some elders believe.

Mayalogue is the presentation of some ideas for telling the world that Indigenous cultures create knowledge, as do any other cultures on earth. To this effort, I propose the development of an interactionist theory of culture from the trialogical relationships (human-nature-supernatural), which pervades Indigenous worldviews.

We need the development of social and humanistic theories of cultures that will be useful in this process of world renewal. In this context, Native ideas and worldviews are basic to the construction of this holistic and cosmocentric paradigm.

ANTHROPOLOGICAL THEORIES AND INDIGENOUS PEOPLE
TWO

IN THIS CHAPTER, I will briefly discuss the history of anthropological theories, particularly "evolutionism," which helped to placed Indigenous People in a powerless position throughout the centuries. Since the early twentieth century, when anthropology developed as a scientific discipline, a series of theories were put forward to explain human behavior all around the world, particularly those that considered Indigenous People as exotic creatures living a primitive life so distant from the advancement of Western civilization.

The prevalent paradigm of the late nineteenth and early twentieth centuries was the evolutionist theory, which was so damaging to Indigenous People who were classified as "primitives" and less evolved savages. This was due to the misinterpretation of Indigenous behavior, since they were more attached to the land and practiced an egalitarian mode of production and subsistence. In other words, the fact that Indigenous People did not overexploit their environment to accumulate wealth was considered a backward and "primitive" behavior. According to this racist interpretation, it was necessary to teach them the value of gold and the importance of private property, greed, and individualism, which was praised as an evolved behavior. Instead, the values of communalistic ownership and respectful relationships with the land and the environment were seen as a less evolved behavior.

In this way, unilinear evolution became a racist theory that placed Indigenous People in a timeless past. It was a doctrine that considered them inferior and uncivilized, as adults exhibiting childish behavior. Under this condition, Indigenous People needed to be controlled or dominated by those who were civilized, the greedy conquistadores and colonizers who invaded Indigenous territories. Unfortunately, the stereotypes developed during this period of time have persisted until now. In the case of the Indigenous People of Guatemala, the Mayas have been called "*indios*," a pejorative term meaning backward people. This categorization justified the enslavement and exploitation of Indigenous People since the Spanish invasion, colonization, and postcolonial period (Smith 1980). The discrimination and racist treatment of Indigenous People in Guatemala continues today, as they are still seen as savages and whose rights as human beings are still denied. Why do we think that Indigenous People were the one who suffered the most during the internal armed conflict in Guatemala (1960–1996)? The reason was that Indigenous People were considered inferior and as such they were destined to disappear (Montejo 1991).

From this racist evolutionary perspective, Indigenous People are still seen as unevolved creatures whose brain and growth were stunted, leaving them far behind the "civilized" and modern globalized world of the twenty-first century. To be Indigenous for them is to be "inferior"—creatures so persistent in their traditionalist ways of life that they have been placed at the margin of development and denied the rights to education and full participation as citizens in the countries where they survive.

Under this marginalization, Indigenous People have not been heard, and their voices claiming for freedom and justice have been ignored for centuries. In some cases, others have managed to speak for the Natives, such as the case of indigenist anthropologists. In Latin America, *indigenismo* became a national project in some countries in which Indigenous cultures were valued while developing national policies for the assimilation of the Indians. A friendlier version of *indigenismo* was the one that truly helped Indigenous People to tell the world about their centuries of suffering under colonial rule, up to now (Stavenhagen 2001; Batalla 2002; Varese 2006). Throughout the Americas, Native people have suffered injustices under tyrants who have ruled the modern nation-states, where they have been reduced to reservations, marginal communities, or as ethnic surviving minorities.

Since the sixteenth century, Bishop Bartolomé de las Casas was the first to defend the rights of the Indigenous People of the American continent. For this reason, he earned the title of "Defender of the Indians," as he defended them in the court of Seville, Spain, against royal historian Juan Ginés de Sepúlveda (Las Casas 1974). The most damaging argument of Sepúlveda against the Indians was that these "savages" committed the worst crimes against nature such as cannibalism and human sacrifices. Without placing a foot on the so-called New World, Sepúlveda condemned the Indians as cruel and irrational beings, who needed to be subdued by the Spaniards who supposedly had a superior culture to those bloodthirsty savages.

At the same time, the Creationist paradigm preached by missionaries penetrated so deeply into the mind and soul of Indigenous People. The categorization of Indigenous People as a "burden" to society and as a failed race in the eyes of God was repeated to the "Indians" throughout the centuries. They were told by Christian missionaries that they must obey colonial authorities and suffer patiently, since that was the will of God. In other words, some missionaries tried to convince Indigenous People that their sufferings were necessary at the hands of their "conquerors," who were placed by God in charge of those savages who lacked human morality, religion, and a civilized life.

With the expansion of colonial empires all over the world, more and diverse cultures were found; still, they were all piled up into the same net and called "primitive" cultures. In this process, anthropology became a discipline that intended to explain the complexities of human cultures from a comparative perspective. Then, the concepts of high and inferior, or civilized as opposed to primitive cultures were developed. Of course, the West classified itself as a superior race compared to the rest of the world. This was then, the development of the evolutionist theory, which praised the progress of the West while arguing that the Natives were still living in a backward and decaying world (Langness 1985).

Evolutionism was the first systematic body of anthropological theory applied to the study of human cultures and behaviors, mainly those of Indigenous People who have become the object of anthropological study. As stated by Lewis Henry Morgan in his *Ancient Society* (1877), the basic premise of evolutionary theory was the issue of progression, or that cultures must pass through different evolutionary stages: from savagery through barbarism to civilization. By the second half of the eighteenth century, the conceptions of Natives as being "primitives," or less evolved creatures, was cemented and Indigenous People were situated at the bottom of the evolutionary scale. Since then, in anthropological literature, Indigenous People were widely called "primitives," while others with more visible material cultures such as the Mayas, Mexicas, and Incas were considered in between savagery and barbarism. In this way, evolutionism placed a stigma on Indigenous People, characterizing them as inferior human beings who needed to pass through the other stages to fully evolve. In other words, their brains needed to grow and evolve to become fully human and achieve civilization. This conditioning of the so-called primitives, at the bottom of the evolutionary scale, contributed to the total domination, exploitation, and enslavement of Indigenous People, with a blatant negation of their human rights.

Another evolutionist anthropologist who perpetuated the image of Indigenous People as true savages was Edward B. Tylor. This anthropologist was interested in the spiritual world of the Natives or what he called primitive religion. He argued that "the savages or barbarians did not distinguish subjective from objective experience or between imagination and reality" (in Langness 1985:20–21). He, then, popularized the notion that Indigenous People did not distinguished between dreams and realities, as they believed that everything had souls. This concept is called "animism" by anthropologists, or the belief that all objects, indiscriminately had souls and that Indigenous People lived in a constant state of fear. Again, this misinterpretation of Native American religion and spirituality gave rise to the belief that Indigenous People lived in a fantastic world of spirits and phantoms. Later, some evolutionist thinkers such as James Frazer argued that Europeans were, in ancient times, at the stages of the now living "savages," so the Natives (called primitives) must pass through unilinear stages—from magic to religion to science—to become civilized. By using the comparative method and the evolutionary stages, Europeans were interested in knowing how far they had advanced compared to those primitives that they placed at the bottom of the evolutionary scale (Langness 1985).

As a major theory developed during the nineteenth century, evolutionism had a strong impact on all societies, not only on that of scholars, but that of postcolonial authorities and the public of Western Europe. The idea of the inferiority of Indigenous People became a true doctrine, and scholars used the term *primitive* to name Indigenous People and non-European cultures all over the world. This naming was transformed into a racist treatment of Indigenous People, a problem that they have endured for centuries. In other words, Indigenous People have struggled for centuries to get rid of this grotesque misrepresentation and denigrating colonial images. And as stated by Vine Deloria, "For American Indians, the struggle of this century has been to emerge from the heavy burden of anthropological definitions that have made Indian communities at times mere laboratories for political and social experiments. Indian advocates are often very bitterly attacked by scholars when they question these experiments and articulate their own ideas which clash with accepted orthodox and comfortable interpretations about tribal people developed by academics" (Deloria 1997:51).

The major implication of evolutionism in the construction of later racist theories about Indigenous cultures is the assertion that "savage" people's backwardness was the result of their unevolved brains or their lack of mental capacities to think as adult human beings. In other words, the minds of the savages (Indigenous People) are illogical, in contrast to the logical and rational mind of Caucasians. This racist assumption was expressed in the measurement of Indigenous skulls to show that Natives supposedly had smaller brains than Westerners (Gould 1981).

The powerful influence of evolutionism continued throughout the nineteenth century, until Franz Boas came across Native Americans in Alaska and recognized the particularities of Indigenous cultures. From his personal field experience, he took a different approach from his predecessors and argued that Native people have their own ways of life and that Westerners did not have the right to look down at them. In this way, Boas got more involved in understanding and learning from Native cultures, to the point that he instituted fieldwork as an ethnographic method to document Indigenous cultures (Boas 1896), in order to write about them from facts and not from assumptions or the imagination. In this way Franz Boas challenged the evolutionary paradigm and argued that there were no primitive minds, but that human beings were the same anywhere in the world. He argued that Native Americans or Indigenous People have particular or distinctive cultural traditions, a conviction that gave rise to his argument for historical particularism.

The recognition that there were diverse cultures, with particular histories all over the world gave rise to the concept of cultural relativism. In other words, Indigenous People have distinctive worldviews from which they explain their existence and make sense of their lives in relation to the land and their environments. This is how: "Boas' fieldwork experience, along with his relativism, apparently led him to perceive particular cultures, in the plural, and to appreciate that each one had a unity, coherence, and history of its own" (Langness 1985:50).

This position changed the reductionist view of evolution and allowed for multiple worldviews and cultures—that each culture is unique as a viable way of life, since people have lived these ways for millennia and have survived as unique cultures in harmony with their natural environments. To probe his argument, Boas sent his students to different regions of the Americas to document Indigenous cultures that were supposed to disappear soon. This project of rescuing the remnants of the past (salvage ethnography) brought samples of living cultures throughout the continent that were so intriguing, thus showing that Indigenous cultures were not remnants of the past, but healthy living traditional cultures extremely well adapted to their environments. From this, I argue that those traditional communities had their own philosophy of life that was based on an interactionist mode between humans, nature, and the supernatural world, thus informing this trialogical approach to cultures, as will be shown in Mayalogue.

Franz Boas's more humanistic explanation of cultures left a vacuum in cultural theory, as evolutionism was undermined by the new emerging anthropological social science under Boas and his students. Soon other anthropologists were looking for a grand theory for explaining the workings of the mind in the production of cultures and on the different ways humans expressed themselves. For this purpose, most universities had to train students (anthropologists) to become experts in the four subfields of anthropology: archaeology, linguistics, ethnology, and physical anthropology, although, up to the 1990s, physical anthropology maintained the evolutionary racist tenets within the discipline at some universities. It was a short period of time in which historical particularism developed as an alternative to evolutionism. Obviously, there was criticism against this anthropological approach, mainly based on the argument that it was antitheoretical; that this Boasian school failed to develop a concise body of theory for explaining "culture" after attacking cultural evolutionism (Wax 1956).

I believe, the work of Boas and his students was immensely positive, and the fact that they tried to get rid of a grand theory (evolution) was a superb task for these scholars to undertake, thus focusing on the local knowledge of particular cultures before generalizing. It became clear that evolutionist theory, as applied to cultures, misrepresented Indigenous People by creating a false interpretation of their cultures through fixed stages.

Then, a new team of British anthropologists, namely, Radcliffe Brown and Bronislaw Malinowski, pushed the discipline forward, proposing a functionalist theory by comparing and making use of the organic analogy. That social systems work the same way a human body and its organs function, each part contributing to the totality. In other words, to have a healthy life (body) each part must contribute to the harmonious functioning of the system as a whole. Unfortunately, Radcliffe Brown and Bronislaw Malinowski only made reference to the human body as a metaphor for the functioning of culture. They did not take humans as an integral part in the development a wider systemic theory, as Native people conceptualize themselves in a tri-dimensional web of relationships proposed in Mayalogue. Obviously, these anthropologists developed these ideas by observing Indigenous People's ritualistic relationship to nature and the spiritual world, but they did not care for the human-nature and supernatural relationship witnessed in traditional cultures. They tended to treat each part of the system separately as kinship systems, agriculture, religion, political life, organizational systems, and so on. About this atomization of culture, Lewis Langness has said that "a natural science of society must recognize the natural system, discover its structure, and perceive how each part function in relation to the system" (Langness 1985:70).

With the decline of functionalism, anthropologists recognized their failure in not considering the totality of the system, as they concentrated only in the study of cultural segments. On this, Radcliffe-Brown writes: "While no complete science of culture is possible by itself, you can have an independent scientific treatment of certain aspects, of certain portions of culture. They will not give you the final scientific conclusions, but they will give you a certain number of quite important provisional ones" (Radcliffe-Brown 1957:108).

In terms of Indigenous knowledge and the development of Mayalogue, we can take this argument as a fundamental one. Functionalists began to study separate aspects of cultures and developed subdisciplines in anthropology. Their specialized research on segments of cultures became generalized and their findings were considered as representative of Indigenous cultures as a whole. Obviously, the web of relationships represented by the body metaphor—cells, membranes, blood tissues, organs, and systems that formed a unity—was not applied in the social sciences. This metaphor should have been useful if applied to human cultures as a web of relationships that includes religion, language, dreams, agriculture, hunting, praying, dances, rituals and ceremonies, and so forth. All these aspects form human behavior or cultural expressions, according to functionalists. Unfortunately, they tended to explain segments of cultures as representing the whole, and not as "provisional ones," to come to scientific conclusions as mentioned by Radcliffe-Brown.

For Indigenous People, human cultures respond to the interaction between other forces of nature and the environment. In other words, you must recognize the relationship between culture, nature, and the supernatural world. In this way we can have a more complete picture of how Indigenous People conceptualize and live their own cultures as part of a larger system.

While Bronislaw Malinowski worked on his version of functionalism, Radcliffe-Brown also worked on the same ideas creating his anthropological branch of structural-functionalism. Obviously, the idea of basic needs was fundamental in the development of these theories, and in a way functionalism and structuralism continued to view Indigenous People as "primitives" who were engaged solely in making sense of their environment for existentialist purposes, as they extracted their living from nature and fulfilled their basic human needs.

The structuralist theory was a development from philosophical dualism of the early eighteenth century, namely, the debate on idealism and materialism. The reductionist approach to the study of cultures from these opposing philosophical perspectives made a general division in anthropology by creating cultural materialism and cultural idealism. A major proponent of cultural materialism was Marvin Harris, who applied Marxist theory to cultures as presented in his major anthropological work, *The Rise of Anthropological Theory* (1968). Marvin Harris followed the materialist approach proposed by Julian Steward, mainly cultural ecology and its techno-environmental conditioning. For the first time, anthropologists who followed evolutionary theory reflected on the influence of the environment or the ecology on the construction, conditioning, and the development of material cultures for human survival. The cultural materialists, such as Marvin Harris, gave secondary importance to the role of ideas in creating or developing cultures. They did mention the importance of the environment or the ecology, but only as resources to be harnessed for economic reasons to fulfill the material needs of individuals.

While cultural materialism was a reductionist approach to cultures, the other side of the philosophical debate (idealism) developed another theory of culture known as structuralism, which was championed by French anthropologist Claude Lévi-Strauss. Lévi-Straussian structuralism was based mainly on the interplay of binary oppositions as a universal form in which the mind works. As a scholar influenced by evolutionism, Lévi-Strauss used the comparative method to show how far Western thought of today had developed from "primitive" societies or living savages, as he called them (Lévi-Strauss 1966).

At this same period (1960s–1970s), a new form of ethnographic description developed from linguistics, which was called the new ethnography. This new approach, which took into consideration Indigenous classificatory systems, evolved into what linguists and anthropologists called ethnoscience. This part of the structural-functionalist paradigm (ethnoscience) will be used in part to develop the interactionist aspect of Mayalogue, or the interweaving of emic and etic approaches in writing ethnographies.

Interactionism here is developed by finding the interplay between materialism and idealism, as shown in some major works such as that of Michael Taussig (1980) and Victor Turner (1967), whose work I consider fundamental in understanding the dynamics of cultural changes and transformations through a dialectical process. As a Native anthropologist, I will also make use of the empirical model to develop a more balanced view of culture, in which interactionism is the key concept for developing a definition of culture and society from a Native American or Indigenous perspective. In other words, emphasis will be given here to the emic or the insider's perspective in cultural analysis. Only by presenting this point of view, which has always been marginal in major anthropological works and theories, we will move forward to a more integrated concept of culture that is supraorganic in a way that responds to what can be called the universal collective consciousness.

Lately, from this intellectual and philosophical debate on cultural idealism, another anthropological current was developed, which has had a tremendous impact in the field during the 1980s and 1990s, namely, symbolic or interpretive anthropology. Two of the major stars of symbolic anthropology were Victor Turner, with his work *The Forest of Symbols* (1967), and Clifford Geertz, with *The Interpretation of Cultures* (1973). The interpretive development in anthropology was truly a powerful moment in the social sciences, as the ideological part of cultures was given primacy, thus considering culture as a system of symbols to be approached from various levels of interpretation. Victor Turner's *The Forest of Symbols*, based on Ndembu culture of East Africa, is the most important book to be used for developing an Indigenous theory of cultures. Turner explains how symbols and rituals are adjusted to the social processes as a cultural adjustment to the environment from which the symbols are extracted for ritual purposes. For Victor Turner, the analysis and description of a cultural tradition must consider the three levels of interpretive action. That is, the positional, operational, and exegetical levels of cultural interpretation, giving importance to what people do with the symbols and not only what they say about it (Turner 1967). In Mayalogue, I pay attention to the symbolic analysis proposed by Victor Turner, as I develop the exegetical level of analysis while showing the dynamic interaction between the emic and the etic approaches in anthropology.

One of the most important exponents of interpretive anthropology today is Clifford Geertz, who has used the ideological paradigm so heavily in his symbolic analysis, considering cultures as the product of ideas and the mind. Clifford Geertz is among the anthropologists who have come across major ideas (web of relationships) that can be used to explain Western failure in the recognition of Indigenous People's biocentric approach to life and cultures. While explaining his concept of culture, Geertz stated, "Believing, with Max Weber, that man is an animal suspended in webs of significance he himself has spun, I take culture to be those webs, and the analysis of it to be therefore not an experimental science in search of law but an interpretive one in search of meaning" (Geertz 1973:5).

If we analyze Geertz's definition of culture as a semiotic one, we find out that first, there is a continuity of thinking on the philosophical idealist-materialist dichotomy that has been in debate for centuries. Then, considering "that man is an animal suspended in webs of significance he himself has spun," we come to understand humans as animals entangled or captured in their own traps. The concept of "web of significance" is important here, because it is a symbolic representation of multiple relationships that exists: person to person, person to family, person to society, and person to the outside world. Once again, there is no reference to the interactive relationships with the natural world—the reciprocity and interrelationships between humans and humans, humans and nature, and humans with the supernatural or spiritual world. And if humans have spun the web themselves, then this is a human-centered action, and this action is unidirectional—humans conditioning and deciding solely on everything.

The Native experience tells us that humans respond to the calls of nature and accommodate themselves as much as they can, fulfilling their basic needs, but they are dependent on the webs that nature and the supernatural world also spun on them. There are then, mutual relationships and junctures between nature and cultures, as humans cannot live without the gifts of earth and the blessings of cosmic life and elements (sun, wind, and rain).

Finally, Geertz tells us that analysis of culture should be "not an experimental science in search of laws but an interpretive one in search of meaning." Again, this last part of his definition makes claims for the binomial opposition between nature and culture—objectivity (science, law, norms) as opposed to the subjectivity of symbols and meanings that are always supposed to be separated.

As Geertz's major work, "The Interpretation of Cultures" has been influential in the training of modern anthropologists; it is healthy for anthropology and the social sciences to bridge not only the separation of mind and body, subjective action, and natural law, but also to understand the connectedness that exist between humans and nature, and humans and the spiritual world. If we consider cultures in this trialogical way, we at least can give it its place and its importance in human thought and action as a holistic and unified concept of culture.

With the development of symbolic anthropology and cultural materialism, we can see that the philosophical dualist debate has continued into the 1970s and 1980s, while materialist approaches have changed to make some room for ideological symbols to explain the changes in ideologies because of colonialism, postcolonialism, and imperialism in the Americas. On this side of the fence, we have the classical work of Erick Wolf, *Europe and the People without History* (1982), and *The Devil and Commodity Fetishism in South America* (1980) by Michael Taussig, mainly on the dialectics of fieldwork. Here, the capitalist mode of production took over the precapitalist mode practiced by Native people, which was based on reciprocity and respect for the natural world.

While dealing with the development of scientific theories during the eighteenth and nineteenth centuries, Thomas Kuhn argued in *The Structure of Scientific Revolution* that anomalies and conflicts are important movers of profound changes: "Let us then assume that crises are a necessary precondition for the emergency of novel theories" (Kuhn 1962:77). In the case of anthropology, Postmodernist theories alerted on the problems of misrepresentation, while promoting critical revisions of ethnography. The purpose was to accommodate the struggles of Indigenous People and minorities as a way out of this "crises of representation" (Marcus and Fischer 1986).

At this point in human history, the social sciences and the humanities have developed theories that attempt to explain from an outsider's perspective how the Indigenous minds work in producing their cultures. Indigenous People have been constantly represented as "the other," separated from the white mainstream society. In this way, their cultures have been interpreted in relation to the outsider's hegemonic cultures and worldviews. During the 1980s and 1990s, anthropology went into a major revision, starting with the criticism of anthropology as a colonialist enterprise (Said 1978; Asad 1988; Faris 1988; Clifford 1988; Pratt 1992). In this camp we have the contribution of major anthropologists who showed that anthropology continued to be a colonialist discipline. One of these scholars is Edward Said, whose criticism in *Orientalism* can be applied to the ancient cultures of the Americas and their living descendants today (Said 1978).

The forefront critique of anthropology as a colonial discipline was carried further by Talal Asad and his collaborators in *Anthropology & the Colonial Encounter* (Asad 1988). That anthropological works served other interests besides knowing cultures, such as that of the colonial administrators and rulers. In this volume, James Faris argues that "If our science doesn't change with our politics, we can hardly be of much intellectual help in struggles against various manifestations of imperialism. Not only must the content and application of our science change, but also our theory and methodology" (Faris in Asad 1988:154).

The critiques of anthropology continued, and some scholars developed the branch of applied anthropology and later a more militant branch called *Antropología Comprometida* (Carmack, 1988; Manz, 1995). By the 1960s and

1970s, most anthropologists working in Latin America had come across Indigenous movements of self-representation, if not self-determination, which is still a distant goal to achieve. Convinced of their position as intellectual intermediaries between the people whom they study and the Western world of university communities, some dedicated their time to join efforts to speak up for those oppressed Indigenous communities, instead of just doing traditional fieldwork. Major figures in this struggle and promoters of anthropology of liberation were Rodolfo Stavenhagen (2008), Stefano Varese (2006), Bonfil Batalla (2002), Robert Carmack (1988), Carol Smith (1990), Kay Warren (1998), among many others who have become some of the most important non-Native scholars committed to the anticolonialist fight. Many younger scholars like them have become supportive of the Maya in the struggle for their rights and self-determination. On this strong commitment for a liberating anthropology, Stefano Varese writes, "British anthropologist Kathleen Gough and UC Berkeley professor Gerald Berreman had led a devastating critique of mainstream anthropology and its political quietism and moral abstinence on the central issues of war, social inequality, counter-insurgency politics, political repressions and human rights abuses" (Varese 2006:34).

In sum, Indigenous People have lived many centuries of neglect, while Western scientists continued to create theories and representations that ridicule or dehumanize them. In other words, none of the intellectual contributions of Indigenous People to human sciences have been valued or taken seriously. To maintain this intellectual control over vast populations of the world, Eurocentric doctrines have been imposed considering Indigenous People as inferiors and lacking intellectual capacity for producing knowledge. "Among the notions central to this worldview is the racial construction of white privilege. Decolonization, therefore, involves the questioning of the racial and evolutionary bases of colonial power, and how these have tended to underlie the construction of knowledge" (Mallon 2012:2).

Finally, the postmodernist approach was developed during the 1980s and 1990s, as a devastating critique against the continuous colonialist practice by anthropologists who were sticking to major Western paradigms. The major proponents of the postmodern critique in anthropology were George E. Marcus and Michael J. Fischer. They argued in *Anthropology as a Cultural Critique* (1986) that anthropology has maintained its Western power and authority over Native populations they study, who are still mainly subjects of Western colonialism. The postmodern critique was a stone in the shoes of traditional Western scholars who were comfortable in their fields, while applying theoretical paradigms that misrepresented the life and existence of Indigenous People. It was then a rupture in the traditional way of practicing anthropology that provoked major revisions and critical exposures. "Consequently, the most interesting theoretical debates in many fields have shifted to the level of method, to problems of epistemology, interpretation, and discursive forms of representation themselves, employed by social thinkers. Elevated to a central concern of theoretical reflection, problems of description become problems of representation" (Marcus and Fischer 1986:9).

The distancing from Western hard sciences and restrictive theories that deny interaction and inclusion of Native knowledge as appropriate lessons and experiences to live by gave strength to environmental studies. In turn, this emerged from the traditional forms of cultural ecology, ecology and religion (Rappaport 1979), and the nature and culture dichotomy.

The postmodern debate made possible the development of innovative approaches to culture and society by some modern social scientists. They now recognize and use Native knowledge or Indigenous epistemologies (Varese 2006; Descola 1996), as a tool for better understanding human relations with nature and the universe—all this, because of current Indigenous leadership in writing and resisting the continuous imposition of Western forms of knowledge that has maintained intellectual colonialism (Tuhiwai-Smith1999; Deloria 1999; Montejo 2005). Through the years, a strong support has been received from some scientist and anthropologists who have sided with Indigenous People's liberation ecology (Tedlock and Tedlock 1975; Grim 1991; Knudson 1991; Suzuki and Knudson 1992; Descola 1996; Varese 2006).

Other scholars have been more involved with current Indigenous issues and activism through media production, such as TV educational shows with Indigenous People (e.g., the Kayapo) supporting Native Nations and their struggle for self-determination. The work with cultural survival of anthropologist Maybury-Lewis, Guillermo Bonfil Batalla, and Rodolfo Stavenhagen in Mexico, among many others, are good examples of how anthropologists and institutions can work hand by hand in support of the struggle of Indigenous People around the world against racist scholarship (Stavenhagen 1996).

The opportunity to enter into a field of Native studies not restricted by a totalizing theory, has been propitious for rethinking Indigenous forms of knowledge and epistemology. It is a positive moment for Indigenous thinkers who want to contribute to the social sciences and humanities with Native knowledge that has not been considered important or not taken seriously in the past. In other words, Indigenous People have followed ancient teachings and moral values that enforce their attachment to the land and their respectful relationship with everything that exists. This trialogical relationship—human, nature, and the supernatural—is a Native understanding common to Mesoamerican cultures. In the case of the Maya, there is a pan-Maya base culture that is still practiced today, which provides unity in the diversity of Mayan cultures (Warren 1998; Montejo 2005). From this global point of view, Mayalogue focuses on Maya ideas and theories of knowledge, stemming from ancient and modern Maya civilization.

FIGURE 2.1. Mapa Lingüístico de Guatemala.

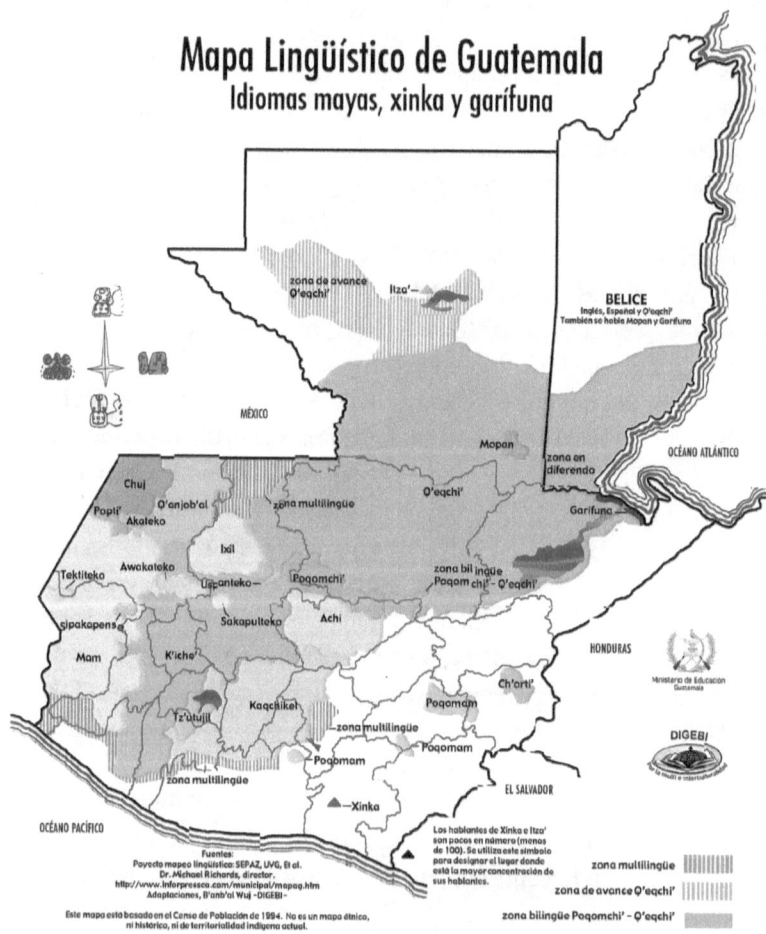

DECOLONIZING MAYA HISTORY AND CULTURES

THREE

AS I LEARNED IN GRADUATE SCHOOL from my mentors about the current trends in anthropology, I was also thinking about other ways of explaining human behavior from an Indigenous perspective. For me, it was necessary to study and be aware of the many anthropological theories proposed for the study of cultures. Indigenous organic intellectuals must be grounded in their culture and be at the forefront of the current struggle for intellectual decolonization.

I remember some Native American friends objecting to my training in anthropology. "How come you joined the white man and became an anthropologist?" I remember saying, "You cannot criticize what you don't know well. You must know the field, its theories, and methods to do constructive criticism. If you are not happy with what they do, then, present your own ideas and propose a new way that must include native ideas." And this is the reason for Mayalogue.

To criticize without a solid and alternative proposal does not help to decolonize the Native world. So, the question remains: Why think about the possibility of developing a Native theory of cultures? Or why should we bother to search for other ways of interpreting social reality from an Indigenous perspective? Can Indigenous People teach us new ways to think in conjunction with communities of persons, humans, and nonhumans that inhabit the world? As I have mentioned earlier, Indigenous People of the Americas have been neglected and their ideas or contributions have not been recognized for the past five centuries. They have been called backward Indians who needed to be assimilated or eliminated as the modern world takes over their lives and their resources. Some even think that Indigenous People are incapable of making reasonable use of their resources, so their lands are invaded for "development" projects. The Latin American states and transnational corporations only want to see obedient and passive Indians. When they resist, they are seen as "bad Indians" who are opposed to progress, or even worse, as subversives to be eliminated.

Another reason for presenting some ideas or Native theories at this point in history responds to the prophetic time known as the 13 B'ak'tun, or the end of the fifth millennia Maya, which occurred on December 21, 2012. This event sparked new concerns for the future of the world and all forms of life that it supports. Truly, major changes are already occurring on earth such as climate change—for example, melting of the glaciers, as well problems in other regions of the cosmos. Just as an old man told me in dreams, "The universe is infinite and perhaps changes are now occurring among the stars in the sky that will affect us. Look up," he then said. I looked up in the sky and focused my vision on the Andromeda galaxy and the Aries constellation, where he said changes have already started. Obviously, these cosmic events will not affect us in millions or billions of years, except by major catastrophes that may originate from earth itself, in relation to the sun.

According to the Nahua legend of the Fifth Sun, or the Maya myths in the *Popol Vuh*, major cyclical changes have already occurred on earth. The coming of major and painful changes was referred to by the Mayas as *k'ayilal* (extinction) or massive destruction of life on earth. These myths have been repeated in the oral tradition of Indigenous People, so that people may react and reorient their actions and their ways of life within these profound universal changes.

The ending of the Maya millennia or 13 B'ak'tun marked the beginning of a time for correcting humanity's wrong doings against itself and nature all over the world. For this reason, this is also the appropriate setting for the development of innovative theories following the common sense of respect and reciprocity, rather than greed and irrational exploitation of natural resources on the planet.

Of course, there have been major Indigenous contributors to human sciences and philosophies on this continent, but they have been mythicized to a point that their contribution to human knowledge has been categorized as myth and folklore. These Native philosophies and worldviews could have helped in a better understanding of Native cultures if they had been respected and valued instead of destroyed or demonized.

In ancient America we have major philosophers and wise men whose legacy have persisted until now, but whose names are not mentioned as major figures in the development of universal sciences and philosophies cherished by the Western world. This is the case of the Iroquois prophet and diplomat Deganawidah or "The One Who Knows," founder of the League of Nations, which was based on the philosophy of peace, unity, and democracy. The teaching of Deganawidah was unique in the "New World," and it influenced major thinkers such as Lewis Henry Morgan, whose work in turn also influenced the philosophical thought of Karl Marx and other Marxist theorists. Deganawidah's contribution to world peace and his legacy for the construction of real democracy and unity among the six nations is a very good example of the intellectual contribution of Native leaders and prophets. His proposal for a peaceful world was based not only on the absence of war, but on the development of a confederacy that could protect human beings, the land, and resources. This was a way to please the Creator, as the Haudenosaunee (Iroquois) replicated the universe in the longhouse, thus sanctifying their territories that provide for their living. Deganawidah's teaching and philosophy of life was based on the trilogy: humans, nature, and the supernatural as a cosmic unity that must be nurtured though prayers, songs, ceremonies, and rituals for its maintenance and proper functioning.

While creating the League of Nations, or the Iroquois Confederacy, Deganawidah left his teachings on how to maintain unity by giving reverence to the land or Mother Earth. He instructed the chiefs that whenever they had a United Nation's council, the Onondaga who had the role as that of the Speaker of the House.

> Shall make and address and return thanks to the earth where men dwell, to the streams of water, the pools, the springs, and the lakes, to the maize and the fruits, to the medicinal herbs and the trees, to the forest trees for their usefulness, to the animals that serve as food and give their pelts for clothing, to the great winds and the lesser winds, to the Thunders, to the Sun, the mighty warrior, to the Moon, to the messengers of the Creator who reveal his wishes, and to the Great Creator who dwells in the heavens above, who gives all things useful to men, and who is the source and the ruler of health and life. (Peterson 1990:76)

In Mesoamerica, a similar prophet and statesman also emerged and left behind great teachings and commandments that continue to be cherished by Indigenous populations. This is Quetzalcoatl, or the Plumed Serpent, also known by the Mayas as Q'uq'ul-kan. He was the architect for the revision and establishment of the ancient Maya calendar and its cyclical prophecies. As in any ancient civilization, the birth of the prophet and philosopher was predicted through a prophetic dream. Hueman the Elder foretold the emergence of a great king and ruler, so he prepared the Toltecs to receive the great ruler Quetzalcoatl. But prior to the coming of Quetzalcoatl, "Hueman wrote the axioms of the ancient knowledge, the metaphors and the philosophy, and recorded all the astrological knowledge, architectural data, and secret arts of his time. After summarizing everything, he sealed the book and branded it Teomoxtli" (Diaz 2002:2–3).

Hueman the Elder was then a philosopher and a prophet, and the above account tells us that the Toltecs did have science, which was not separate from religion, politics, and the counting of the days. This must have been a well-established Native theory that guided the life and action of all the people through rituals, ceremonies, games, and festivals to celebrate this interrelationship or cosmic unity.

Quetzalcoatl, or Q'uq'ul-kan, was a great ruler and prophet. He was persecuted by factions of the Toltecs and traveled to Chichen Itza in the Maya land. There, he was received with honors and he helped to build the cities, bringing peace and sharing knowledge with the people. "In each place he searched for knowledge among the elders and the wise ones and studied their beliefs, customs, and ways of life. That is how he perfected his own wisdom" (Diaz 2002:137).

The Quetzalcoatl presented here was a prophet, a philosopher and a wise ruler. He did not impose his view, but was willing to learn from other cultural traditions (the Maya) to perfect his wisdom. We can then, definitively say that ancient cultures of Mesoamerica shared their cultural traditions, and they were civilizations that practiced a way of life that was respectful of other people in relation to their environment and the spiritual world. The knowledge of the ancient Toltecs generated by thinkers such as Quetzalcoatl, who created the arts, writing, the calendar, poetry, and sacred stories of creation were continued by the *tlamantini*, or "wise man and woman" and the *tlahcuilo* (painter or scribe). The knowledge and wisdom of these elders were documented by Bernardino de Sahagún in the *Huehuetlatolli*, as part of the Florentine Codex (León-Portilla 1999).

Once again, we can insist that the understanding of Native people's world, life, and existence is holistic and totally linked to the supernatural realm. For example, agriculture is a human activity that needs the rain, a natural element. But the rain is also petitioned to Hunab' K'uh, so that it is measured to avoid an excess or the lack of it, if not, it could also cause suffering and destruction. This was the role of the prayer-maker, who is the intermediary between the supernatural beings and humans. In this context, the action of planting is not, then, an isolated activity but part of a series of events and rituals that involve the mountains, the heavens, prayers, and songs by the specialists for softening the will of K'uh, the lord of thunder, lightning, and rain. This reciprocal relationship between humans, nature, and the spiritual world is what the early missionaries witnessed in Mesoamerica among the Nahua and the Maya. So, by not understanding the sacred dimension of these ceremonies, the missionaries persecuted them as devil worshipers. This is how the rituals and knowledge of Indigenous People were condemned and satanized for getting rid of this millennial religious practice of the Maya. Unfortunately, no attention was given to this universal theory of unity, respect, mutual understanding, compassion, and reciprocity, which explains the daily life of Indigenous People in relation to the other beings and the natural world. This is the global framing that guided their action in relation to other living beings with which they share life on earth.

In Central Mexico, missionaries like Hernando Ruíz de Alarcón collected material on curing practices and incantations for every human action on earth. These prayers had to do with health, suffering, illnesses, happiness, war, famine, agriculture, fishing, hunting, travel, politics, and economics. These missionaries did not collect this knowledge for learning from them, but for rooting out their traditions, knowledge, and religious practices. Since then, cultural practices and religious beliefs of Indigenous People have been seen as barbaric—something that needed to be controlled by the civilized European conquerors and colonists. In his *Treatise*, Hernando de Alarcon wrote about Indigenous beliefs and traditions in this way.

> The ignorance or naiveté of almost all the Indians ... is so great according to general opinion; all are very easily persuaded of whatever one might want to lead them to believe. Thus, because of their ignorance, they had, and have, much a variety of gods and such different modes of adoration that, having resolved to ascertain the basis of their beliefs and what they all are, we find as little to get hold of as if we tried to squeeze smoke or wind in our fist. (Ruíz de Alarcón 1986:43)

As we can see, early missionaries were the first one to misunderstand Indigenous cultures and traditions. They were predisposed to attack and destroy Native religious traditions and spirituality because they thought Indigenous People were heathens, never exposed to the word of God. So, what was a culturally viable way of life for centuries or millennia became a major problem—something to get rid of, according to early missionaries and colonists. Unfortunately, early anthropologist took these reports at face value and continued to devalue and misrepresent Indigenous cultures and worldviews.

Referring to this holistic and contrasting worldview held by the Natives in terms of their spirituality, Andrews and Ross wrote the following:

> A further distinction between Christianity and the Native religion lay in their fundamental view of the physical world. The dominant Western view held the non-biological world to be filled with lifeless objects. The Native view held it to be full of animate beings—clouds, fire, and so forth. Consequently, two very different perspectives on causation were in contrast. To the Natives, whatever had happened would happen as the result of one's relationship to these entities. The world is seen not as random and accidental but has supremely ordered—supernatural involvement was the natural order. To the Westerner, however, the world lacked this comprehensive, supernatural flavor. (Andrews and Hassig 1984:22)

While Ruíz de Alarcón collected samples of Nahuatl incantations and prayers related to curing rituals he called curiosities and superstitions, another missionary, Diego Durán, engaged in learning the language and interviewing the elders to document the antiquities of their ancestors. The reason for documenting thoroughly the Indigenous cultures of Central Mexico was to understand them, as a step to eradicate what he called the Natives' idolatry. To Diego Durán, the knowledge system of these Natives was equated with a great disease that has contaminated them for centuries or millennia.

Fortunately, not all missionaries were so eager to destroy Indigenous cultures like Diego Durán among the Mexica, or Diego de Landa among the Mayas. Another Spanish missionary, Fray Bernardino de Sahagún, dedicated most of his life to documenting Nahua history and culture through systematic questioning and interviews with the elders. The knowledge of the elders was called *huehuetlahtolli*, or the ancient words. In this effort he came to understand and value ancient Mesoamerican religion and philosophy.

The work of documentation done by Sahagun was unique because he himself, being a priest, could document and save what others were destroying and condemning as the devil's trick among the Indians. Sahagún was the first to argue that "the truth, wrapped in the vestments of myth and considered to be the product of wisdom, is symbolically attributed to Quetzalcoatl, the personification of wisdom" (León Portilla 1999:29).

In other words, Sahagun understood the uniqueness of Mesoamerican ideas and he gave a place to this knowledge in his own ethnographic writing. In this way he showed the importance of the accumulated knowledge of the Mexicans, which was being destroyed by missionaries and by the colonial government. Fray Bernardino de Sahagún did extraordinary research on Nahua culture, writing historical, ethnographic, and linguistic works that he compiled into multiple volumes called the *Florentine Codex*. For his contribution in rescuing and doing research on Native knowledge, religion, languages, and cultures, Bernardino de Sahagún was called the "first ethnographer of the Americas" (León-Portilla 1999).

In the Mayab' or the Maya region in Central America, the same cruelty and perverse actions were taken against the Indigenous People. Despite the king's order to document the histories and cultures of the Indians, as well as their belief systems and antiquities for knowing more about their origin, the missionaries persecuted them, destroying their knowledge and cultures. Among them, Bishop Diego de Landa was the cruelest missionary who managed to destroy the ancient knowledge of the Mayas. After burning their books and libraries in Yucatan, he defended his malevolent action by saying: "They contained nothing but the teachings of the devil, so I burned them. And the Indians took it with great pain" (Landa 1941). Obviously, the Mayas cried and were in despair when they saw the books containing their teachings, arts, science, and literature being burned. This ethnocidal action was purposely carried out to leave an entire civilization without history—an orphan of knowledge. The books of *Chilam Balam of Tizimin* refer to the anguish and sorrow that the Mayas felt by the burning of their books.

> With rivers of tears we mourned our sacred writings amid the delicate flowers of sorrow in the days of the katun (11 *Ahaw*) ... When they had succeeded in reducing the population, the compassion of heaven set a price upon our lives. Should we not lament in our suffering, grieving for the loss of our maize and the destruction of our teachings concerning the universe of the earth and the universe of the heavens? (Makemson 1951:3-4)

After committing this unspeakable action and cultural ethnocide, Bishop Diego de Landa tried to rewrite the Maya's history and culture. He tried what Bernardino de Sahagun did among the Mexicas of Central Mexico—gathering the most knowledgeable elders for eliciting information about their antiquities (*payat tzoti'*), but the elders did not respond. They were fearful of Landa because of his previous actions, so they desisted from informing him about their knowledge, writing, and culture. Nevertheless, a couple of young informants were convinced, and with their help he created the now-known Landa's Alphabet, which was an attempt to understand Maya hieroglyphic writing. Later, a few old men gave Landa some information on their ancient ways of life and histories, so that Landa could document their histories in his: "*Relación de las Cosas de Yucatán*" (Tozzer 1941). This is an important account, which provided firsthand information on what was left of their science, religion, and writing systems. Landa refers to their dedication to the sciences, religion, and the writing of books for educational purposes as follows: "They provided priests for the towns when they were needed, examining them in the sciences and ceremonies, and committed to them the duties of their office, and the good example to people and provided them with books and sent them forth. And they employed themselves in the duties of the temples and in teaching their sciences as well as in writing books about them" (Tozzer 1941:27).

After committing such an atrocity, Diego de Landa was repentant, and he tried to rescue what he had destroyed, such as the hieroglyphic writing system. Unfortunately, not much was revealed to Landa after his attack against Maya culture. His informants only gave him glimpses of their sophisticated writing system, as well as memories of their histories, sciences, and antiquities.

According to what Landa had stated above, Maya science and knowledge was passed on from generation to generation through a systematic education in the *kuyum* (school) or centers for higher education. For them, education was practical, since the purpose was to use it in everyday life. In other words, Maya education was not just informational, but mostly experiential. The way they applied their sciences to real life could have been a major foundation for a global theory of Maya culture, but much of their scientific knowledge was lost, and transformed throughout colonial domination and forced conversion to Christianity. As Luis Enrique Sam Colop, a Maya scholar, said about the transcription of the original *Popol Vuh*, "Here, we have to warn that, those who transcribed the text into the Latin alphabet, they did it under religious persecution, and even then, they left as a legacy this text, which is unique in its genera. That this document was later copied by Ximenez, a priest who came to believe that the author of that book was the devil himself" (Sam Colop 2008:14).

Fortunately, not everything was lost, since much has been documented in the ethnographies written by anthropologists during the first half of the twentieth century. It has become necessary to reread these early ethnographies to understand the continuity of Maya knowledge and sciences.

As I think of a Native theory of culture, the work of Peruvian Felipe Guaman Poma de Ayala comes to mind. His works of resistance and his contribution to the knowledge of Inca culture under colonial rule was the most powerful historical and methodological contribution by a Native intellectual. In other words, we can consider Guamán Poma de Ayala's magnificent work *Nueva crónica y buen gobierno* (1615) as a forceful testimony of indigenous Andean cultures under destruction by war, diseases, and forced labor in the mines. Guamán Poma de Ayala was outspoken against the silencing of Andean culture and the elimination of their traditional ways of life during the colonial period (Andía Chávez 2002). So, in a process of validating Indigenous cultures and languages in their own terms, Guamán Poma de Ayala took the task of transposing oral tradition into the written text to prove that the Incas had a powerful organized culture and rulership before the coming of the Spaniards.

Unfortunately, Guamán Poma, as a convert to Christianity, followed the early missionaries who argued that the Incas were descendants of the sons of Adam or Noah, although, he used the historiographical method to argue that despite their origin, they were not inferior to the Spaniards. He argued that the Incas were a very organized society with strict laws of government that controlled and ruled human behavior. Guamán Poma de Ayala can be considered the first auto-historian of this continent who wrote his *Nueva crónica* to show that the Andean Natives were intelligent beings with rights as original inhabitants of these lands.

Consequently, Guamán Poma suffered persecution and exile because of his denunciation of the abuses against the human rights of Indigenous People of Peru. As in Mesoamerica, the Indigenous People of the Andean region were exploited and enslaved by Spanish missionaries, *encomenderos* and official authorities (Andía Chávez 2002). His methodology of illustrated passages on his book was developed to visualize these abuses, so that the king could see the reality and react with pity and compassion to stop these abuses against the Natives. The *Nueva crónica* can be considered an early contribution to the field of Native American studies, which allowed for the self-representation of the Natives in search of human dignity and respect for their ancient knowledge and cultures.

As I have mentioned earlier, Native Americans or Indigenous People of the Americas had major Native exponents in the sciences and humanities in the past, but their contribution have not been recognized as positive or valuable contributions by Western academics. Most often, Indigenous contributions have been ignored or rejected, despite evidence that they have developed their sciences, architecture, philosophy, religion, agriculture, mathematics, ancient writings, perfect calendars, and astronomy, like the Mayas.

Knowing that these contributions exist, outsiders or pseudoscholars have created "denial theories" to dismiss Native contributions. By accrediting these great intellectual achievements to non-Natives or even extraterrestrial beings, they are asserting that Indigenous People are incapable of great achievements. In the case of the Mayas, their most brilliant achievements in mathematics, architecture, astronomy, and a most perfect Maya calendar are said to have been given to them by survivors of the lost continent of Atlantis. Other, such as the Church of Jesus Christ of Latter-day Saints (Mormons) said that Maya culture was the product of the teaching of knowledgeable men from one of the Lost Tribes of Israel, and from descendants of Noah, and so on. Others believe that Maya technology, hieroglyphic writing, and the Maya calendar were provided by ancient astronauts who once helped the Indigenous People of Mesoamerica (Von Daniken 1968; Jose Argüelles 1987).

> From the time of Columbus to the present day, unending stream of Western writers have concocted fanciful explanations for the origin and cultural achievements of the Mesoamerican Indians. We refer to them as Romanticists because their ideas have been highly speculative, and for the most part based on preconceived religious notions about how the world ought to be. Almost all these explanations are ethnocentric, rooted in the belief that cultural sophistication could only be achieved by Europeans, and therefore Mesoamerica's cultural developments must have resulted from ideas originating outside the region. The romantic explanations of Mesoamerica have not stood the test of time, but they continue to be proposed and to have ardent followers even today. (Carmack, Gasco, and Gosen 1995:22)

There is then, a continuous negation of the humanity of the Indigenous People and their supposed incapacity to produce intelligent discoveries, or to create a sophisticated culture as that of the Mayas, Incas, or ancient Nahuas. The current critical moment in Maya history, or the closing of the fifth millennia, *Oxlanh B'ak'tun*, has been a fertile moment for these pseudoscholars who continue to propose denial theories. For example, some argue for the ending of the world and a time when the children of light, or the ancient Mayas, will return from their thousand-year trip through the galaxies. These denial theories are racist statements that negate the human abilities of Indigenous People to produce knowledge. In other words, these theories negate Indigenous intelligence, arguing that they are incapable of creating something worth of admiration such as the achievements of ancient Maya civilization, which still marvels and amuses scholars and researchers today.

Contrary to these racist arguments, the writing of Mayalogue or the theory of interrelationships is an effort to show and value the persistence of Native intellectual traditions that hopefully will become more recognized and cherished in the centuries yet to come.

MAYALOGUE: THE TREATY OF MAYA IDEAS   FOUR
Q'inal: Time, Life, and Existence

WE HAVE DISCUSSED, briefly, the development of anthropological theories, mainly those that have historically restricted the cultural and scientific expression of Indigenous People from the inside. These theoretical developments served mainly the purpose of explaining Indigenous cultures' "backwardness," compared to the progress and success of Western civilization. In other words, the scientific study of mankind was simply a comparative study of the advancement of the imperial world in comparison to the rest. Anthropological theory of the twentieth century erred in part because of its own bias, and because it did not consider that other cultures such as the Nahuas, Mayas, and Incas had greater civilizations in the past. The general image imposed on millions of people of this continent was that of the naked and uncivilized Indian. If early missionaries had not burned the ancient books of the Mayas and kept destroying their knowledge throughout the centuries of colonization, we might now have a more accurate description of their sciences and a different appreciation or image of their descendants. According to Walter Mignolo (2011), the disqualification of Indigenous knowledge in America occurred because of the "Management and control of knowledge (for example, theology and the invention of international law) that set up a geo-political order of knowledge founded on European epistemic and aesthetic principles that legitimized the disqualifications over the centuries of non-European knowledge and non-Europeans aesthetic standards, from the Renaissance to the Enlightenment and from the Enlightenment to neoliberal globalization" (Mignolo 2011:49).

As we can see, some theories proposed here have mentioned the existence of internal structures, functions, and sometimes the ideological ways of how Native cultures work. But at the end, these theorists have decided to configure Native cultures within a Eurocentric cultural frame of mind, thus restricting the free expressions of Indigenous worldviews.

Here, I will mention some of these hints of recognition by early scholars about Indigenous paradigms that were only observed, but not developed into mainstream theories of culture. One reason was that these Native ideas were blurred by colonial domination, of which anthropology was a part, thus, showing the failure of the social sciences by not weaving into their proposed cultural theories Native ideas that are still relevant and useful.

This was the time when Native ideas were still vibrant in the so-called closed corporate communities (Wolf 1957), which were not totally open to the outside world. These are the places, or Native communities where early anthropologists worked and spent long periods of time doing fieldwork. This close contact or interaction called participant-observation could have had a more positive outcome, if only the researcher came to do fieldwork with the intention of learning from the Natives. But instead, Western researchers or anthropologists brought with them their own mainstream theories and tried to interpret Native accounts fitting the data to please their mentors, while disfiguring Native cultures in the process.

I have always argued that we must work within the politics of Indigenous People and stop these biased modes of representation (Montejo 2005). The "authority" of the ethnographer who has been successful in cementing his interpretation as the truth must change. It is time for local knowledge (Geertz 1983) or Indigenous truths to be accepted in the Native's own terms. I suggest that if anthropologists really want to learn while doing research on Indigenous communities, they simply must consider Native knowledge as real knowledge and not as superstition, folklore, or weird ways that causes foreigners to experience disgust and "culture shock." Yes, culture shock has been used to describe this form of contempt for Native cultures and the rejection of their ways of life as described by anthropologists who come out of fieldwork as heroes/heroines, triumphant over "wild and uncivilized" Natives. Unfortunately, the result of fieldwork and the processed information called ethnographies rarely returns to the communities studied, on the argument that Native s are mostly illiterate and do not read or care about written reports. In other words, anthropologists abandon the communities studied as soon as they are done collecting information. Even in this century, most researchers do not care why the Indigenous People they have studied continue to live in poverty, neglected by their governments. Anthropology, then, did not have much cultural, political, or economic impact that could benefit the Indigenous communities studied for more than a century.

In the case of the Mayas, it is important to read early ethnographies such as that of Oliver La Farge (1931), Ruth Bunzel (1952), Robert Redfield (1964), among others, who documented more pristine cultural information during the first half of the twentieth century. These ethnographies describe more accurately the way of life and thinking of the Mayas just before the massive intrusion of technologies, transportation, and even Protestantism.

Currently, the training of young anthropologists focuses more on the classical ethnographies and theories in anthropology by consecrated figures in the field. Most of the time, students and new scholars are happy to read each other's work and forget to read the original ethnographies, which are documents that provide firsthand information on the ways of life and ceremonies that are still practiced by the Mayas today. I am not suggesting that modern ethnographies are not important, but if we must penetrate the deeper meanings of Indigenous cultures, we must read Native accounts, early anthropological ethnographies, and modern interpretations of these cultures. So, in terms of interpretation and (re)presentation of cultures, anthropologists must be careful and respectful in describing ceremonies if allowed, since these are the truths practiced by Indigenous People. In other words, they believe and live their own ceremonies and for them, a ceremony does what they say it does. In other words, they don't need an interpreter to tell them the meanings of what they are saying or doing.

From a Mayalogical point of view, this tri-dimensional multilogue between and among humans, nature, and the supernatural realm is the best way for Indigenous People to practice their belief systems in relation to everything else that exists. This is the case with the Navajo Nightway, a healing ceremony, which is a good example of this cosmic unity that must be recognized, invoked and reenacted for restoring health and balance with the world.

> Thus, the Holy People do not themselves 'cause' illness. It is violation of humans of prescribed order and proper ceremonial observances and attitudes, conditions of balance, beauty, harmony, and peace that brings about illness. This order, these ceremonial observances, these proper social relations have been set down by the Holy People in Navajo history.

Illness is disorder, unbalance, and ugliness. Violation may, of course, sometimes be unintentional or committed through ignorance; re-balance and re-order come through appropriate and proper appeal to the Holy People. (Faris 1990:14–15)

As we can see from the Navajo worldview, the reason of illness and the consequence of putting together actions for restoring the stolen balance are important for recognizing the trialogical relationship. This is what Mayalogue, emphasizes with the concept of *komontatism*, which refers to the interrelatedness between communities of humans and nonhuman persons. Also, we recognize that human peace, harmony, happiness, and balance can be altered into illness or unbalance for violating the norms, rules, and prescriptions of behavior established by the Supernatural (Holy People). This illness is then the result of a disrespectful rupture of the proper social relationship either with humans, nature, or the supernatural world. This philosophy of life or interrelatedness (*salap*) is universal and the foundation for the behavior and action of Native people in the Americas and all around the world.

BASES OF MAYALOGUE

I used the term *Mayalogue* as a treaty of ideas and knowledge system, stemming from ancient and modern Maya civilization. This body of knowledge produced by the Mayas has been dispersed in Native texts, hieroglyphic writing, ethnographies, history, and literary production through time and space. Little by little, this Maya knowledge is fading away and it needs to be documented and presented as a valid body of cultural traditions that must be synthesized. For a long time, these scientific, philosophical, and cultural systems have been seen as fragments of a decaying Maya civilization. But for modern Mayas, their culture is still alive, and it constantly creates and re-creates itself. Thus, paraphrasing Eric Wolf (1982), to me cultures are not static, but dynamic ways of life that are always in a constant process of construction, dismantling, reconstruction or renewal. In this way, Maya culture carries out and produces a body of knowledge that is "logical," just as any other culture or civilization around the world, so that Maya culture is then Mayalogical.

The voices and point of view of the Natives must be allowed and respected in the anthropological practice. Experts in Maya culture such as anthropologist Dennis Tedlock have understood this situation as he proposed a different approach to the study of cultures he called "dialogical anthropology" (Tedlock 1987). That anthropology should not be a monologue in which, after fieldwork, it is the sole task of the anthropologist to process and interpret the data collected and write the ethnography. In this way, the Natives are not allowed to talk, so any reference to them appears only as brief notes or appendixes to the main text or ethnography. Dialogical anthropology shows a hermeneutical process in which dialogue must be initiated at the field and continued up to the writings and productions of ethnographies.

As we can see, "dialogical anthropology" advocates for multivocality. That is, to give voice to the Natives, while listening to them and including their points of view in the ethnographic writing. We must make sure that this dialogue is not only between anthropologists and Natives, but has Tedlock has stated: dialogical anthropology is not a dialogue between two individuals but a "dialogue across cultures."

Despite its interactive role, one of the limitations of dialogical anthropology is the persistence of a conditioned dialogue between and across cultures. Here the anthropologist as an authority is still the one who initiates a "dialogue" or questioning that is geared toward his or her own anthropological research project. But Mayalogue proposes a trialogue or the *komontatism* approach to cultures (*a community of beings and their relationships*), where Indigenous People understand themselves as part of a whole in a continuous process of reciprocity. This is a trilogy of equal power and responsibility in the interaction between humans, nature, and the supernatural world.

FIGURE 4.1. Interrelationship as equals between humans, nature, and the supernatural to produce meditated action reciprocity.

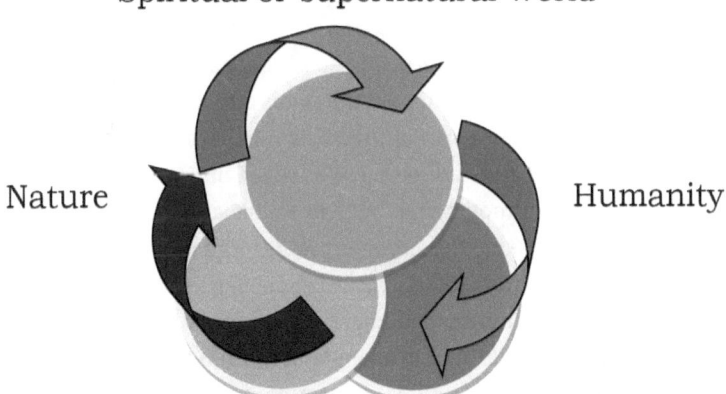

In Mayalogue I present the cultural concept of unity in diversity, or the power relation between and among the three elements fundamental to life in which no one is more important than the other. Here, the three elements interact and contribute equally to the production and continuity of life *q'inal*, as well as the maintenance of the whole. We must understand culture as a forceful relationship among the three fundamental categories: humans, nature, and the supernatural world, which are generative of life and existence. Each part or element individually affects the other and vice versa. So, to have some harmony, we must observe and comply with the rules and norms of conduct established by the ancestors as we live and experience life in our communities.

The failure in the observance of one of these generative elements, mostly the supernatural, can alter the harmony or rhythm of life and create conflicts that can affect societies and nature, thus causing world imbalance. There must be a reciprocal relationship between and among these three entities if we want to maintain healthiness, peace, relative harmony, and happiness in our mutual survival.

The tendency to see cultures from a Mayalogical (*komontatistic*) perspective, which is an Indigenous theory, has not been explored and discussed as a theory at all. One of the reasons, as mentioned above, is that Native people are still seen as "backward people" who lack the capacity for developing a sophisticated civilization as in the West. In this way, their profound and reciprocal relationship with the natural world has been labeled animism. Animism has been defined by early anthropologists as a primitive stage of the mind by which "savages" gave spirits to everything, as they fear the unknown.

Obviously then, there has been a long and historical distortion of Native cultures to the point of disfiguring the Native image of a normal human being. This racist discrimination that has treated Indigenous People as inferior beings must be eradicated as we recognize that humans are equal everywhere in the world. Another reason is that there have not been that many Native scholars who have questioned the status quo in anthropology, while also being critical of their own cultures. The role of the Natives in the ethnographies have been reduced to that of a "smart informant" for justifying the authority of the ethnographer, or "bad informants" to explain failures of the ethnographer in eliciting and interpreting ethnographic information.

Sometimes, the anthropologist as a social scientist has come to a personal conclusion, far removed from the Indigenous cultures studied. This is due to the pressure to be scientific and to adapt or accommodate (force) their data within a theoretical framework that is current or popular at his or her time of research and ethnographic writing (Marcus and Fisher 1986). With this, I am not saying that existing theories on cultures are all good or are all bad, but they are intellectual instruments that can be used to generate an ample array of possibilities for explaining, describing, presenting, or representing different cultures and worldviews with which we have contact and interaction. This is the case of Mesoamerican cultures, which interacted and shared major ideas prior to the coming of Europeans, such as hieroglyphic writing, the vigesimal system, the calendar, life centered on corn, and so forth. "With this interaction, Maya culture has received, undoubtedly, influences from outside but in generality its particular worldview is maintained, because its essence lies in Maya culture itself" (Yojcom Roche 2013:64).

A culture, then, cannot be understood from the library, from the office desk, or from sporadic visits to the community. Indigenous worlds such as that of the Mayas revolve around the cyclical Maya calendar, which has established special days for human activities, natural elements, animals, supernatural beings, heroes, and ancestors. There are ceremonies that are sacred and secret, performed in isolation or at midnight where intruders are not allowed. But if intruders are to be present, the ceremonies are modified. Indigenous cultures are very complex and must be respected as any other Indigenous or non-Indigenous traditions around the world.

For this purpose, there is a need to revitalize Indigenous cultures, starting with showing respect for the elders and their cultures—respect for their rights to live and their peaceful coexistence with other creatures on earth with whom they share the breath of life. In other words, Native knowledge should encompass the recognition of these fundamental forms of mutuality and reciprocity—the idea of a global community that transcends into an integrated whole: humans, nature, and the universe of the sun, moon (supernatural beings). Through this Native model or Mayalogue, we will approach the world of the Mayas and other Indigenous cultures elsewhere.

We have an enormous amount of works written by scholars (anthropologists, sociologists, linguists, epigraphers, etc.) about Maya culture, but what is lacking or missing is a concrete explanation of Maya worldview stemming from Indigenous or emic point of view. We need a broader analysis of Maya culture, knowledge systems, and their traditional lifestyles in relation to their natural environment and the supernatural realm. Much Maya knowledge and its epistemology has been lost or not given the importance that it deserves. But as a Maya, I am interested in searching at the heart of my own culture, hoping to rescue and give life to what is in danger of disappearing —or at least, to bring awareness to our existence as Indigenous People, giving importance to our cultures within this modern world of technology, which is moving us further away from human feelings and more toward the automatization of the world.

One major argument to develop in this work is the idea that for Mayas, human beings come to life with a special mission to fulfill. To be humans is not to dominate, control and overexploit nature as we have been led by Western capitalist world economy and industrialization. Western thinkers have cheered their triumph over the natural world by claiming that "We are able, through scientific thinking, to achieve mastery over nature" (Lévi-Strauss 1978:6). By agreeing on this view of human achievement that can affect the future of humanity, we have come to limit our mental powers, because we reject Native worldviews as nonscientific, and in consequence, not worth a systematic attention.

Mayalogue is an attempt to explain in a unified picture the traditional patterns or ways of life among the Mayas of Mesoamerica, and to synthesize Maya knowledge from the insider's perspective. I hope to provide Indigenous and non-Indigenous People a conceptual framework that will help to understand the ways of life of Indigenous People that have been disturbed by Western colonialism. I can affirm that Mayas have a respectful approach to life, its reproduction, and its maintenance. For them, everyday-life activities have a spiritual significance because they incorporate the individual, the community, the environment, and the spiritual world. This is explained by Rigoberta Menchú when a newborn child is cleansed and integrated to the community. "Four candles are placed on the corners of the bed to represent the four corners of the house and show him that this will be his home. They symbolize the respect the child must have for his community" (Menchú 1984:12).

Similarly, the construction of a house in Maya communities was the replication of the four corners of earth and the universe. The place for its construction must be sanctified, and the four poles at the corners of the house are supposed to be the four corners of the universe, called the *skanh txukut* in Jakaltek cosmology. The idea of the four corners and four directions, as mentioned in the *Popol Vuh*, is a Mesoamerican concept known and used by Nahuas and Mayas throughout the centuries or millennia. According to Thomas Ward, "It becomes clear that some pre-Hispanic parceling found ways to survive in the Hispanic Christian world. In a central Mexican context, these four subdivisions respected the standard Mesoamerican quadrilateral layout of the world" (Ward 2018:63).

FIGURE 4.2. Sacred House of the Prayer-maker at *Ch'imb'an*, San Miguel Acatán, Guatemala.

Other activities such as the tending of the cornfield or the counting of the days in the Maya calendar, all respond to cosmological principles that govern the life of humankind according to the Maya worldview. The meanings of this complex representation of life or the reasons for being humans can be explained in terms of Maya epistemology. Maya ways of knowing and learning emanates from a collective or cosmic consciousness not yet totally understood by the global society.

In this text we also use the concept of *komontat*, which is a Jakaltek Maya term that refers to the sacred land and territory set aside for the cultivation of the people's corn. This corn is used to feed the people during communal ceremonies and the sacred authorities throughout their yearlong service to the community. The *alkal-txah*, or "sacred authority" is a politico-religious office destined to serve God, the community and to make sure that the land and nature are protected and respected following the ordering of the days from the sacred Maya calendar. We can argue that *komontat* is a model of coordinated effort that unifies human activity with production, which must respond to the needs of the community and that feeds the people, honoring the ancestors during their gathering for religious festivities.

Having said this, the Native exegesis to follow, will be a deconstruction of the most significant treasure of ancient Maya thought, the *Popol Vuh*, or the *Sacred Book of the Mayas* (Goetz and Morley 1950). This ancient text provides a solid foundation for Mayalogue, as well as the sacred Maya calendar or the *b'isom tz'ayik* (instrument for counting the days), also called here the "great unifying idea." I am aware of numerous publications and interpretations of the *Popol Vuh*, and I refer to some of them (Tedlock 1996; López 1999; Sam Colop 2008; Quiróa 2011), which are very useful references. But my purpose here is to make relevant the trialogical sequence—human-nature-spirit—which are evident in Maya ethnohistorical documents such as the *Título de los Senores de Totonicapán* (Carmack and Mondloch 1983), *Memorial de Sololá* (Otzoy 1999), and the *Rabinal Achí* (Tedlock 2003). Even in the context of a pre-Hispanic war among the Rabinal and the Quiche nations, the captive Cawek of the Forest People makes a speech giving farewell to his mountains, thus showing this strong connection argued in Mayalogue.

> Lord Five Thunder
> If I may be allowed
> Before Sky
> Before Earth
> To speak my words now
> In your teeth, sir
> In your face, sir:
> Now give me thirteen score days
> Thirteen score nights.
> I have yet to say farewell
> To the face of my mountain
> The face of my valley
> Where I walked
> Where I moved
> On all four edges
> In all four corners
> In the course of searching
> Striving
> To provide myself
> With meals
> With morsels. (Tedlock 2003:118–19)

The *Popol Vuh* is a text that may have been written in Maya hieroglyphs in pre-Hispanic times (Tedlock 1996), but as we already know, the missionaries burned the books of the Mayas, destroying their accumulated knowledge through time. Fortunately, a copy of this ancient Mesoamerican text survived destruction and was transcribed from Maya hieroglyphic writing to Maya language using Latin characters. That is how, Francisco Ximénez, the parish priest of Santo Tomás de Chuwila' (Chichicastenango) found the manuscript on the attic roof of his convent, so he took the job of translating it into Spanish, sometime between 1701 to 1703. The Ximénez manuscript did survive the colonial period in Guatemala, but it was taken out of the country and now it is housed at the Newberry Library of Chicago, waiting to be repatriated one day to Guatemala.

MAYALOGUE AND THE COSMIC UNITY OF LIFE:
THE *POPOL VUH*

As in the case of Guamán Poma de Ayala who recorded the Inca Empire's history, the anonymous author of the *Popol Vuh* was an educated Maya who followed the doctrine of the Christian missionaries. But unlike Guamán Poma, he wrote down the sacred stories of creation to show the antiquity of the inhabitants of the land. In this way he defended their rights and territories that were being parceled among *encomenderos, missionaries*, and Spanish captains of war. The one who wrote the *Popol Vuh* was apologetic to the missionaries, while carefully stating that he was just writing down the ancient traditions, under the law of God and Christianity "because now the *Popol Vuh*, as it is called, cannot be seen anymore ... The original book, written long ago, existed, but its sight is hidden to the searcher and to the thinker" (Goetz and Morley 1950:79–80).

This statement of a "hidden text" can be interpreted in many ways. Literally, the *Popol Vuh* may have been buried or hidden in a place, because of missionaries burning the books of the Mayas (e.g., Bishop Diego de Landa). Or it is the metaphor of what is hidden in the pages of the text and not revealed, which is evident here in this statement: "its sight hidden to the searcher and the thinker."

The *Popol Vuh* has been translated in most languages of the world and read and reread by anthropologists, Mayanists, and all sort of scholars. But the meanings and teachings encoded in the *Popol Vuh* remain largely hidden to the modern searchers and thinkers. Most modern Mayas, not to mention the anthropologists or Mayanists, cannot interpret the teachings and lessons provided in the *Popol Vuh* as our ancestors did, since we don't believe or practice it anymore. For example, the Maya calendar, which is still among us is largely ignored and considered an esoteric instrument useful only to "shamans" or Maya priests. In other words, we do not follow it as our ancestors did. We don't live or follow the rules, the designs, the omens, and the predictions or prophecies established to clear and prepare our path toward the future. We can say that this knowledge is implicit there in the book, but it remains hidden from our sight.

To focus on the Mayalogical relationships expressed in the *Popol Vuh*, we will discuss the creation of the first human beings, showing the failures and achievements of those who helped the Creator. There were several trials in the process of creating human beings, but in each one there was consultation, dialogue, collaboration, and joint decision. "They talked, then, discussing and deliberating; they agreed, they united their words and their thoughts." These words from the *Popol Vuh* teach us that major decisions should be discussed, agreed on, and even consulted to the Hearth of Heaven or Creator. In other words, nothing occurs without a consultation or collective decision for action. This process of democratic participation is called *lah-ti'*, literally to compare the mouth, which in Jakaltek Maya language means to compare or balance ideas and discourses to reach a consensus or a unified decision for action.

Here, the power of the words of creation is like that of the Christian Bible. "Earth, they said, and instantly it was made" (Goetz and Morley 1950:83). Then, the land was populated with trees and plants that covered the surface of earth. In this order, earth, plants, and trees were created first. "Then they made the small wild animals, the guardians of the woods, the spirits of the mountains, the deer, the birds, pumas, jaguars, serpents, snakes, vipers, guardians of the thickets" (Goetz and Morley 1950:84). But the helpers of the Creator were not happy to see earth without those who will nourish and give thanks for life to the Creator, so they decided to create the first human beings. First, they created the men made of mud, but they were not intelligent and did not respond to their mission on earth, so they were destroyed by water. Next came the men made of wood, who multiplied and were originally obedient, but then forgot their mission to protect life on earth, so they were punished for their misconduct. Thus, the *Popol Vuh* establishes the eras of human development and the continuous process of world building, world maintenance, and world renewal after the end of each era. What follows is a major teaching or lesson to be drawn from the *Popol Vuh*, a sacred text containing ancient Maya wisdom that reinforces my arguments in Mayalogue.

The second intent in creating human beings was the joint decision of the grandfather and grandmother Xpiyacoc and Ixmucane (mythical human ancestors), in consultation with the Hearth of Heaven, Heart of Earth (the Creator). All agreed that human beings must be made of wood. This was a successful creation since the people made of wood multiplied and populated the surface of earth. But then, the problem arose when they forgot their Creator and lost their souls and minds. They became selfish and destructive of their own environment. They lost their ways and forgot to nourish their Creator, and so they were punished and destroyed by a flood. A black rain fell from the sky by day and by night, while their dogs and utensils rebelled against them and punished them for their abusive behavior against the natural world.

> Then, there came the small animals and the large animals, and sticks and stones struck their face. And all began to speak: their earthen jars, their griddles, their plates, their pots, their grinding stones, all rose up and struck their faces. "You have done us much harm; you ate us, and now we shall kill you," said their dogs and birds of the barnyard. And the grinding stones said: "We were tormented by you; every day, every day, at night, at dawn, all the time our faces went *holi, holi, huqui, huqui*, because of you. This was the tribute we paid you. But now that you are no longer men, you shall feel our strength. We shall grind and tear your flesh to pieces," said their grinding stones. And then their dogs spoke and said: "Why did you give us nothing to eat? You scarcely looked at us, but you chased us and threw us out. You always had a stick ready to strike us while you were eating. "Thus, it was that you treated us. You did not speak to us. Perhaps we shall not kill you; but why did you not look ahead, why did you not think about yourselves? ... At the same time their griddles and pots spoke: "Pain and suffering you have caused us. Our mouths and our faces were blackened with soot, we were always put on the fire and you burned us as though we felt no pain. Now you shall feel it, we shall burn you," said their pots and destroyed their [wooden men's] faces. The stones of the earth (*tenamastes*), which were heaped together, hurled themselves straight from the fire against their heads causing them pain. The desperate ones [the men of wood] ran as quickly as they could; they wanted to climb to the tops of the houses, and the houses fell and threw them to the ground; they wanted to climb to the treetops, and the trees cast them far away; they wanted to enter the caverns, and the caverns repelled them. So was the ruin of the men who had been created and formed, the men made to be destroyed and annihilated. (Goetz and Morley 1950:91–92)

There are many lessons and teachings to be learned from this story of the wooden men. If the argument in Mayalogue is a tri-dimensional dialogue between the Creator, humans, and nature, here we can see the rupture of this collective consciousness of respect, thankfulness, and reciprocity that must exist as a norm for a balanced existence on earth. The creator allowed the men of wood to multiply, but then they forgot their mission to serve humanity and God by respecting the lives of other members of creation. Here we can see the overpopulation on earth and that humans became abusive to their natural environment and to the animals that served them for food and survival.

When I read this passage to my students in a class on Native American religion and philosophy, some students commented that it was funny, it was interesting, and it was nonsense. How can jars and pots talk? Others thought that those are stories of the past, nothing more than myths and folklore. Very few said that these stories were not that old, and they still have a message for us today. Effectively, we are now living in a world that has become far removed from the spiritual world, and the focus is on material wealth and accumulation. The *Popol Vuh* establishes that earth, trees, and animals were created first and that human beings were later created with the help and support of plants (corn), animals (the crow, the fox), and Grandfather and Grandmother, who responded to the Creator's will. This message from the *Popol Vuh* establishes that human beings do not have supremacy over the rest of creation, but that they are an integral part of it.

In the same way, we can interpret the actions and attitudes attributed to the utensils that attacked their owners—the grinding stones, pots, and jars getting mad and hitting the faces of the men made of wood as a punishment for disrespecting their tools and utensils that were there to facilitate their daily life. It was a common practice among Maya artisans, pottery makers, and so on to blow their breath on their hands (*xhuh-nhelaxi*) when manufacturing or handling something, because they knew that an object being created would have a mission to serve humans. With this act, they are infusing the original breath of creation into the objects being manufactured or created. In other words, for Indigenous People, everything has a "spirit of creation" throughout its life span because of the service that it provides. Of course, this respectful relationship with objects and utensils is being forgotten, as people now see their tools and instruments as material objects that can be discharged at any time. Consumerism is so powerful, and most households now are accumulating many objects, even if they don't really need them. For example, most people are not happy with just one or two TV sets. They want one for every room in the house, a bigger one, a newer one, placing in the garbage a used one, even if it still works. There is an exaggerated abuse and overuse of resources, and is done not because of a real need for an object, but because of the wasteful behavior of those greedy individuals who do not care for future generations.

But there are also some people, like myself, who get used to their objects and learn to appreciate the service they provide to us. In the case of the pots and jars, how many times we forget these objects on the stove without water, burning them and getting rid of them just as old and useless objects. Then, we simply go to the store and buy another one, without thinking that with our carelessness and wasteful behavior we are contributing to the depletion of our natural resources. This brings us to what Michael Taussig (1980) has said about the conflict of worldviews experienced by the Andean tin miners of Bolivia whose precapitalist mode of production (use value) was changed to the capitalist mode of production (exchange value). The clash of worldviews resulted from the development of capitalist economy, which transformed what was natural (modes of production and social relations) into bad or evil actions—the enslavement of Indigenous People as forced labor in the tin and silver mines of South America.

Another good example of a respectful approach to nature is a practice among the Huichol Indians of Mexico. When the Huichol Indians go to the mountains on a pilgrimage to gather peyote for their religious ceremonies, the guide advises the followers to collect the peyote in the most appropriate way. "Brothers and sisters take only what you need. Why take more if what you have is sufficient?" (Furst 1969). They said this because in previous years, the hippies went down to pick up as much peyote they could, leaving the Natives without it for their ceremonies.

So, the lesson to be learned from the *Popol Vuh* is that we must take care of our utensils, using more reason; we must take care of animals and other living beings that we share life with on earth. They must be protected and taken care of, especially the dogs, since they were domesticated by men to serve as companions during their journeys or to protect their houses and families. For this reason, dogs are very important in Maya culture and they must be taken care of because of their special mission to serve humans. According to Maya mythology, dogs protect human beings during their lifetime and after death. It is believed that the dog helps the spirit in its journey to the afterlife. If people want to enjoy eternal peace at *kamb'al* (the place of death) after leaving the world, they must be nice to their dogs and treat them appropriately during their lifetimes. The dog helps the person or soul to cross the river of death and continue its journey to the resting place (Montejo 2020).

The *Popol Vuh* teaches us the appropriate way of treating pets and other animals that live with us. For this reason, the story of the dogs punishing their masters becomes an implicit teaching and norm that reinforces respect and reciprocity with other living beings. In the same way, the story of men

FIGURE 4.3. Dog dancer during the Patron Saint's festivity.

made of wood is a metaphor for men whose heart and mind have become senseless (dry) without human feelings and compassion. In conclusion, this section of the *Popol Vuh* teaches us about the violent ending of another great cycle of life on earth, as a result of the abusive and destructive behavior of those human beings.

This is a major teaching that has persisted through time in Mayan communities. The belief that objects are at the service of humans does not mean that we should abuse and be wasteful of our resources. As I have mentioned above, for Indigenous People, objects have souls of creation or manufacturing. If we overexploit our resources, these same objects can be dropped on us and make us suffer the consequence of our actions (e.g., excessive production of garbage). An unbalanced world will create major changes that will affect human life on earth due to floods, earthquakes, acid rain, pandemic diseases, and even the danger of a nuclear war. These are some of the problems facing humanity at the end of the Maya fifth millennia or the closing of a great Maya cycle *13 b'ak'tun*. This ending is the beginning of another set of *thirteen b'ak'tuns*, which is also the beginning of an era that will bring major violent changes.

This is not only the preaching of New Age followers who are now announcing the violent end of the world because of human's wrongdoing. Instead, this philosophy of life has been preached and passed on through the oral tradition by the elders as a way of educating their children and their society in the past. Even those elders who have never traveled outside of their communities have complained about the destruction of their homelands. This is the case of Chan K'in of Naha', who has condemned the destruction of the Lacandon rainforest by Mexican loggers and ranchers. Chan K'in complained to the sky and said: "The roots of all living things are tied together. When a mighty tree is felled, a star falls from the sky; before you cut down a mahogany you should ask permission of the keeper of the forest, and you should ask permission to the keeper of the star" (Perera and Bruce 1982: back cover).

This highly poetical and philosophical thought comes from a Maya prophet who has lived all his life in the Lacandon rainforest and who understood the deepest form of gratitude, respect, and compassion for every living being on earth. In other words, this is truly one of the best examples of Mayalogue or the cosmic consciousness with constant dialogue among and between humans, nature, and the universe.

For the Mayas and most Indigenous People, the world around is a living being, and they are not worried about interpretations or coming out with cultural theories to explain their human behavior. We could say that the Mayas' preoccupation or what takes their full attention as presented here in Mayalogue, is life itself. Any discussion on culture must be transported to the concept of life, how the three components interact appropriately to produce action. In the same way, when these norms or natural laws are not followed, then human action produces violence, unbalance, illness, or death.

So, the basic concept to deal with in terms of Mayalogue is the concept of life or *q'inal*. This term has multiple meanings that have to do with *q'inh*, the sun. The word *q'inh* is also used to name something that is young and in the process of developing as a fruit. *Q'inh* is also a festival, happiness, and enjoyment—the festivity of life. Then, the term used for time is *q'inal*, which means existence, time, life, ages, and eras. The vibrant interaction of the sun *q'inh* or *komam tz'ayik* (father sun) which gives heat, so that earth produces and give life to humans, plants, animals, rivers, lakes, mountains, and so forth. *Q'inal* or life, then, is the result of the dynamic interaction of the sun (blessings from the supernatural world), the actions of human beings following the rules of respect, and protection to those who cannot defend themselves such as earth or the environment, and the animals whose survival depends on the actions of human beings.

Traditionally, the ethnographies produced by anthropologists have mostly focused on "cultures," which is what they care for as outsiders of Native communities. They take culture as an isolated item, dissecting different aspects of it such as language, art, religion, economy, and so on. Then, they describe or interpret what they see or write about as if this represents the totality or ethos of that community being studied. But for Native Americans, the tangible culture is only one part of the totality that produces action. If a Native is knowledgeable of the canons of his Indian nation, he or she will act to produce a global action that includes that dialogue between the natural and supernatural worlds. In this regard, consider what Chief Seattle said in his letter to President Pierce in 1870, while looking in despair the destruction of the ways of life of his people. He asked,

> Will you teach your children what we taught our children? That the earth is our mother? What befalls the earth befalls all the sons of earth. This we know: the earth does not belong to man, man belongs to earth. All things are connected like the blood that unites us all. Man did not weave the web of life; he is merely a strand in it. Whatever he does to the web he does to himself. (Chief Seattle, in a letter to President Franklin Pierce [1854], 1993)

The idea that everything is interrelated is a common doctrine among Indigenous People all around the world. The profundity of this philosophical thought has not been studied or understood appropriately, because it has not been documented thoroughly either. Mayalogue demonstrates that we humans have a common origin with all that exists, that we all are related, and that we have a common destiny; although we should not fall into the common stereotype that presents Native elders as extreme wise men who always speak with beautiful or poetic words, like Chief Seattle. Instead, we must learn that the messages in the words of famous elders are seeds of ecological concerns that must move us to action. In other words, we all need to respond to this cosmic consciousness and universal truth that whatever we do to other living beings we do to ourselves.

MAYALOGUE

FIVE

From Oral Histories and Traditions
to Written Ethnographies

FOR INDIGENOUS PEOPLE, the word is a source of power and the histories and teachings passed through oral traditions are, obviously, the knowledge of a culture that needed to be maintained and promoted for future generations. The oral form was the main method used by Indigenous People to teach and communicate their knowledge and all sorts of information, from the sacred to the profane. It is then, curious that early anthropologists, knowing that most information was to be gathered from oral accounts, devalued this important method. For them, oral tradition was unreliable and so they imposed their method of questioning and eliciting information they called ethnographic "fieldwork." This is how ethnographic fieldwork became the source of anthropological "adventures into the wild," conquering unknown cultures from which they emerged triumphant with an ethnographic report. Ethnographic fieldwork was a challenge for the young anthropologist who must survive "cultural shock," and return home with a prize, the ethnographic information collected from "dangerous savages." The importance is always given to the West's imposition as they intruded communities and carried out interviews, collecting some oral accounts that needed to be processed later out of context, and far removed from the places of action or Native communities.

We can argue that, instead of giving the oral tradition a rightful place within ethnographic writing and methodology, the storyteller or the so-called informant's account disappears in the finished text. At this point, all information provided is transformed and becomes the anthropologist's "interpretation" of the culture being studied. The Indigenous provider of anthropological information is reduced to an "informant," mentioned in the introduction of the text where the anthropologist claims that he or she had the good fortune to come across a "very intelligent" informant, thus justifying that he or she has produced a well-informed ethnographic report. For example, Ruth Bunzel (1952) mentioned in her ethnography that she had to choose some "intelligent informants" over other less intelligent ones. The selection of an "informant," she mentioned, was important for the outcome of the interviews and storytelling. "The fact that an anthropologist continues to work with an informant, there must be mutual trust, respect and interest. If the informant is hostile, generally inhibited, bored, insecure or stupid, the relationship is inappropriate, he dries up as a source of information, and the anthropologist takes a better informant" (Bunzel 1952:24).

I mention the above problem with anthropological fieldwork, because the role of oral histories and traditions has been taken for granted. The telling of stories is considered "natural," by foreigners, so Indians must tell their ways of life to strangers whose job is to make sense of these "primitive" cultures. In other words, Indigenous oral histories are confused with regular myths and legends, a mixture they called folklore, or the fantastic projection of the "primitive" mind. For most anthropologists, only a few of those stories "make sense," so it has been only through the work of interpretation by anthropologists that those stories make any sense. This process of interpretation by an expert then becomes the only important voice that emerges over the data collected during fieldwork.

Unfortunately, the plans for fieldwork and the resulting knowledge accumulated are not shared between anthropologists and community. Traditionally, the ethnographer considers gathering as much material as he or she can obtain, dictating the rules and agenda to follow in their research. For example, no anthropologist would first explain his or her community's worldviews to the Natives, explaining their relationship with the natural world and universe before requesting information on the same subject from the Natives. The fact is that most anthropologists do not even know much about their own culture's worldviews because of the lack of beliefs and even spiritual relationship with the natural world and human communities that characterize modern industrial societies.

This has been the case in the study of Maya culture throughout the early twentieth century. Starting with the description of ancient Maya cities by John L. Stephens and the drawings or illustrations by Frederick Catherwood (1841), the interest for ancient Maya civilization continued up to now. A great number of antiquarians and researchers, including archaeologists, epigraphers, linguists, and anthropologists came to the Maya land to carry on research and fieldwork. In this way important information was gathered by early anthropologists who spent time doing fieldwork in Maya communities. This is how during the early 1900s, the documentation of oral histories about Maya antiquity intensified. Since the common belief was that Indigenous cultures were destined to disappear, early anthropologists went to the field in response to Franz Boas's request to do extensive fieldwork before the Native's way of life disappear (salvage ethnography). They collected stories from Indigenous languages, which later became an important source for understanding Indigenous beliefs systems and cultures in a process of change. This was the time when Indigenous People were more traditionalists and less assimilated into the modern world.

Therefore, the classic Maya ethnographies are important, because at that time (early 1900s) most Indigenous communities were still isolated, without roads, schools, and modern technology. This isolation from the outside world created a linguistic barrier that strengthened what Eric Wolf called the "closed corporate community" (Wolf 1957). From the stories provided in these ethnographies, we can affirm that Indigenous People were still very much engaged in the maintenance of their worldviews, despite the centuries of neglect and discrimination throughout the colonial and postcolonial world. In these ethnographies we can find sample stories that sustain my arguments for the existence of a cosmocentric worldview among the Mayas.

Among the most influential anthropologists during the early twentieth century was Oliver La Farge, who studied the Jakaltek Maya and published his ethnographic results in *The Year Bearer's People* (1931). La Farge became interested in studying Jacaltenango because he was told that in this Maya town, the people continued to celebrate the Year Bearer ceremony, which is an ancient, pre-Hispanic ceremony dedicated to celebrating the Maya New Year. In the ancient Maya culture of Yucatan, described by Bishop Diego de Landa, these Year Bearers were called the Bacabs who are said to be placed at the four corners of earth by God to sustain the universe. This is an ancient belief system that had continued up to the time when La Farge visited Jacaltenango in 1929, thus collecting the names of the four Year Bearers revered by the Jakaltek Maya according to their Maya calendar: Watanh, Q'anil, Ah, and Chinax.

FIGURE 5.1. The Maya Year Bearer.

According to the Jakaltek diviners that informed La Farge, the character of each Year Bearer is different. For example, Watanh is said to be good for everything, so when he is carrying the year most things happen to be fine throughout the year. The second one, *Q'anil*, is the patron of merchants, but he leans more toward conflicts, war, and droughts. On the other hand, *Ah* is more supportive of good weather and good agricultural production, while Chinax, the fourth Year Bearer is said to be more caretaking of Mother Earth, animals, plants, and life on the planet.

The name of each Year Bearer, which is a name of a day in the calendar, comes from the name of sacred and mythical ancestors. Each one has a different characteristic that are manifested during the year in which they are in charge. According to Jakaltek cosmology, humans must be prepared to support the difficulties and live prepared, knowing what to expect in accordance to the symbolic "load" carried by the Year Bearer ruling the year. To have a good year and avoid danger, problems, and misfortunes, it is important to practice a religious system that promotes and nourishes a good relationship between humans, nature, and the Creator. It is only by pleasing God and living in harmony with all living beings that life is more meaningful, despite the multiple problems such as wars, famines, diseases, and so on that affect humans. If the ceremonies are practiced as a way of remembering the ancestors and giving thanks to the Creator for the breath of life, then the year will be more bearable.

For the maintenance of this complex way of life that integrates all institutions such as religious-philosophical, political, or agricultural activities, the prayer-maker (*alkal-txah*) or *sacred authority*, plays an important role. The *alkal-txah* is the politico-religious authority in charge of daily activities directed to sustain the heavens, God, and the ancestors. At his side, we can find the elders or *Principales* who have served the community in previous years and act as advisers to the prayer-maker or sacred authority. Finally, at the *popb'al nha* or sacred house of the *alkal-txah*, there is always a major diviner (*ahb'eh*) who is the most knowledgeable man or women in charge of counting the days of the Maya calendar and instructing the *alkal-txah* on the most appropriate way for guiding and serving in this sacred office.

Traditionally, the *alkal-txah* is elected a few days before the Maya New Year, so he starts his duty for a year, totally dedicated to serve the people and his community, thus, putting aside any of his own business or interest such as planting corn. When a prayer-maker is elected, automatically his house becomes the sacred house or *popb'al nha*, and his wife becomes the sacred mother. Following the rules of gender complementarity, she takes charge and is consulted by women for keeping up with the sacred ceremonies where women participate throughout the year. Once the people elect a new *alkal-txah*, usually a person who has excelled in his voluntary service to the community, he must accept and obey the rules step by step. If someone is repentant and tries to avoid this sacred service or mission, then the person will become sick, have an accident, or die suddenly. This is a sacred office that must be fulfilled with all one's heart, including a pledge of sexual abstinence during the full year of service to God and the community. Failure to follow the rule would bring disaster to the community, and it is the *alkal-txah* who must pay for the wrongdoing, so he may be jailed, or expected to pay a fine, depending on the gravity of the sin committed against this sacred office.

During the Maya New Year, all minds are concentrated on receiving the information from the *ahb'eh*, the wise men or diviner who provides the information or prophecies of the year. As the term *ahb'eh* means, he is the one who shows the path or the road to follow throughout the year in terms of ceremonies and human activities, paying close attention to the Maya calendar. Another important figure in the assembly of the prayer-maker is the *ninq'omlom*, or the "sacred speaker" who is the expert in prayers and poetic discourses. He must recite the ancient prayers with a poetic language called flowered words, which is a metaphorical and esoteric language full of symbolic meanings. The poetic language of the *ninq'omlom* is the most appropriate ancient discourse or poetic language for addressing and convincing the divinities. This is a very delicate task and it must be done by a specialist, so that it is forceful enough and convincing to God, the angels, or the ancestors being addressed. In other words, the positive or negative outcome of a petition depends on the effectiveness of the *ninq'omlom's* delivery of the message. Then, the *alkal-txah* or prayer-maker will also petition for a good agricultural year, for travel, business, hunting, and so forth. The trilogy—humans, nature, and the spiritual world—is always integrated into a cosmic unity that is dictated by the omens and the prophetic designs of the days, according to the sacred Maya calendar.

For example, on March 15, 1927, the Maya New Year date (*7 Ah*), Oliver La Farge participated in the ceremony by burning his candles as the people did in front of the church. "That morning, or earlier in the day, the people went to place candles at the foot of their fruit trees and cornfields, as well as in their houses and on the patios" (La Farge 1931:186). This ceremony mentioned by La Farge, which involved "placing candles at the foot of their fruit trees," confirms our argument that the Maya calendar unifies everything—that humans concern for their well-being extends toward their fruit trees and animals, as a way of maintaining life on earth and balance with the universe. These activities are carefully explained by the *ahb'eh* or diviner, who interprets the designs or omens of the days and years as well as the *k'altun* (20 years) and *b'ak'tun* (400 years) cycles.

The maintenance of this sacred covenant between humans, nature, and the supernatural world was the main concern for daily activities by the layman and specialists during the early 1900s. This is what anthropologist Charles Wagley observed among the Mam Mayas of Santiago Chimaltenango in 1940. "Through this knowledge, which only they know, the *chimanes* control the religious life of the laity. The *chiman* is the mediator through whom, in important matters, the layman reaches the supernatural" (Wagley 1949:68).

According to Wagley, the role of the ritual specialist and diviner is to mediate between the supernatural and the people of the community. In turn, they must follow the rules for living in a Maya society, while accommodating themselves to their natural environment from which they make a living. Those community rules are mostly conditioned by the supernatural, since they must follow the norms established by God and enforced by the owners of the hills or mountains spirits. Unfortunately, the term *chiman* (from shaman) was equated with that of the witch or *brujo*, so these wise men who carry the ancient knowledge of the calendar have preferred to go under anonymity. Because of their esoteric knowledge and their expertise in interpreting the signs and omens from the days of the Maya calendar, the so-called *chimanes* or *ahb'eh* were persecuted by the churches as witches and devil worshipers. For this reason, most communities were left without this Maya calendar expert, who guides the road or the path toward a harmonious life with nature and the supernatural world.

Like Wagley among the Mam, and La Farge among the Jakaltek, Ruth Bunzel found among the K'iche Maya that the Catholic religion and Maya religion were so tightly integrated, forming a unity or Native religion that cannot be differentiated as either Catholic or Native. The prayers and ceremonies of the K'iche were a form of dialogue and communication with the supernatural world, particularly the concept of *Mundo*, or the Heart of Heaven and Heart of Earth according to the *Popol Vuh*. "The general adoration of earth and its products is associated with certain days in the ancient calendar, mainly the Maya days *Ixh* and *Q'anil*. In a very preeminent form, *Ixh* is the day of earth, of life, and of all living beings, as opposed to the world of the dead. This day is special for giving thanks for inhabiting earth" (Bunzel 1952: 93).

Ruth Bunzel's ethnography about the K'iche Maya of Chichicastenango provides numerous oral accounts that refer to the need to maintain balance and unity between human beings, nature, and the supernatural world. The respect and reciprocity between humans and earth, while being thankful to God for one's own life must be the center of all human ceremonies. Failure to do this can cause misfortune for the individual, and/or illness that will threaten his or her own life. Those who do not observe these sacred relationships move away from their moral commitment for a corporate survival. The disrespect and abuse of nature is an insult to the spirit or guardian of earth Juyu-tiq'aj, which means "lord of the hills and valleys." Among the Jakaltek and Q'anjobal, the guardian of the mountains and valleys is called naj Witz-ak'al, or Tzuul-taq'a among the Q'eqchi' Maya of northern Guatemala, always meaning guardian of the hills and valleys. Earth and its guardian Witz-ak'al is the central axis on which life takes place, and ceremonies must be performed to give thanks for one's own well-being. In other words, we humans must be thankful for the gift of life given to us to be enjoyed during our brief existence on the face of earth.

Continuing with the assertion that Maya people throughout Mesoamerica practiced a unified worldview that is cosmocentric, we have some comments by Calixta Guiteras-Holmes, who worked among the Tzotzil Mayas of Chiapas, Mexico. "In the Pedrano world view the whole of the cosmos is animate, making it impossible to separate its parts from the powers that rule over them. The air belongs to the world and to man's body. It is the vehicle for good and evil and of thought" (Guiteras-Holmes 1961:286).

So, while some early anthropologist made brief reference to Maya ideas of unity with the natural world and understood the importance for maintaining peace and harmony with the natural forces through rituals and ceremonies, others neglected such teachings and decided to keep up with their traditional research in the four subdisciplines of anthropology.

Later, close to the end of the twentieth century, modern Mayanists became more centered on the living cultures and on the process of assimilation through which these cultures were underway because of modern political and economic control. Among these scholars we can mention Nancy Farriss, whose project focused on the colonial and present struggle of those living descendants of the ancient Maya of Mesoamerica. In her words: "Very little exists on the Indian side of the story: that is, how they viewed and responded to European domination as opposed to what merely happened to them" (Farriss 1984: ix-x).

In her work *Maya Society under Colonial Rule* (1984), she argues that there is a magnetic field that maintains the integration and cohesiveness among Maya people, which has an ecological base. This ecological base can be explained from a Maya perspective, which has been the base for preindustrial agrarian societies. To understand Maya life and its collective survival through five centuries of Spanish colonialism, Nancy Farris provided the following explanation, which I quote extensively, and which supports the Native concept of Mayalogue:

> As can be expected of an agricultural people inhabiting a tropical forest environment where biological recycling is especially rapid and obvious, the Maya ecological model was an organic, circular one, in which all creation was mutually dependent, feeding itself in endless cycles of decay and renewal. In a region where the life-renewing rains are so uncertain, it is also not surprising that this cyclical rhythm was not to be taken for granted and that man as part of the system was expected to do his share to keep it going. The Maya conceive of survival as a collective enterprise in which man, nature, and the gods are all linked through mutually sustaining bonds of reciprocity, ritually forged through sacrifice and communion. This collective enterprise provides the organizing principle of Maya society, incorporating the individual in widening networks of

interdependence from extended family through community and the state and ultimately to the cosmos. (Farriss 1984:6)

The interrelatedness of the natural world, the people and the universe as practiced by the Mayas was severed by the hardships, enslavement, and sufferings that brought Spanish invasion and colonialism. There is a myth that in ancient times, earth was connected to heaven with an umbilical cord through which nourishment passed between earth and heaven. This cosmic connection was maintained through the ceremonies and appropriate action taken by Mayas in their prayers for all living beings with whom they coexist. This mythical union or umbilical cord was named *kusansum*, and according to oral tradition, it was ruptured because of the Spanish conquest and invasion of Indigenous lands. Alfonso Villa Rojas refers to the *kusansum* as the white road that was suspended in the sky and which connected the ancient Maya cities in the past. "This road was made of a long rope (*sum*) which supposed to be a living thing (*kusam*), and from its mid-section or center blood emerged. It was through this living rope through which nourishment was sent (from heaven) to those who inhabited the sacred temples now in ruins. Perhaps for some reason this rope was cut, and all the blood spilled down, until that rope [or umbilical cord] disappeared forever' (Villa Rojas 1945, 1978:438, my translation).

Nancy Farriss presents an important metaphor for nourishment, reciprocity, and survival with the umbilical cord. But she also mentioned that the Mayas complained because they were not able to freely perform their rituals and ceremonies in their ancient sites, as they were persecuted by missionaries and colonial authorities. The rupture of the *kusansum* or cosmic umbilical cord is then a great metaphor that explains a major change and attack against the Mayas' worldviews. According to this myth, the connection between Indigenous People and the Creator was ruptured and their prayers and poetic discourses of gratitude for life elevated to Hunab' K'uh as nourishment to God, was transformed into desperate complaints and petitions for survival under such inhuman conditions. Colonial authorities placed the Indigenous People under the *encomienda* system of forced labor, which combined with pandemic diseases and wars, decimated entire populations (Lutz and Lovell 1995; Lutz and Dakin 1996). This colonial exploitation and forced labor caused extreme poverty in the Native populations of Guatemala, a condition that persists even today in the twenty-first century.

Despite these sufferings, Indigenous People maintained their conscious action and connection to earth and the universe, while struggling for their collective existence on earth. It has been a difficult task, but there are many Native scholars now working for the construction of a more positive image of their cultures and Maya civilization. In this effort, one of the most important Indigenous struggles now is the process of dismantling the myths of inferiority and backwardness placed on them. Meanwhile, a revitalization of Maya culture must take place by producing important texts and ideas for intellectual decolonization, as is the case with Mayalogue.

ORAL TRADITION: A PERSONAL EXPERIENCE

For the Mayas, there is a classification of speeches in different categories of verbal behavior. This model or Native taxonomy of verbal art is well described by Gary Gossen (1984), and his model can be applied to any Maya language and oral tradition in the Maya region. In this way, storytelling and verbal performance is not done spontaneously without direction, but following a structural pattern that must be followed, depending on the kind of stories to be told. There exists the category of *antivo k'op*, or *payat tzoti'* (ancient words). This category is related to ancient historical and mythical events of creation, and the ancient deeds of the First Fathers and Mothers (ancestors) of the great Maya nation. There is a category of animal stories "*yik'ti'al nixtej noq'*, which I tried to follow and develop in my work on Mayan fables called *The Bird Who Cleans the World and Other Maya Fables* (Montejo 1991).

I was nine years old when I started my formal education with the Maryknoll missionaries, who built a boarding school in Jacaltenango, Western Guatemala. Coming from a very small Maya village (La Laguna) close to the Mexican border, I carried with me in my head, a whole world of teachings, myths, and fantasies that connected me to the land of my ancestors. As a child I have learned many stories from my parents, the elders, and from older children in the village. My childhood was a fantastic world in which normal activities such as traveling, working in the cornfield, going to the river to swim or to the forest to fetch firewood, and so on were always connected to fantastic stories that molded our behavior and maintained us in close contact with nature. At an early age, children already knew where to go to listen to certain stories, since there were storytellers, men and women, in each Maya community. Usually, there were old men who specialize in telling stories, so we male children always accompanied our fathers whenever they gathered to tell stories early at night, as it was a tradition to visit neighbors before going to sleep.

There were no radios, TVs, or other forms of distraction in the village, so storytelling or just playing in front of the chapel was the way to spend time before going to sleep. Since I was born and raised in a poor Maya family, the house of my parents was a *jacal*, like all the houses in the village. These *jacales* had thatched roofs with wood posts standing vertically as a fence that served as a wall. There was no need for windows in these houses, because we could see from the inside to the outside without any difficulty.

During the nights, you could see the stars or the moon at the horizon from inside the house as we lay on the sleeping mat on the dirt floor. The nights were very peaceful since there were no cars and no electricity. I remember those nights of full moon, when I used to wake up at the middle of the night and peer through the wooden walls toward the place where my father's mule was tied to a tree. I have always wanted to catch by surprise "*el sombreron*," while he made bridles with the hair or tail of the mule. It was the belief that this mythical creature (the size of a child wearing a big hat like a Mexican charro) only appeared at night and liked to play with horses by making bridles on the animal's hair or tail. The bridles made by *el sombreron* were like the Gordian knot, which was impossible to untie. So, every time I woke up at night and there was a full moon, I always tried to surprise this mythical figure that was so prevalent in Maya folklore when I grew up. I have seen these bridles made on the hair or tail of horses, and sometimes the owners of the horses must cut these bridles with scissors, since they were impossible to untie.

Now that I think of my childhood, I can still remember those mythical moments that filled my life and my dreams with awe and mystery. At this early age, the children could enjoy the Maya folktales, myths, and legends that they were told, learning at the same time the name of places and the guardian spirits attached to them. The most important one, of course, was Witz, the owner of the hills, who was also the guardian of the animals. Lately, the image of Witz was transformed into that of a white Ladino man who accumulates wealth inside the hills or mountains. Witz is said to give wealth to those who request it from him, but the person making the deal also gives his soul in exchange, and that of his children who are fed with this forbidden wealth or gifts from the devil. These types of stories were so common when I grew up; we learned the name of the mountains surrounding our communities and each guardian assigned to it by the Creator.

Besides the storytelling and other forms of oral histories, dreams were also important as the medium for obtaining certain knowledge about nature and the world around us.

One night, during my childhood, I had a very interesting dream which I told my parents as we were eating breakfast in the morning. In my dream,

I saw myself fetching firewood in the forest that existed around the village. As I was looking at the trees, a magpie flew to the lower branch of a tree, just in front of me. The bird looked beautiful with its black, white, and blue feathers, but I was also concerned because in our culture, this bird was said to have the power of witchcraft, which could affect another bird or even human beings. While I was watching the bird, this magpie started to talk to me as if it was a person. "Young man," it said, "I have come to see you because I want to give you a gift." "What kind of gift?" I asked. And the bird said, "The gift that I want to give you is that of knowledge that goes beyond what regular human beings achieve by themselves. I want to give you the gift or power of the occult, so that you can solve problems in the easy way and penetrate the unknown."

I got scared when the bird said that I could learn the magic of witchcraft, so I immediately said, "No, I don't want your gift. Give it to someone else, but I don't want it for myself," I said. Then the magpie said, without altering its voice, "I understand that you fear the unknown, but you should know that this power can be used for good or for bad purposes, whatever the circumstance is. For example, if there is someone causing you problems or someone who is abusive to nature and makes you mad, you just say the words '*kobak*' and the person will start to feel pain and will get sick, depending on the intensity of your desire or the power of your words. Now, if the person has corrected his action, you can take away the illness that you have placed inside his body by saying the words '*kiki.*'"

I stood there listening to the magpie as it explained to me the process of achieving knowledge of the secret kind that not many people can achieve in life. After listening to the magpie, I then replied, "No, thank you, this is a kind of power and knowledge that I am not interested in." And the magpie insisted: "Don't be afraid and don't be unthankful. This is a power and knowledge that I cannot just offer or give to anyone."

"Thank you, but I don't want it," I said, so, the magpie got a little bit unhappy and said, just as it flew out of my sight, "Too bad, you don't like my gift, but someone else will take it."

As a child, I have seen the magpie truly becoming a mad bird. I have seen it waiting for other birds to lay down their eggs, and then it will go there to eat them in the nest. The children in my village also knew that this bird can change the way it sings, especially when it is in the process of bewitching another bird. The magpie is said to magically place worms under the wing of a bird that soon will have problems in flying. This is what we children believed when we grew up, and that's why the magpie is not an edible bird among our people.

The dreams, then, helps to understand the forces of nature. Definitively, this methodology of in-depth observation of nature has been fundamental in the creation of knowledge and passing on those stories from generation to generation. But, here I also want to emphasize that Indigenous People use dreams as an important method for obtaining knowledge of the world, particularly about the past, the present, and the future.

In those days, I remember that children like me paid attention to these stories and could see and feel nature as a living being. So, they were totally immersed in the mysteries of nature and the world around them, and these stories, legends, myths, and fables were taken as teachings that described and explained human relationships to nature and the supernatural world. The Maya children were open minded and they themselves tried to make sense of the complex world around them. The information inculcated through the stories remained in the mind of the listeners because they were always surrounded by a halo of mystery. This is how children achieved information and knowledge that comes from different sources concerning the natural and the supernatural world.

Obviously, other information and knowledge of the world came from dreams as children at an early age were immersed into a fantastical world inhabited by people, ancestors, and spiritual beings. Certainly, these stories and the close contact with nature have changed for children today, because of the modernization of the world through the media, Western education, and technology.

At an early age then, I was truly living a full life of that of a Maya child, as I felt free to move in my own limited world and community where I grew up. Any opportunity was used to scold a child with a story as mysterious and profound as is life itself. For example, I remember my father scolding me because I cut a little tree as I was trying my sharpened machete. "Son, don't cut the little green trees whenever you please. When you do that you are cutting short your own life and you will die slowly" (Montejo 1991).

Other times, my father would become more serious or mad to the point of disciplining his children with punishment. I remember walking in the path carelessly, so I tripped down and fell to the ground. He immediately turned back and looked at me with a serious face, shouting: "Watch your way ... cabron"! My father was mean and harsh when disciplining his children, as he too was coming out of a difficult world of poverty and forced labor that he lived and endured when he was growing up during the 1920s.

As a child, I learned how to plant corn and beans. I also knew how to take care of the mule and help my parents in bringing firewood to the house.

After doing my duty or contributing to the work at home either peeling the corn cobs, or taking care of my youngest brothers and sisters, I would go to the patio of a chapel to play soccer with the children of my age. This was the routine of my life until I went to the Catholic boarding school run by Maryknoll missionaries in 1960. The boarding school separated me from my parents, my community, and my familiar landscape, where I used to be in close contact with nature. Despite the harsh discipline in the boarding school, I went through my primary education with happiness as I did well and earned scholarships every year for being a good student. After graduating from sixth grade with the Maryknoll missionaries, I then moved to the city of Sololá for middle school and to Antigua Guatemala for high school, until I graduated as a schoolteacher in 1972.

As I grew up with one foot in both worlds, I could still remember that world of my distant childhood (Montejo 2021). Little by little I found myself in a real and changing world, an ontological world of conflicts and struggles. From this experience, I argue for a Native epistemology based on my personal observation of the world, the sky, and nature—all this with awe and respect for the spiritual world, which is a living cosmology.

I mentioned this anecdote from my childhood because I believe that oral histories or traditions in Maya communities play an important role as a method for teaching and obtaining knowledge from the community and from the natural world around us. But, of course, the most important instrument for passing on the information is the Native language itself. By speaking the Jakaltek Maya language and learning original stories from this language, I could value the importance of maintaining Indigenous languages as tools for understanding cultures and the production of knowledge. Most importantly, now that I want to talk and write about an Indigenous theory and forms of Native knowledge, I present myself here as a storyteller and as a Native scholar, since I value storytelling as an important method for obtaining knowledge and sharing useful information about the world. Most of the information presented here comes from oral tradition and the methodology of telling stories, particularly the mythification process, which I will discuss later in this book.

Obviously, in the present industrialized world in which we are living, storytelling has become something of the past, even for Indigenous People in small villages. The youth are not interested in the histories of their communities, but in the fashions that are coming out from industrialized societies and where Indigenous communities are targeted as markets for these products. The youth have become more communicative lately, because of the cell phone, but the content of their discussions does not revolve around traditional knowledge. Most Maya children and adults are now more interested in TV programs and are not learning their Native language because they consider it without value in the modern world. Among the Hopi, for example, "Perpetuation of traditions must battle imposed institutions like schools and missions, supermarkets, wage-labor, television and other forms of cultural imperialism. These have had a profound effect. Many Hopi children do not understand the Hopi language; prefer heavy-metal over Hopi songs. Coke and Big Macs over yoyuwolo ..." (Whiteley 1998:169).

In Maya rural communities, the only ones who practice certain forms of storytelling are the day-keepers or Maya diviners, who maintain the sacred tradition of counting the days and their omens. This is a more secret practice, since some of them now have books where they read and consult the names of the days and omens for the appropriate ceremony to perform. But as we know from antiquity, even if the Maya had the ancient books or codices that they consulted for their prophecies, they still had to pass the information on verbally to the people who gathered in the plazas to listen to these sacred messages.

This practice of orally communicating in public the omens of the year continued among the Jakaltek and Q'anjob'al Maya until 1932, as reported by Oliver La Farge (1947). Although, the text was written in a variety of Nahuatl language, this one was read out loud to the public at the time the sacred authorities took power as in ancient times. The time and contents of the discourses have changed, but the practice of reading out loud to the public gathered for "receiving" the Maya New Year continued. In other words, as the Maya people had to survive under harsh punishment by the missionaries, other texts were adopted masking Maya beliefs under Christianity. This is clearly exemplified by this text recorded by La Farge among the Q'anjob'al Maya of Santa Eulalia, which was read in public while the new authorities of the community took office. This Nahuatl text memorized and delivered in a Q'anjob'al Maya community started with a Catholic salutation.

"Jesús, María y José y del Hijo y del Espíritu Santo,
Dios todopoderoso.
Sempualis
he metonalis

> quemoquesames
> De noviembre del año
> ypan y elbites Santa Lucía
> y tuchibasques tu cabildo
> tebantin regidores
> ytexcupa alcaldes y regidores
> mochintin oficiales tochinamil ..."
> (La Farge 1947:144)
> Translation:
> "Jesus, Mary and Joseph, and the Holy Spirit,
> All powerful God
> Twentieth
> day of this month
> quemoquesame (?)
> of November of the year
> on the feast of Santa Lucía
> we shall make our court,
> we Regidores
> concerning Alcaldes and Regidores
> and all officials of our chinamitl (village) ..."
> (La Farge 1947:144)

The ceremonial speeches were made from very long memorized ancient texts, full of metaphors and esoteric meanings, which was the characteristic of symbolic and poetic sacred languages. There was a concern for eloquence in the poetic delivery of refined thoughts, so it was as if presenting aromatic flowers to the Creator. This eloquence was achieved by using different literary devices such as metaphors and couplets to produce "flowered words." In this way, the *ninq'omlom* or the speaker of the cargo office, could deliver the collective thoughts or prayers from the community. The intention was to please God, so that the Creator may send his blessings over the whole community of humans and nonhumans that live on earth.

What follows is another short text from the Tzotzil Maya of Chiapas, showing the importance and power of the flowered words for maintaining good relationships, communication, and reciprocity between humans, nature and the spiritual world. This is a fragment of a text or prayer by a newly elected cargo-holder so that he is successful in his duty or service to San Juan, the patron saint of the community of Chamula.

Have mercy, my Lord
great San Juan
great patron.
How much I come before your feet,
how much I come before your hands,
with my spouse,
with my companion,
with your guitar,
with your gourd rattle,
with your servant;
the musician.
With your servant
the gruel-maker,
with your servant,
the cook with your shot guns,
with your cannons.
Your children are gathered together,
your offspring are gathered together,
for you to see,
for you to witness.
Great San Juan,
great patron.
Now you are to be delivered at my feet,
now you are to be entrusted to my hands,
now I am your new servant,
now I am your new attendant.
I shall be as father to you,
I shall be as mother to you,
for one year,
the same as for each day,
great San Juan,
great Patron.
There is incense for you,
there is smoke for you.
I shall embrace you,
I shall carry you,
for one year,
the same as for each day.
(Gossen 1974:203–5)

ORAL TRADITION AND INDIGENOUS METHODOLOGIES

More recently, the Indigenous method of storytelling was taken advantage of by anthropologists, folklorists, and historians for gathering information and writing their ethnographic reports on Indigenous communities. Oral histories are then, important, because they reflect the collective experience and behavior of those who maintain strong relationships with their environment, while observing the taboos or moral norms established for dealing with the supernatural world. We can think of the oral tradition or storytelling as a web of connections that extends into Native cultures, places, and the spiritual world, as all stories are connected to something else in the web of life. This is clearly stated by Angela Cavender while referring to Lakota oral tradition. "I have come to realize that while I have a clear sense of the difference between myth and true stories according to my culture's standards, our oral tradition is a kind of web in which each strand is a part of a whole. The individual strands are most powerful when interconnected to make an entire web, that is, when the stories are examined in their entirety" (Cavender 1997:108).

This web of relationships in the oral tradition can be approached more clearly from Maya classificatory systems, or a Native taxonomy. Among the Jakaltek Maya, this universe of oral histories and traditions can be classified in different categories through the Maya language. Once again, the language is instrumental in the description and representation of Native cultures from the inside, or Native perspective.

In Jakaltek Maya language, storytelling is called *ik'ti'* (*ik'* = old, ancient, antiquity, descendancy, heritage; and *ti'* = the mouth), literally meaning "retelling old stories by words of mouth." The compound word *ik'ti'* also means ancient history, or storytelling, something of the past that has become history and it is told by word of mouth. This was a method of socialization by which people contributed with pieces to the global history of the known region, always in relation to the community, nature, and the spiritual world. Since children and adults are part of the community and live within their demarcated geography or territory, they know the names of the places mentioned in the stories. They also know the names of animals, trees, rivers, mountains, old roads, ruins, and caves, so, the storyteller passes on firsthand information to the listeners about the landscape and sacred geography of the region.

For this, modern researchers now recognize that storytelling is an old and effective method of passing on cultural information within a traditional community.

As a form, it is no wonder that narrative is the primary means for passing knowledge within tribal traditions, for it suits the fluidity and interpretive nature of ancestral ways of knowing. (Kovach 2009:94)

Due to the facilities by which Native people, mostly elders and the experts on specific roles in society, tell stories, either ancient or recent, or as they create new stories out of their personal experience and knowledge, they can help anthropologists understand Indigenous communities by doing fieldwork. While people were eager to tell their stories, and pass on their knowledge to those who requested it, the anthropologists did not consider Native knowledge to be significant enough for it to be catalogued as real "knowledge." Instead, they gather the stories as mere "information" and they processed it, while getting rid of the essence of the stories—that aspect that is relational to the global environment (human and nonhuman). If the researcher wanted to gather knowledge and not just information, he or she could certainly find out that even in the smallest story the Native collaborator informs about the world around him or her and the way the culture works in relation to everything else. In other words, a story can be the blueprint for Native epistemologies and certain stories are used as key elements to elicit knowledge of different fields of human inquiry and disciplines.

For this reason, much is needed to be done in documenting knowledge from the insider's perspective. Fortunately, at the present, there are many Native scholars writing from inside their cultures and producing auto-ethnographies, while others are still engaged in the long-standing critique of anthropology (Marcus and Fischer 1986; Asad 1988), as part of the struggle for decolonization and self-determination (Smith 1999; Vine Deloria 1997).

On the practice of cultural critique, the postmodernist tide in anthropology has long emphasized ethnographic writing and reporting as storytelling (Clifford and Marcus 1986). Ethnographic reporting is, ultimately, the manipulation of oral histories and traditions provided to the ethnographer as a researcher. This "information" is in turn processed and given the name of ethnography, which is a written text to fulfill the needs of Western scholars who have faith in written texts as "the truth," while rejecting Indigenous oral histories and tradition as unfaithful accounts full of distortions. But for Indigenous People, the oral tradition is not fixed in time, as it is a vivid part of their daily life in community. So, the important instrument for passing it on to younger generations is the Native language. "Through language we make those ideas walk, and fly and shine; we share our feelings and our knowledge and memories. Our stories and songs should be remembered, as they also teach us valuable lessons" (Young Bear 1994:16).

And these teachings begin early in the life of the individual as Rigoberta Menchú mentioned in her testimonial biography. When a pregnant woman goes to the cornfield or to the forest to fetch firewood, she talks to the child in her womb, showing and explaining that he or she must learn how to respect the natural world and not to abuse the different forms of life. "This is very important. We say, 'We cannot harm the life of one of your children, we are your children. We cannot kill any of your creatures, neither trees, nor animals'" (Menchú 1984:58).

As I mentioned earlier, in this age of modern technology and formal education, oral tradition and storytelling has become less important. Children are busy with video games and other electronic instruments and are not paying attention to the elders or to anyone who may have a story or something to say about community values. This is observed among Indigenous People almost everywhere around the world today. For example, Peter Blue Cloud has noticed this lack of interest in storytelling among the Iroquois in modern times. "There are not as many Mohawks sitting around a campfire at night. Most of the ones that I know are sitting around a T.V. set in the living room" (Blue Cloud 1987:42). The oral tradition was basically a form of teaching through stories that are passed from elders to younger generations. Klallam poet Duane Niatum also refers to the teachings received from his grandfather as follows:

> I think one of the things you have to respect the fact that in the natural world the animals and the plants have a position equal to your own. I think that was a very important training. You must respect that world and know that you share the same world and that means that there is a mutual dependency. When you take from nature you should give back something. You're only allowed to take your fair share. This way was the original and traditional training. (Niatum 1987:199–200)

We can argue that Indigenous People all over the world have given the same value and importance to the oral tradition as a source of truths and knowledge from their own cultures. So, in terms of universal or cosmic relationships, we can observe that "the whole worldview of the Indian is predicated upon the principle of harmony in the universe" (Momaday 1987:180). The oral tradition is, then, a Native method used to produce, teach, and pass on Native knowledge and lessons about human relationships with the natural word and the cosmos.

NATIVE METHODS FOR DOCUMENTING HISTORY — SIX
Oxlan B'en: The Cyclical View of Time and History

IN THIS CHAPTER, we will focus on the importance of time and space for explaining and understanding Mayalogue. For the Maya people, the concept of time is an everlasting moment that is past, present, and future. In other words, there is a continuous dialogue between the present and the past to construct or prepare for the future. As I explained earlier, *q'inal* is life, is time, and is the existence of all things on earth and in the universe. The Jakaltek Maya say, "*itzitzal sat yib'anh q'inal*" or be alive on earth. *Q'inal* is a spatiotemporal idea that is ever present in the universe, just as the sun is present with its light and heat to produce life on Mother Earth.

For the Maya, time is not linear as in Western worldviews, where history is something that has happened in the past, and thus becomes distant as time goes by. Instead, time is cyclical and it is the Maya calendar that establishes the cycles that repeat themselves in periods or cycles of time. The day cycle (*kin*, or *tz'ayik*), the month cycle (*ahaw*), the year cycle (*haab'*), the twenty-year cycle (*k'altun*), and so on, until the long count or cycle *b'ak'tun* (400-year cycle). Then, thirteen times the *b'ak'tun* is the great cycle of the 13 *B'ak'tun* (5,200-years cycle). This great cycle of 13 *B'ak'tuns* goes into counting another greater cycle, the prophetic one called *Oxlanh B'en*, meaning "to go back and forth thirteen times." According to this sequence of cyclical periods there is no 14 *B'ak'tun*, but the integration of the *b'ak'tun* cycles into the *Oxlanh B'en* cycle (13 × 5,200 = 67,600). The current question is, what is the actual counting toward the *Oxlanh B'en* at this moment? Are we starting the greatest cycle *Oxlanh B'en*? Are we at the middle or at the end of it?

As we explained earlier, the evolutionist paradigm was fundamental in the development of racist and discriminatory practices against Indigenous People. And the conditioning of Indigenous People as backward or primitive has to do with time and space. This distancing or division between "us" and "them" or the usage of the term *the other* marks the conscious and continuous differentiation of the "West from the rest." This is what Johannes Fabian (1983) has called the allochronic distancing, in which Indigenous cultures have been studied as "primitives," encapsulated in a changeless past. No wonder Indigenous cultural traditions and knowledge such as those expressed in Mayalogue have been considered irrational.

In this way, Indigenous People were automatically considered inferior just because they practiced a distinctive and more egalitarian way of life, compared to those foreigners who studied them. They were considered less evolved and needed more time to develop a larger brain and think reasonably: "More profoundly and problematically, they require Time to accommodate the schemes of a one-way history: progress, development, modernity (and their negative mirror images: stagnation, underdevelopment, tradition). In short, *geopolitics* has its ideological foundation in *chronopolitics*" (Fabian 1983:144).

In this context, Johannes Fabian argues for the recognition of the "Other" as a person living at the same historical moment in full as a person. just as the Western researcher is also living the now and today, or the ethnographic present (to be in time), which Johannes Fabian calls "coevalness."

Mayas have not escaped this fate, particularly by early archaeologists who have focused their attention on Classic Maya archaeology, so they have invented much of the history we now know about the ancient Mayas. The arguments have been that the ancient Mayas have disappeared and have nothing to do with the present "Indians," thus severing the present or contemporary Mayas from their ancestors. For this reason, when we talk about the Mayas, our mind goes back toward the distant past, the time when the "true" Mayas were said to live. So, the present Mayas are lost or placed in a limbo, either fossilized in time as "*indios*" (a colonial creation) or marginalized as "people without history" (Wolf 1982).

For the Mayas, time and space are considered to be a process of continuous change, produced as a result of interaction among the trilogy: human-nature-Creator. And this interrelatedness is maintained as a cosmological working model through ceremonies as fixed in the sacred Maya calendar. There is, then, a different conceptualization of time, compared to the West, where time flows as an eternal unilinear current divided into the past, present, and future. Instead, for Mayas time is cyclical or a recurring sequence of event that moves as a spiral that overlap its edges at certain points in time and space, and these cyclical conjunctures share the same cosmic environment or characteristic that we call destiny—not the same actors, but similar situations, and supposedly similar outcomes; although if we learn from the past we can change and redirect our destiny to a more positive action or historical moment in time.

The Mayas have been counting time for millennia, so after observing the events within the cycles of time, *tun* (one-year period) and *k'altuns* (twenty-year period), up to the *b'ak'tun* and *B'en*, which marks the ending of all previous cycles, the patterns of events became clear, so the future could be prophesized with some accuracy. This is how Mayas foretold the future, such as the Spanish invasion of the Maya land according to the *Chilam Balam* texts. Since previous invasions had already occurred in the past, other similar events were expected to occur almost in the same way when a prophetic cycle was completed. The case of the Spanish conquest is a good example. "Whether or not the Maya were expecting this particular invasion, Spanish action followed patterns familiar enough to suggest that history was repeating itself. And since the Maya's entire view of time was based on the conviction that each of their twenty-year *katun* periods repeated itself with the same recurring events at 256-year intervals ... the suggestion must have had a compelling force" (Farriss 1984:21).

This cyclical view of history is also discussed by Victoria Bricker in terms of the cyclical prophecies documented in the book, *Chilam Balam of Chumayel*.

> THE FIRST KATUN 8 AHAU
> It was in 8 Ahau
> that Chichen Itza was destroyed.
> Thirteen folds of the katun (256 years) had passed
> when Chakanputun began;
> they were in their homes for that katun period.
>
> THE SECOND KATUN 8 AHAU
> It was in 8 Ahau
> that the people of Chakanputun were destroyed
> by the Itza people.

And they came to seek their homes again.
For thirteen folds of the katun
the people of Chakanputun
had settled there
in their homes.
This was the katun period
when the Itza went
beneath the trees,
beneath the bushes,
beneath the vines
in such misery.

THE THIRD KATUN 8 AHAU
It was in 8 Ahau
that the Itza people were destroyed
in their homes again
because of the treachery of Hunac Ceel;
because of the dispute
with the people of Izamal.
For thirteen folds of the katun they had live there.
And they were destroyed
by Hunac Ceel
because of their being asked those Itza riddles.

THE FOURTH KATUN AHAU
It was in 8 Ahau
that there occurred the smashing with stones
within the fortress
of Mayapan;
because of the capture of the fortress,
the destruction of the stronghold;
because of that confederation
in the city of Mayapan. (Bricker 1981:7)

The above quotation from the *Chilam Balam of Chumayel* provides the most clear and eloquent use of the prophetic cycles of time in Maya life and history. A prophetic cycle that will bring events closer or parallel to a previous cycle is the thirteen-fold of a *katun*, meaning 13 × 20 = 260 years (although in the text above the total of years of the thirteen-fold is given as 256 years). The time and the year will be similar, but the actors and events will not be the same, although they will have the same characteristics or effect on the population. If there was war or famine during the previous thirteen-fold of a katun, then the Mayas would expect the same event—war, famine, or disease at the ending of another cycle. Of course, the idea that events tend to repeat themselves at intervals of time called *katun* (*k'altun*) is well known among the Mayas. Then, follows the great cycle documented by the ancient Mayas as the 13 *B'ak'tun*, which occurred on December 21, 2012. Finally, there is the *Oxlanh B'en*, or the ending of all great cycles.

To my understanding and following the model or repetitive actions and prophecies, the ending of the 13 *B'ak'tun* marks the beginning of major changes that will affect the world as it did in previous *b'ak'tuns* in the past. The questions that follow are: will humanity reach the ending of the 13 *B'en* and survive into the future? Why is the 13 *B'ak'tun* important as a prophetic time in Maya history? Does it mark the beginning of the end in *Oxlanh B'en*? Many of those interested in this prophetic cycle thought that the end of the world would occur at the exact day of the closing of the 13 *B'ak'tun* (12/21/2012). But the prophecies do not give exact dates, so we can take the 13 *B'ak'tun* as the beginning of the major changes and destructions yet to come.

For the Mayas the concept of time and space is very important, not only in ordering different events and eras of existence on earth, but also in everyday life activities such as with prayers, telling stories (oral tradition), and the documentation of local, national, or even world events. For example, the time that most Maya elders of Guatemala still remember and talk about is the period during the dictatorship of President Jorge Ubico ("*stiempo ubiko*"). This tyrant government presided by General Jorge Ubico, who ruled Guatemala with an iron hand was one of the most painful periods in Guatemalan history.

Since the Guatemalan elite considered Indigenous People to be poor and backward Indians, they were condemned by discriminatory laws of indenture, forcing them to do free labor in the construction of roads and railroads used by national and transnational companies to move and export their products. Definitively, the Mayas suffered exploitation and violence during this period in Guatemalan history (1931–1944), which pushed them into extreme poverty.

Obviously, the young generations did not lived or experienced such painful and dramatic times in history, so it became necessary to develop a method for fixing those events into modern history. In this way, the young people were required to remember and learn about the suffering of their recent ancestors, because there were no written records left behind by them. For this purpose, the name of the hero or the villain to be remembered becomes immortalized through myth. In other words, the Maya concept of cyclical time and history becomes relevant in the continuity of ancient knowledge to be passed on from one generation to the next by using two major historical devices: the telescoping of time and the "mythification" process.

THE TELESCOPING OF TIME

The Maya people use a method to place or infix in history certain extraordinary individuals or figures that they want to elevate to the category of heroes or supernatural beings. This process or Indigenous method for infixing modern heroes into history can be called the "telescoping of time." This is a process that has been mentioned by some anthropologists, but not recognized or developed as an Indigenous method for weaving history through time. This is a Native way of documenting historical events that are considered extraordinary and that must be fixed in the mind of future generations for centuries or millennia into the future.

The concept of "telescoping of time" or the temporal distortion of events is mentioned by Victoria Bricker (1981), as she identifies Indigenous cyclical histories and ethnic conflicts among the Mayas of Guatemala, Chiapas, and Yucatan, Mexico. Through her major work: *The Indian Christ, the Indian King: The Historical Substrate of Maya Myth and Ritual* (1981), we come to know about Maya heroes from ancient pre-Hispanic time period woven into modern historical events and integrated into the oral tradition. In other words, the names of heroes from ancient time continue to be used by storytellers to document the deeds and heroism of modern figures that need to be canonized into Maya oral history and traditions. This is a way to immortalize heroes who have sacrificed their lives in wars, fighting to save their people from annihilation—be it by war or by pandemic diseases. The definition of this concept, the "telescoping of time" can be explained as follows: "The folklore of ethnic conflict among the Maya covers a time span of at least two thousand years. As new conflicts arise and become history, they are mentally fused and confused with other conflicts, their structural components squeezed into the pigeonholes of the timeless folklore paradigm. The only distortion necessary to achieve this result is the telescoping of time" (Bricker 1981:9).

In the definition provided above, we can clarify that this process is not a distortion of historical events, but a process of weaving recent events into ancient ones that have the same or equivalent value or importance to become part of history. And this history for illiterate people must be passed on through a process of mythification. The telescoping of time is then a process in which selective aspects of history are fixed into the cumulative deeds of a culture or people, and then brought back and forth to be accommodated into the appropriate myth-history that is already known by the community. Like the lenses of a telescope used here as an analogy, we can bring distant events nearer (to the present), while recent events are pushed further into the past. In this process of spatial and temporal accommodation they achieve the status of a sanctified myth to be accepted and integrated into the community's history. This has been the case with mythical figures such as Cuauhtémoc in Mexico, Tupac Amaru in South America, and Tecun Uman and Kanek among the Mayas. The same case with Quetzalcoatl, the "Feathered Serpent," a name used by lords and rulers through time, who was even considered a deity among the Toltecs and Aztecs of Central Mexico. Let me exemplify this process of immortalizing heroes with a Jakaltek Maya myth from the oral tradition.

In 1931, anthropologist Oliver La Farge mentioned in his ethnography a short legend about a Jakaltek Maya hero called Xuwan Q'anil. The storytellers were reluctant to tell the story to La Farge because they said the hero could get angry if his name is mentioned, since he was not just a regular human being, but a hero with supernatural powers. His sanctuary is located on the top of the Q'anil Mountain, and at this place he has lived forever, protecting his Jakaltek people as an immortalized hero. The Q'anil Mountain is located at the south of the town of Jacaltenango, and it continuous to be a major Maya sanctuary.

In 1977, I started to collect fragments of the Q'anil legend, which was vanishing because of the process of *Ladinization* (de-Indianization). The reason I became interested in weaving back the full story of el Q'anil was, because I saw young men being captured and forced to serve in the Guatemalan army. "Indian" soldiers were needed to be sent to a possible war against England for the case of Belize, its colony.

During the 1970s, the conflicts escalated when Guatemala requested that England leave Belize and not to interfere in Guatemala's effort to recuperate it as part of its territory. Instead, England placed a claim on Belize, based on a treaty signed between Guatemala and England in 1859. This treaty allowed England to exploit the natural resources of Belize, then a Guatemalan territory, on the condition that England would construct a railroad for Guatemala starting from the Atlantic coast to Guatemala City. But England did not comply with the terms of the treaty and did not build the railroad. Instead, England continued to exploit the resources of Belize, claiming it as its colony.

FIGURE 6.1. The Q'anil Mountain and sanctuary of the Man of Lightning.

The call for enlisting young men for an army to prepare for war to defend Belize against a military superpower, such as England came as a surprise in Mayan communities. The parents of those taken to the army and some Maya priests started to visit the sanctuary of Q'anil, asking for his protection. Q'anil was a warrior himself, who had helped to defeat the enemy in a distant war by transforming himself into lightning. This epic-legend of El Q'anil was a part of history that each Jakaltek Maya person knew since childhood, thus learning about their identity and about their cultural heroes (Montejo 2001).

This is how the legend of Q'anil was revived again, since the belief was that no Jakaltek man should die in combat in foreign lands, if protected by our hero Q'anil, the Man of Lightning (Montejo 2001). It happened that, while

Guatemala and England were busy in reclaiming Belize as each country's territory, Belize itself was engaged in obtaining its own independence from Guatemala and from England. Fortunately, the war did not occur because England decided to facilitate the independence of Belize, which became a new nation in 1979.

The process of accommodation of heroes within cyclical time periods or the mechanism called telescoping of time can be demonstrated with the legend of El Q'anil. The method of telescoping of time is an intrinsic element necessary in the process of documenting by memory Maya oral histories that are also cyclical in scope. In other words, the telescoping of time is a process of weaving recent events into ancient ones in the cosmic great cycle of time. To start with, Q'anil is a name of a day in the Maya calendar. For the Jakaltek, Q'anil is also one the four Year Bearers mentioned by Oliver La Farge in his description of the Jakaltek Maya calendar. Q'anil is then an ancient name used in Classic Maya period, possibly a great Maya hero whose name was also immortalized in the Jakaltek Maya calendar. Just as La Farge mentioned: "It could be that this myth which have acquired so many modern characteristics, be an ancient pre-Hispanic tale; that it may refer to a man, who originally had the name of the day" (La Farge 1931:121).

It should be also mentioned that Tzeltal Maya oral tradition refer to the four Year Bearers, including Q'anil, as actual human beings and warriors who have lived in the ancient past (La Farge 1931).

The name Q'anil and the lightning man appears throughout Maya ethnohistorical books such as the *Popol Vuh, Annals of the Kaqchikel, Titles of the House of Nehaib*, as well as in Maya oral tradition. According to the *Annals of the Kaqchikel*, a man came to the *Kaqchikel* lords who was subjugated by Pedro de Alvarado, conqueror of Guatemala in 1524, and said: "I am the lightning. I will kill the Spaniards; by fire they shall perish. When I strike the drum, depart [everyone] from the city; let the lords go to the other side of the river. This I will do on the day 7 *Ahmak* [August 26, 1525]. Thus, that demon spoke to the lords" (Recinos 1980:129).

Similarly, the following account written by Mayas during the Spanish conquest documents the presence and action of the lightning man. "The indigenous people who could not kill *Tonatiuh* [Alvarado] and the Lady that protected them [Virgin Mary] returned and again sent another captain who was capable of turning into lightning bolt, and this Nehaib went to confront the Spaniards as a lightning bolt" (Recinos 1983:86).

In this story translated by Adrian Recinos from the original Maya text "*Titles of the House of Nehaib*," the lightning man was not successful, because of the presence of another supernatural being, the White Lady (Virgin Mary) who protected the Spaniards. Here comes the rupture of Maya cosmology and the imposition of Christianity, which also changed and transformed their cultural beliefs into a syncretic religious belief system.

One last sample of the process of telescoping of time that I want to present here to illustrate this important device in Maya oral tradition is the case of the folk hero Erasto Urbina among the Chamula, or Tzotzil Maya of Chiapas, Mexico. Anthropologist Gary Gossen argues that to document events or history among the Tzotzil Maya, there is a process of manipulation to change history for accommodating new situations. On this process, Gary Gossen states that "Pre-existing patterns usually provide raw material for any culture change" (Gossen 1974:241). And to explain this selective change and accommodation of certain segments of Native history, we have from Gossen's category of recent true narrative the case of a Ladino (non-Indigenous) hero who entered the realm of Tzotzil Maya history as personification of previous heroes in Mexican history.

Don Erasto Urbina was a Ladino of San Cristobal de las Casas, Mexico, who after his death entered the realm of heroes, saints, and supernatural beings. This process will be mentioned later as the process of mythification of Maya leaders and heroes. The reason why Erasto Urbina entered Maya folk history as a hero was because, despite not being a Maya person, he was a protector of the Indians, as he respected Maya language and culture. In other words, Erasto Urbina supported the struggles of Indigenous People for their rights, as he protected them from the rage of Ladino authorities who continued to exploit and discriminate against them for centuries. "Urbina enforced in every way possible the law in the 1917 Constitution called Ley del 6 de enero, which guaranteed the freedoms and rights of indentured servants and peons. In 1936 he founded the Sindicato de Trabajadores Indigenas, which raised a furor among landholding elements in Chiapas by acting as a contracting agency for highland Indian labor in the lowland coffee plantations and trying to provide the best possible conditions for the Indians" (Gossen 1974:241).

For Indigenous People it was unusual that a Ladino person could really side with the Indians and be trusted as a friend. Erasto Urbina was one of these good Ladinos, who became a hero for the Tzotzil Mayas, as he fought for their rights against a powerful system that historically has kept them in servitude as a cheap labor force. Erasto Urbina lived during the mid-twentieth century, but his deeds on behalf of the Chamula of Chiapas have impressed them to the point that Urbina was fixed into the history of the Mexican Revolution of

1915. Of course, this is a historical event in which he did not participate. Gossen documented some texts from the oral tradition in which Erasto Urbina is credited for solving the problems that gave rise to the Mexican Revolution. And on the issue of mythification or the process of becoming a mythical figure through supernatural action Urbina was also "credited with a kind of mystical partnership with San Cristobal in saving the San Cristobal Church from destruction by the Carrancistas" (Gossen 1974:242).

In this way, Erasto Urbina as a good Ladino man became a hero and was credited with supernatural power, a precondition for entering Mexican history, thus joining the rank of heroes who have become national figures during the Mexican Revolution. This is clearly a process of telescoping of time, in which the Mexican Revolution was brought to the present, to fix Erasto Urbina into the preexisting historical pattern and then push it back to become part of a global history by joining the Mexican revolutionary heroes celebrated by Mexico.

THE HALO OF MYSTERY AND THE MYTHIFICATION PROCESS

As I have mentioned above, Q'anil may have been a Maya hero who has been immortalized as a day name and year bearer in the Maya calendar. This name, Q'anil, has been repeated or reused by successive Maya leaders or heroes throughout the centuries or Maya millennial history. Each new Q'anil has been recognized as having supernatural powers and becoming a hero by defeating the enemy that threatens the life of the entire community. In this cyclical view of time, history repeated itself, so new heroes arose and performed extraordinary deeds, being immortalized under the name of the previous one. The event in which the hero has excelled must have been of an extraordinary nature, in which he had made the ultimate sacrifice: offering his own life to save his people from evil. This is the ultimate action or sacrifice that count: that out of selfishness a hero fights for what is right—that is, to save his community from danger and ensure the continuity of life on earth. This is an extraordinary task of heroism that fulfills the requirements for being immortalized. Xuwan Q'anil, the Jakaltek Maya hero, performed this extraordinary task. The following is an excerpt from *El Q'anil: Man of Lightning* (Montejo 2001):

> Xhuwan stood under the shadow of the k'uh saying:
> "Father Q'anil, give me your powers."

Q'anil answered, surprised,
"Tell me, Xhuwan, why do you ask for my powers?"
"Tomorrow my brothers will go to fight a war
in aid of an oppressed people far from here.
As the fame of the warriors of Xajla'
has reached their ears, they now ask us
to fight the enemy that uses strange weapons
and fights from the sea, under the waves.
But our battalion is made of sorcerers.
They are not warriors! What can they do?
We bearers will perish with them in that sea,
because they all can do is turn themselves
into ferocious beats or strange creatures
that will be targets for the enemy on the beach.
Therefore, Father Q'anil," Xhuwan declared.
"I want to offer my life for those people.
It matters not that my blood be spilled
and that I never return to this land,
as long as they achieve peace and are saved.
Thus, I wish to perpetuate the name of my people.
Give me, therefore, the powers I need and long for
so, I may depart tomorrow with the morning star."
Hearing this touching tale and request,
the great k'uh responded, saying:
"Are you willing to leave behind all that you have
and never return to your town
or change your mind once you have the powers?"
"I have already made that decision," Xhuwan said.
"Then lie down and receive my powers."
Xhuwan lay down, and at that moment there was
a great thunderclap, and many lightning bolts
lit up the darkened sky.
The voice of Q'anil was heard through the lightning.
"Arise and put on this yellow shirt
that holds all the powers you ask for."
As Q'anil spoke,
Xhuwan stood up and rubbed his hand with satisfaction.
(Montejo 2001:18–19)

From the above fragment we realize that there is a ritual in which the old hero Q'anil transfers the power and name to the new Jakaltek hero or young man called Xhuwan. At this point, Xhuwan is called also Q'anil as he receives the power of the lightning—a powerful weapon that he uses to destroy the enemies and save his people. Despite being victorious over the enemy and saving the people, he cannot return to the town as a regular person, and becomes another lightning man who now duels in the mountain, also called Q'anil (Montejo 1991).

In this story, what was needed was the spatiotemporal accommodation of a hero into a historical and cyclical pattern, fixing important events (Jakaltek triumph) into the memory of generations yet to come. The time necessary for the mythification process depends on the gravity or magnitude of the event in which the hero has excelled by giving his life for his people. He must defeat the enemy and achieve the long-awaited transformation, to be free from an oppressive social order. How long does it take for this process of converting a hero into a mythical figure to be forever remembered in the oral tradition? It depends on the storyteller or the one who recounts the event to his listeners, but at least one generation must have passed, or at least five *k'altuns* (100 years).

Another example of a Ladino becoming a hero among the Jakaltek Maya of Guatemala is that of Rafael Carrera. Carrera became president of Guatemala (1837–1865) after the rupture of the Federation of Central American countries under the rule of Francisco Morazán (Woodward 1971). Just like in the case of Erasto Urbina in Chiapas, Mexico, Rafael Carrera came into existence as a legendary figure because he provided support for Indigenous People. As president, he allowed them more freedom to move and to revitalize their cultures, which were decimated during the colonial period. In other words, Rafael Carrera recognized the plight of Indigenous People who were forced to work as cheap laborers in *finca* plantations of the southern coast of Guatemala. In Central America, during this period there was a conflict of ideologies between the two existing political parties, Conservatives and Liberals, on how to develop these countries. The Conservatives were more supportive of the native peasant population, while the Liberals wanted a radical change, which included selling the native's communal lands to foreign investors.

Most of Rafael Carrera's life was unknown to the Indians, but the story that was popularized was that he was a poor man who dedicated himself buying pigs in Mayan villages and selling them in the market of big cities.

"El era un cochero" (He was a pig merchant), the people said. This was the opposition's way to denigrate this strongman (*caudillo*), whose leadership was approved by the Indigenous population that defended them from the elite or ruling class.

In real life, Rafael Carrera was an army man, a general who became a very charismatic leader who united Indigenous communities on his behalf, as he sought power in Guatemala. He was persecuted and took refuge in Mexico, but continued to work in building his army from the border town of Comitan, Chiapas, while he got into contact with the Jakaltek Maya people of Western Guatemala. His strategy was to identify himself as an Indigenous and poor peasant who wanted to liberate those of his own condition. He visited Maya villages in Western Guatemala, asking leaders to support him and giving them positions as captains or commanders in his own rebel army.

According to Jakaltek Maya oral tradition, Carrera was tested by the Jakaltek authorities to verify if he had the gift or the required qualities for becoming a great leader. The test for Carrera was to find a bottle of rum with some arrows that the Jakaltek authorities had hidden somewhere in a cliff at the outskirts of town. According to Maya tradition, a good leader must have the intuition and the ability to solve problems in the shortest period of time. If he could find the hidden bottle and the arrows, then the Jakaltek, who were known to be excellent warriors, would join his army and fight on his side. The story tells us that Carrera found the hidden bottle and the arrows without much difficulty and within the required time limit, so the Jakaltek approved his leadership and offered him their support as allies. Then, the politico-religious authorities of the town proceeded to make a ceremony of preparation and cleansing of the leader, so that he could march into Guatemala City with the assurance that he would defeat the enemy and become president of Guatemala.

After finding the hidden objects and being cleansed by the prayer-makers in Jacaltenango, Rafael Carrera was taken to the plain in San Marcos Huista, just across the canyon separating Jacaltenango from the village of San Marcos. At this place, the prayer-makers and the diviners collected the dispersed bones of a dead horse and after pilling them together, a powerful *ahb'eh* or diviner hit the bones thirteen times with a stick. When the *ahb'eh* gave the thirteen or last slash to the bones, a white horse rose up from those bones in front of everyone. Of course, this white horse was the materialization of a spiritual horse by the power of the ancestors and God. In other words, this was an extraordinary horse given to Rafael Carrera, so from this point on he became very strong and invincible in battles.

In the same way, the *Jakaltek* warriors who accompanied Rafael Carrera also achieved extraordinary powers here, as they could use only one arrow to defeat hundreds of enemy soldiers. For example, an arrow would be shot from the bow of an archer and fly to the target, crossing not only one or two bodies at a time, but several, before returning to the hands of the one who shot it.

In this way, the Jakaltek Maya helped Rafael Carrera to achive supernatural power by defeating his enemies and fulfilling his mission, which was to deliver the Indians from oppression, servitude, and forced labor which had caused them too much pain and poverty throughout the centuries. Here, Carrera takes the role of Santiago, the patron saint of the Spaniards, who is always represented mounting a white horse while leading the Spaniards to battle. In other words, Carrera passed the test of time and became not only a mythical hero, but a warrior with supernatural powers. His role was parallel to that of Santiago Apostle, whom the Spaniards invoked as their savior before invading Indigenous territories in the Americas during the early sixteenth century.

In this way, by the late 1900s the Jakaltek oral tradition had already mythicized Rafael Carrera as a great hero, enshrouding him in the aura of mystery, and thus, achieving the process of mythification. Rafael Carrera was loved by the people, as he helped them to come out of servitude and did not enslave them during his government, which lasted thirty years.

Unfortunately, Rafael Carrera was overthrown by the Liberals and the pressure on Indigenous People as a cheap labor force continued under the Liberal reform implanted by Justo Rufino Barrios (1871–1885). Once again, Indigenous People were placed under forced labor; under these circumstances, the people remembered Carrera while constructing his mythical figure. Under Rafael Carrera, Indigenous People were real citizens, not the backward and inferior people they were considered to be by previous and successive governments after Rafael Carrera.

In Guatemala, the Liberal government did not consider Indigenous People to be assets to the country, but obstacles to progress. This is how Indigenous People had to endure dictators after dictators, especially Jorge Ubico (1931–1944). This military government subjugated Indigenous People to harsh punishments and servitude. It was after the defeat of Jorge Ubico and the beginning of the so-called ten years of spring with the government of Juan José Arévalo and Jacobo Arbenz Guzman (1944–1954), that Indigenous People were freed from the forced labor. At this time, Carrera had already become a mythical figure as mentioned above.

The legend of Carrera shows the process of mythification like that of Erasto Urbina among the Chamulas in Chiapas, Mexico. Thus, Rafael Carrera as a Ladino is fixed within the Spanish historical event of conquest. The Spaniards believed that Santiago the Apostle fought on their side during the invasion of Native lands, as he had done during the wars to expel the Moors from Spain. These myths have been internalized by Indigenous People on this continent, and they used them in a syncretic way to explain the power of Catholic religion that was imposed on them by Spanish missionaries. This is the case of the image of the White Lady (Virgin Mary), who was said to protect the Spaniards against the "man of lightning" during the Spanish conquest of Guatemala in 1524, mentioned above. In Jakaltek mythology, Rafael Carrera was accommodated into the spatiotemporal pattern of cyclical history through the mechanism or device that we have called the "telescoping of time." In the oral tradition of each Maya community there are many of these legends and myths of heroes who have passed the test of history and have been included in the historical process, to be remembered for posterity. This is the case of *Tecun Uman*, the great K'iche Maya captain of war who was said to have fled as an eagle as he fought against Pedro de Alvarado, the conqueror of Guatemala. So, when a mythical figure is surrounded with this halo of power and mystery, the hero becomes immortalized, and his memory perpetuated into the oral tradition forever.

MAYALOGUE

SEVEN

Ohtajb'al: Maya Knowledge and Epistemology

THE HEGEMONY OF Western philosophical traditions over Indigenous beliefs systems and forms of knowledge has been deeply enforced through all disciplines taught in schools, as if science and knowledge belong only to the West, from which it traces its ancient genealogy. For example, the Greek term *epistemology*, meaning *episteme* (knowledge) and *logos* (study of) have been universalized as the appropriate term to be used to refer to the Western concept of knowledge. In other words, the tradition of using Greek or Latin etymologies only emphasizes that scientific and "legitimate" knowledge can only come from the West. In this way, other explanations of what knowledge is and how it is produced, coming from other cultures than Greek, are not taken into consideration. We come to take as natural that science and philosophy, as well as the origin of words and etymology, can only derive from the ancient Greek, as originators of all knowledge. But, as we know, other ancient cultures and civilizations such as that of the Maya have also developed sophisticated terms for explaining the production and nature of knowledge they called *ohtajb'al* (*ohtaj* = knowledge) and (*b'al* = accumulation of). The reason is that the West has had the power to diffuse its ideas and worldviews, while rejecting as untruthful the knowledge systems of other cultures. Regarding this practice, I have said in previous works that Native scholars must start using the terms traditionally used in their cultures for academic purposes, even if those who are not Natives are not familiar with those terms equally valuable as ancient Greek terms.

Currently, we are encountering more and more books and writings that emphasize the distinctive ways that Native Americans think and produce knowledge. In other words, with the growth of the field of Native American and Indigenous Studies, and the continuous struggle for the decolonization of knowledge among Indigenous People, new works are emerging, and they point to the fact that "Indigenous epistemologies are action-oriented. They are about living life every day according to certain values" (Kovach 2010:62). All this has to do with place and language, as humans relate themselves to the material world and that of ideas (meanings), and to the supernatural world. To know is to understand our responsibilities as humans and recognize the "dignity" of other living beings, while constructing a world of respect, peace, and brotherhood.

To discuss Maya knowledge and epistemology (*ohtajb'al*), it is then fundamental that we start with the Maya calendar, which for the Mayas is the source of all knowledge, action, and appropriate rituals for living a full life on earth. But before entering into the discussion and analysis of the nature of Maya knowledge and how it is produced, let me discuss some of the anthropological and linguistic developments in the past that almost opened the opportunity for a more serious understanding of Native cultures and Indigenous worldviews. This is the case of an important development during the 1960s called the "new ethnography" (Sturtevant 1964), when ethnographers and linguists applied linguistic models of analysis to produce ethnographies. They argued for the need to elicit units of analysis and classification from the insider's or emic perspective, and this extension of the new ethnography was called "ethnoscience."

The development of new ethnography, or the rigorous approach called ethnoscience, was an attempt to validate Native knowledge and classificatory systems as different ways of classifying the world around. With this, there was hope for rethinking new ways and methods for writing ethnographies. This was a response to the increasing critique of anthropology during the 1960, which was truly Eurocentric and colonialist in its mode of research and analysis. Unfortunately, the field's insistence on being scientific and objective turned Indigenous cultures and people into objects to be studied, as if in laboratories. In this process, their abilities to think and produce knowledge were dismissed. From these biased explanations, Indigenous People were neglected, while others created grotesque misrepresentations of their cultures. In other words, instead of creating a multivocal text from insider and outsider's perspective, ethnography became more of an instrument to popularize the stereotypes of Indigenous People (e.g., the Kayapo).

I believe it is important to resuscitate the proposed new ethnography and ethnoscience, since they are ultimately closer to the current projects of rewriting histories and producing auto-ethnographies for Indigenous self-representation. In other words, my discussion here on Maya knowledge and epistemology must refer to previous contributions in the field that were truncated because of the persistent colonialist practice that guided anthropology. The Indigenous voices or the insider's perspective has not been valued by Western "science" that has ignored other ways of knowing and classifying the world. The Western view was considered the only rightful and appropriate way of behaving and being human. Other worldviews and traditions were considered wrong, or it was considered that they needed to be corrected, assimilated, or forced to disappear. For this reason, the latest debate in anthropology focused on the problems of representation.

Obviously, there is a need for an interactionist model for "representing" Indigenous cultures. In other words, Indigenous People must "present" themselves and their own cultures (the Native's point of view) to the readers or academic world, and not to be "represented" by others. Both approaches (emic and etic) are equally valid if we want to keep writing about Indigenous ways of life, but the emic point of view must be elevated to the level of the etic (outsider's) perspective as proposed by the new ethnography. In other words,

> The most important claim of the "new ethnographers" is that they will be able to give more precise descriptions of cultural phenomena than heretofore possible—cultural descriptions that will be modeled on linguistic ones. Just as the linguist works with standard units—in terms of *phonemes, morphemes, phonology* and *grammar*—so, they claim, will the ethnographer be able to find the proper units of comparison. Thus, rather than imposing our own units and classifications on other culture, arbitrarily forcing them, as it were, to have such things economics, politics, or religion as we have done since the very beginning of anthropology, we will be able to elicit their meaningful units and classifications. Perceiving these will give us the "inside" view, the subject's own view of the world and things as opposed to our own ethnocentric and egocentric views. (Langness 1985:115)

The above assertion could have been possible if attention was given to the proposed new ethnography, and auto-ethnography, although, it could have been difficult for ethnographers to master Native culture and languages to describe it from the insider's perspective. The proposed method for writing cultures with attention to the emic perspective was an important proposal, but here, the foreign anthropologists will have difficulties trying to become a Native or think as a Native. The best approach for anthropology might have been to train earlier Native anthropologists who could collaborate with the researcher, instead of the anthropologist trying to become Native him- or herself. Throughout the development of anthropology as a science, Indigenous individuals were not given opportunities to be trained as anthropologists at universities. There was no interest in anthropology for training Natives to become researchers or teachers; instead, they were seen only as storytellers or "informants." A very few exceptions could be mentioned among the Mayas, such as Alfonso Villa Rojas, a Yucatec anthropologist trained by Robert Redfield, who wrote his major ethnographic work titled *The Maya of East Central Quintana Roo* (1945); as well as Jacinto Arias, a Tzotzil trained at Columbia University, whose anthropological work was titled "*The Numinous World of the Maya*" (Arias 1975). It was only until the 1990s that some Maya students were trained in different disciplines, mostly the social sciences, and have become researchers themselves in their own cultures. This is the case of Victor Montejo and his auto ethnography: *Voices from Exile: Violence and Survival in Modern Maya History* (1993).

Another major problem in representation, centered on the complexities of fieldwork and the process of gathering information by using non-Indigenous languages in the gathering and translation of ethnographic material. Knowing the language of the community being studied was the best way to do fieldwork and document Indigenous worldviews. For Mayas, a dialogue or any cultural and social action such as praying, singing, telling a folktale, or even planting, harvesting, hunting, and so on is not an isolated action. It is always the result of cosmic relationships, or a trialogical consultation between humans, nature, and the supernatural world.

Early anthropologists such as Bronislaw Malinowski, Emile Durkheim, Robert Redfield, and so forth, who spent more direct time among the Natives, have recognized many aspects of this respectful approach to nature and the supernatural world. Those days were long gone, when Maya communities were more isolated in the so-called closed corporate communities, while struggling against colonialist domination and forced labor during the early 1900s. Now, other crises have emerged as they continue to struggle against modernization, expropriation, and globalization in the twenty-first century.

To understand Native epistemologies, it is important to understand how Indigenous languages are used to shape cultures and express ideas, thoughts, and Native worldviews. Even if the Native language of the culture being studied is used for research, modern thinkers believe that there are other elements that mediate into the dialogue metaphor mentioned above. "Lacan, and others, have pointed out that in a conversation between two people, there is always at least a third, that is, the mediation of the embedded or unconscious cultural structures in language, terminologies, nonverbal codes of behavior and assumptions about what constitutes the imaginary, real, and symbolic" (Marcus and Fischer 1986:31).

The information presented here in Mayalogue comes mainly from an emic approach, or the process of eliciting meaning from an Indigenous perspective or Native point of view. Victor Turner has argued that the Native's point of view is fundamental to understanding the multiple meanings of dominant symbols. This level of anthropological analysis is what he called the "exegetical meaning," or what we call Native hermeneutics (*tihiloj* = Indigenous interpretation and deconstruction). "The exegetical meaning is obtained from questioning Indigenous informants about observed ritual behavior. Here one must distinguish between information given by the ritual specialist and information given by laymen, that is, between esoteric and exoteric interpretations" (Turner 1967:50–51).

In this statement, Turner recognized the importance of the Native's point of view, but he also recognized that not everyone can tell the story, even if they are members of the same Indigenous community. The role of the specialist should be recognized, and since Indigenous People do not compartmentalize knowledge in different segments, institutions, or action, the ritual specialist then has on his hands a more unifying global story that encompasses the trilogy: nature, humans, and the supernatural world in any of its manifestation.

To achieve and obtain the level of Indigenous interpretation or Native hermeneutics, attention and respect must be paid to Native spirituality, which means not as religion that is localized (institutional), but as a collective and universal consciousness that is present everywhere on earth and the universe. One way to approach Native knowledge, then, is through hermeneutics as stated by Marcus and Fischer: "Hermeneutics similarly became a label for close reflection on the way the Native deciphers and decode their own 'complex' texts be they literary texts or other forms of cultural communication, such as rituals" (Marcus and Fischer 1986:30). This statement brings us again to the dialogue metaphor, a conversation not only between two actors or cultures but with a third party which is omnipresent (the Creator), who expects to be "remembered" and nurtured through prayers, songs, ceremonies. This is a reciprocal interaction needed when taking from nature for the fulfillment of our basic needs. In other words, humans must pray for those who cannot speak for themselves and are dependent of human action such plants, animals, mountains, rivers, and so on. Again, this is a trialogical communication and interaction practiced by Indigenous People for the maintenance of unity and harmony in a more balanced world. For most non-Indigenous People, to communicate with nature or to talk to a tree, for example, is unconceivable or nonsense practiced only by crazy people. But for Indigenous People it is a norm, since all living beings are part of creation and they all are related and interdependent for their universal and collective survival. In explicit terms, we must protect nature from depletion so that earth is always abundant and healthy for future generations yet to come.

The ethnographic text, then, is the key production that can depict accurately a culture if developed in accordance with the Indigenous worldviews, and not from a Eurocentric perspective. But how can we approach other cultures and write about what they do, think, or live if we don't speak the Native language of the community studied? This dilemma has been discussed widely, mainly in the development of anthropological methods for doing research and fieldwork. But above all methodologies, the importance of the Native language is essential and considered a key to opening true dialogue and entering other people's cultures and worldviews. For that reason, anthropologists are required to learn other languages and do fieldwork, but usually they learn the official language of the region or nation (e.g., Spanish) if doing fieldwork in Latin America and not the Native language. A few have tried to learn other's language, but even with this superficial learning it is difficult to deconstruct or *tihiloj* the multiple meanings and layers of symbolic rituals and esoteric discourses. Despite this difficulty, language is still the vehicle that can bring us to a closer contact with Indigenous cultures and worldviews.

I use the Maya concept of *"tihiloj"* which has multiple meanings: to analyze, deconstruct, and interpret the meaning of something that is hidden or not open to regular observation. We can use the metaphor of a tied bundle that we can see from the outside—its size, shape, color, texture, and weight, but you cannot see the content, much less its significance or the information contained in it. You need to open the bundle and see its content so that the information provided, plus your external observation can jointly provide a more accurate description or analysis of it.

For this reason, language for the Mayas is sacred, and it has the power to name and rename things, people, and places. In other words, language for the Mayas according to the *Popol Vuh* is a gift from God and the sacred instrument that connects all parts of creation together through the spoken word. The uses of the language for giving thanks is clearly established in the *Popol Vuh*, as exemplified by the first fathers and mothers made of corn who were thankful to their Creators.

> "We really give you thanks, two and three times! We have been created, we have been given a mouth and a face, we speak, we hear, we think, and walk; we feel perfectly, and we know what is far and what is near. We also see the large and the small in the sky and on earth. We give you thanks, then, for having created us, oh, Creator and Maker! For having given us being, oh, our grandmother! Oh, our grandfather!" they said, giving thanks for their creation and formation. (Goetz and Morley 1950:168)

It is evident, then, that the language carries information and it is used to express internal feelings that can move us to action. We can assert that Indigenous languages are important for understanding and explaining the world around, as well as for giving thanks and celebrating life itself. The term *language* in Jakaltek Maya is *ab'xub'al* (*ab'* to listen, *xub'* to whistle, *b'al* instrument), and *tzoti'* (word), which is a compound word too, meaning "*tzo*" (rattle), as well as "*ti'*" (mouth), which literally means: the "rattling of the mouth" or the mouth producing sounds or words. Language is the major vehicle for expressing Native knowledge and for producing flowered words (poetry), songs, chants, prayers, and so forth. Ritual language is then important for performing rituals and ceremonies that bring peace, harmony, and unity to the trilogy: nature, humans, and the spiritual world. That is why in the *Popol Vuh* God is called Heart of Heaven, Heart of Hearth, which is the powerful web of relationship that unifies the cosmic force that moves earth, the sun, and the universe in great cycles of creation, destruction, and renewal. "In time present, as in time past, language with its wide range of rhetorical, poetical, and musical embellishments, as served as a sacred symbol which allows humans to share qualities with and communicate with gods. In effect, beautifully executed speech and songs are the only substances that the human body can produce that are accessible to and worthy before divine beings" (Gossen 1999:84).

For this reason, the Tzotzil of Chiapas pay much attention to the classification of language into ancient words, recent narratives, language for rendering holy, and language for people whose hearts are heated, and so on (Gossen 1984). A similar language classification exists among the Jakaltek Maya, and this taxonomy can be used to document ancient and modern histories. But for our task here, I will refer to the importance of language for the classification of the world around in time and space. Although, some linguists have argued for the prominence of linguistic relativity that gave rise to the Sapir-Whorf hypothesis, which basically states that there is a strong relationship between language and culture, in a way that language determines the way we think, act, and create cultures.

Other linguists explained Indigenous cognition and classification systems through the universalism of color terminology. Brent Berlin and Paul Kay (1969) proposed a basic color terminology that argues for the evolutionary process of the mind to produce a terminology for colors. According to these scholars, the fact that many Indigenous cultures do not have separate terms for certain colors such as blue or green is because either they don't recognize the difference between these two colors or they do not have linguistic terms to name them. Obviously, this is a misunderstanding of Indigenous classificatory systems, and this assumption cannot be supported by Maya cultural and linguistic data.

The Maya have clearly classified the world into five major (primary) colors, to distinguish the five directions or divisions of earth. From the *Popol Vuh*, we are told that the roads of *Xibalba*, the underworld, replicated the colors assigned to the five directions on earth: the color white for the north, yellow for the south, red for the east, and black for the west, as well as "blue-green" for the center.

The ancient Maya classified the four directions in this order, and this is established in the ancient Maya codex. At the center of the world grows the mythical sacred *ceiba* tree, whose branches reach into the heavens. The Jakaltek call the center on earth *smuxuk txotx'* (the navel of earth), and they call the center on the sky or direction of the axis from the center of earth to heaven *smuxuk kanh* (navel of the sky)—something like the *kusansum* or umbilical cord that united earth with heaven, and through which nourishment passed through in ancient times, according to the Yukatek Mayas (Villa Rojas 1978).

The fact that the Mayas have only one term for green and blue (*yax*), has been used by some researchers to argue that either they have visual problems so they do not distinguish between green and blue, or that the language was not well evolved enough for them to have a distinct name for green and blue. These assumptions are wrong, since the Mayas were extreme observers and developed metaphorical and abstract ideas to name and symbolize things around them. Even a child can distinguish the array of colors from the color

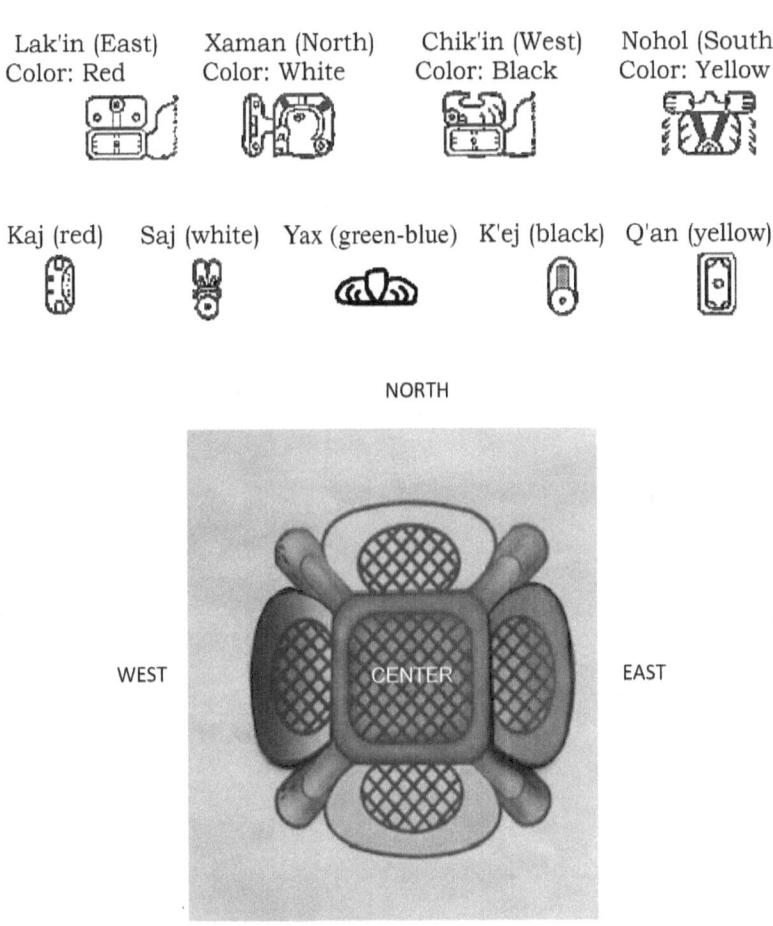

FIGURE 7.1. The five Maya directions and attached colors.

spectrum displayed in the sky by a rainbow. Let me exemplify this observation and explain the different classificatory system used by the Jakaltek Maya in terms of colors, to dissipate this myth of "color blindness."

Any Maya person could, at an early age, distinguish and name the different colors within the Native classificatory system. The key image to be used is the rainbow, which is called *"kaj ch'elep,"* or the dispersion of color through the prism of raindrops (*ch'elep*) stemming from the dominant color red (*kaj*), according to Jakaltek observation. The term *ch'elep* is fundamental in

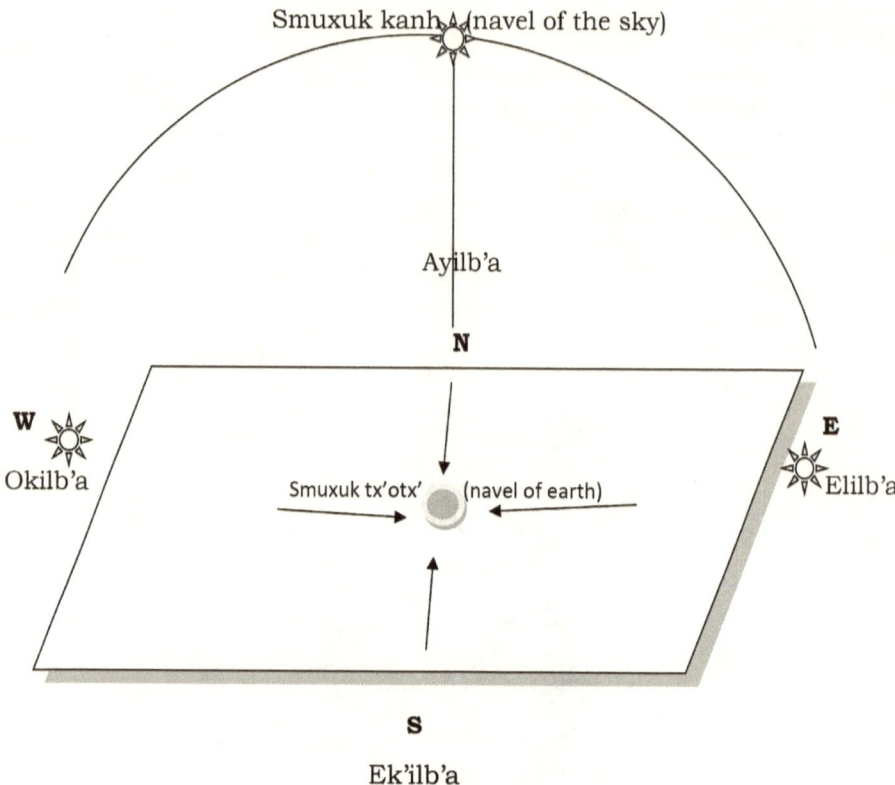

FIGURE 7.2. The Jakaltek Maya universe and directions.

explaining the name of this natural phenomenon, since it implies that there is a display of many colors to observe in the rainbow. Each dominant color split into different tones and intensities, forming this spectrum of colors.

For example, when we used the term *yax* for green and blue, it is not that we don't distinguished the difference between these two colors, but for the Jakaltek, the green disperses from light green to a deeper green that becomes blue. So, to differentiate the spectrum of colors stemming from *yax* (green) to a deeper *yax* (blue), we have a classificatory system that is complex, since each term to be used for the variation of greens or blues come from the texture, dimension, quality, brilliance, opacity, deepness, healthiness, abundance, distance, and so forth. For example, to deal with green or *"yax,"* a speaker of Jakaltek will understand and recognize this classification and what is being referred to by mentally identifying and imagining the texture and other information surrounding the object being named. Thus, in the Maya language, a fertile land is called *yaxlum* (literally: green land). The term *lum* for land is not used anymore, as the Jakaltek now use the term *tx'otx'*.

Here, we present a few possible arrays of colors stemming from the color *yax*, as referred to green. And green is, in turn, the dominant color used to name or classify everything that pertains to plants, trees, grass, fruits, mountains, earth, water, the sky, and so on.

Yax = green (name of the color).
yax waq'woh (strong green), for example, the color of forest trees
yax janjoh (deep green), for example, healthy bushes
yax paq'poh (pale green, not healthy)
yax lanhloh (e.g., healthy cornfield)
yax nhich'noh (a green of a young, not mature fruit)
yax tz'antz'oh (green plantation in extension or distance)
yax kich'koh (green like the inside of a caterpillar being squeezed)

Now, by shifting to the same color *yax* to the domain of the color blue, as referred to water and sky, we can do the same exercise, since the adjective

FIGURE 7.3. The Rainbow (*kaj ch'elep*).

attached to the color's name will provide the speaker with the information required to recognize the object being named.

> *Yax* = blue (primary color).
> *Yax namnoh* (the blue color of the sky),
> *yax hon-oh* (deep blue, referring to profundity of water: lake or ocean blue),
> *yax en-oh* (deep, dirty blue like a pond with algae)
> *yax tz'antz'oh* (deep and brilliant blue)
> *Yax lanhloh* (bright moving blue) like flame of fire.

The classification of a color into its derivate or color spectrum can be done with all the colors. For the sake of showing the complexity of the Jakaltek Maya classificatory system, let's provide a list of possible reds, in relation to the object being described as follows. Red (*kaj*): *kaj maymo* (red of abundant small red flowers), *kaj linhlo* (red as the sunset), *kaj tz'uytz'u* (profound red and shiny), *kaj panhpoh* (color of the spilled blood), *kaj ch'otch'o* (color of the eye after crying), *kaj yolyoh* (color of fruits very ripe), *kaj ch'epch'o* (red of meat when cut), *kaj chub'chu* (red of the lips with lipstick), and so forth. For a non-Native speaker of the language it could be very difficult to identify these colors right away. The development of a complex classificatory system among the Jakaltek and other Maya cultures confirms that there are no "primitive" minds and cultures, and that the universal state of the mind is the same everywhere among human beings. This confirms our argument that there are many different forms of classification used by non-Western cultures to identify and explain the texture and quality of objects that colors the world.

MAYA WAYS OF KNOWING, EPISTEMOLOGY

Most scholars writing on Indigenous knowledge have recognized the relationship of Indigenous People to their environment as a way of producing knowledge about the world. But this same relationship has been seen as a confirmation of the universal "nature-culture" dichotomy predicated by structuralist anthropologists such as Claude Lévi-Strauss. Structuralism was of course a very important theoretical development in anthropology, but for Indigenous People this dichotomy did not mean much. The cosmocentric paradigm was always present in Native human action, as their relationships were always tri-dimensional: nature, humans, and the spiritual world. The different definitions of culture were Western constructs, since for Indigenous People there is no separate human behavior that is relevant if does not respond to the original teachings of the ancestors. Respect and reciprocity with every part of creation was the rule, which was also conductive to a peaceful survival. To develop knowledge from this cosmic unity is to understand the relationship as an integral part of the whole. Nature is not something separate from humans (culture), and distant from the supernatural world. All are part of a totality in which humans share the ethic responsibility to nourish and maintain this cosmic unity. There is a continuous dialogue within the three major structures or realms as shown and presented by the Mayalogue model.

Hopefully, modern scholars will take Indigenous People's concerns for life more seriously and put aside their Western "privileged epistemology" thought to be the only form to explain knowledge. "To understand such a process, one must consider such dimensions as local theories of the working of the cosmos, sociologies and ontologies of non-human beings, spatial representation of social and non-social domains, ritual prescriptions and proscriptions governing the treatment of, and the relation with, different categories of beings" (Descola 1996:85).

The above suggestion is what I intend to do with Mayalogue, as I take Indigenous knowledge in the context of a cosmic unity, which is basic for understanding how Indigenous People (Maya) produce knowledge—not to separate culture, nature, institutions, and events as isolated units, but as part of a global system that is alive and sharing the breath or blessing of creation. Mircea Eliade has come close to explaining this cosmic alliance or unity; in turn, it will be so difficult for Western rationalists to even consider these actions to be a result of a logical behavior.

> The Modern Occidental experiences certain uneasiness before many manifestations of the sacred. He finds it difficult to accept the fact that, for many human beings, the sacred can be manifested in stones or trees, for example. But as we shall soon see, what is involved is not a veneration of the stone in itself, a cult of the tree in itself. The sacred tree, the sacred stone are not adored as stone or tree; they are worshipped precisely because they are *hierophanies*, because they show something that is no longer stone or tree but the sacred, the ganz andere. (Eliade 1959:12–13)

It becomes clear that Indigenous People use nature and their environment for gathering information, ideas, and knowledge. We must learn how to listen to the forest, the birds, the waters, and the animals. By paying attention to Native knowledge and by not imposing privileged Western epistemology as the only right way to produce knowledge, we can have a different appreciation of Native ways of life and learning. Referring to the respectful attitude of the Mayas toward their natural environment, a Catholic priest referred to their spirituality in this way. "It is *religion* without a temple, the earth is the first place, universe if you wish, and where all forms of life exist: Man, plants, animals, and the owners of the mountains. The next universe is where the stars exist, and all the stars are real persons from the earth accompanying the Saints. The Sun, the most important to all beings and the grandmother Moon are here too" (Reina 1984:107).

The extension of human kinship into the universe is presented in the *Popol Vuh*, where Hunapuh becomes the Sun (Father), and Ixbalanke becomes the Moon (Mother), and the Pleiades constellation was formed by the 400 boys killed by Zipacna. This cosmic kinship or sacred myth of creation was established in the *Popol Vuh* with the purpose of reminding human beings that they and other beings on earth depend on the powers of the universe to survive and coexist, always following the rules of respect and reciprocity.

For the Mayas, everything should start with the sacred calendar or the source of "great knowledge," followed with the appropriate ceremonies for each day as practiced by the ritual specialist or *ahb'eh*. In the past, during La Farge's research among the Jakaltek, the calendar (*b'isom tz'ayik*), or *b'isom q'ag'al*, according to the *Popol Vuh*, was known as the sacred bundle containing the information that needed to be interpreted every day for predicting the future. The production and accumulation of knowledge was based on a deeper understanding of the omens of the day, and the prophetic cycles of time interpreted by the diviner or *ahb'eh*, which means "the one who leads the way." As mentioned earlier, the Jakaltek Maya calendar has days dedicated to plants, animals, for traveling, for trading or business, for the ancestors, for ancient heroes, for the wind, for the waters, lightning or thunder, to earth, and God. Humans are then caretakers of nature and they should maintain a constant dialogue (to give thanks, make requests, or just complain) with the Creator for the maintenance of a healthy life for all. The petition is done for the collective and not for an individual, since we all are interconnected. Each part affects the other if there is an imbalance, so the role of human beings must be to follow the sacred norms of coexistence for maintaining relative harmony. For this reason, a peasant will pray and ask compassion for the trees that he will cut for planting his cornfield. The prayers are directed to God, and in the prayers, the cornfield is also recommended to *Witz-ak'al*, so that animals from the wild will not destroy it.

In the communities there are also specialists who will pray for rain and for the well-being of the entire population by following the teachings of the ancestors. Since most Mayas were agriculturalists, they paid special attention to nature while carrying out their slash-and-burn agricultural practice. In the past, before setting fire to the trees already cut and dried, ready to be burned, the Jakaltek Maya used to go through the cleared land making noise and scaring away any animals or birds that were still on the land to be set on fire. This compassionate feeling and practice was documented by Robert Redfield during his fieldwork among the Yucatec Maya of Chan Kom in 1931. According to Redfield, the Yukatek Maya of Chan Kom have a very special relationship with the turtle, an animal related to water and rain. "When the bush is kindled at the time of burning, the pious agriculturalist does not fail to call out, 'Save yourselves, tortoises! Here comes the fire!' (*Hoceneex acob! He cu tal le kake!*)" (Redfield 1964:207).

Human activity, then, should be a conscious action that considers a respectful relationship and recognition of the rights to live of other beings in their natural environment. It doesn't matter what kind of activity was being performed, be it related to agriculture, religion, hunting, travel, building, and so on; every activity was always directed by the *ahb'eh*, in consultation of the Maya calendar for the appropriate day to initiate any activity. The fact is that the Maya calendar (the Great Knowledge) is an instrument for practicing, living, and guiding the production of knowledge through a holistic view of nature. The Jakaltek Maya calendar documented by Oliver La Farge in 1929 is a good example for illustrating how nature, the cosmos (the sacred), and human beings are all interrelated. As recognized by Oliver La Farge, the Jakaltek were still practicing the Year Bearer ceremony, an ancient Maya ceremony mentioned by Bishop Diego de Landa in Yucatan. Unfortunately, La Farge did not speak the Maya language, so he had to use a Ladino interpreter. For this reason, the Native experts or diviners (*ahb'eh*) did not provide him with enough information concerning the nature of the days of the Maya calendar. But despite his limitations, La Farge managed to document the twenty day names from various *ahb'eh* or Maya calendar experts in Jacaltenango. In what follows, I provide a few more pieces of information related to each day, and its importance for a collective survival.

THE JAKALTEK MAYA NAMES OF THE DAYS:
THEIR NATURE AND OMEN

The Jakaltek Maya calendar, which is the continuation of the ancient Maya calendar of the Classic Maya of antiquity, contains the twenty day names forming a uinal (month), or *x-Ahaw* (month) in Jakaltek language as described by Oliver La Farge (1931).

FIGURE 7.4. The Maya Calendar (Madrid Codex).

Imox: The day of women and the First Mother. Dedicated to the art of weaving.

Iq': The wind, prayers for protection against destruction by winds and hurricanes.

Watanh: Year Bearer. A day for celebrating life and wellness. Generally, Watanh is good as a day and as a year bearer. An appropriate day to ask for rain. (Name of an ancient Maya leader or hero.)

Q'ana': The protector against bad will and false accusations. Name of the First Father or ancestor of the Jakaltek. His sanctuary is at *Yula'*, toward the east, and pilgrimages have continued there since antiquity as a constant reminder for the Jakaltek's origin. An informant mentioned to La Farge that *Q'ana'* was an ancient conqueror.

Ab'ak: The day for certain products and species. (A day for achieving secret knowledge, esoteric knowledge and magic.) A day in which a witch can be born.

Tox: A day for being aware of death, illness, and diseases. A day for praying for health and happiness.

Cheh: This is the patron day dedicated to animals. To pray for the abundance of animals, and to honor them for giving their lives to feed human beings.

Q'anil: Year Bearer (yellow power, lightning). It is a day to pray for peace and to avoid war. He is the lightning man and ancient Maya hero. *Q'anil* is the "principal" of the twenty Maya days.

Mulu': A special day for turkeys (the domestication of this bird by the Maya was important not only for their food, but for the sacred offering *Xahanb'al*, which is offered to God during the Year Bearer ceremony.

Elab': A day of justice/the concept of punishment for wrongdoings. This is a special day of remembrance of past destructions by flood and to call for the protection of *Hunab' K'uh*, the Only-One-God.

B'atz': The day of monkeys, generally not a good day; neutral. Also, it is the day and patron of the artisans.

Ewub': This is the day dedicated to wild animals, especially wild pigs (peccary), which were domesticated by the ancient Maya (*txitam*, the pig).

Ah: Year Bearer. This is the day of the farmers, peasants. A day dedicated to the cornfield. Also known as *B'en*. The day and year that closes the great cycles of *Oxlanh B'en*.

Hix: The day of the jaguar. This is a powerful day and its omen is money or wealth. Day to pray for good fortune. A patron day of merchants and rulers.

Tz'ikin: The day of the birds, also for chickens.

Txab'in: A day dedicated to Witz, the guardian of nature (owner of the hills and master of the animals). A day to recognize and admire nature: hills, valleys, rivers, and mountains.

Noj: A day dedicated to earth. A symbolic day for knowledge, understanding, and wisdom.

Chinax: Year Bearer. A day dedicated to the warriors. Chinax was an ancient Maya hero or captain of war.

Kaj: (Red power, thunder), dedicated for the maintenance of balance on earth. The day carries a strong temperament. It is a day to pray for the maintenance of peace and harmony. A day dedicated to think about the elders and ancestors.

Ahaw: A special day for ceremonies, especially for cattle and deer. The day of the Lord. *Ahaw* in Jakaltek means "Lord," "month," and "moon."

The Maya calendar is like a sacred bundle containing the knowledge needed for maintaining the flow of life in the most appropriate way possible. The *ahb'eh* communicates with the patron of the day during divination, and the outcome of that divination conditions the action to be taken for maintaining balance and solving the chaos or conflicts that people generate—mostly by affecting the natural world. In other words, the twenty day names provide the necessary knowledge of how humans must relate to the natural world and the universe. That is why the Maya calendar can be called the "great idea, or the bundle of knowledge," because it contains the pathways for dealing with the trilogy: humans, nature, and the spiritual world as a cosmic unity. Most laypeople do not know the entire messages, meanings, power, and symbolism attached to each sign or Maya day name. For this reason, the *ahb'eh* (the one who shows the path) or diviner dedicates his or her whole life to helping and supporting the prayer-makers and sacred authorities to govern rightfully. This is a special knowledge that is not given by God to just anyone. It is part of the gifts and destiny of those designated to "serve" the community and God, a gift received at birth to become a great diviner or carrier of sacred knowledge that emanates from the sacred Maya calendar. This is the most knowledgeable person in the community, who is commonly referred to as a "shaman" in anthropological literature.

When I grew up in the Maya village of La Laguna, Jacaltenango, I learned many stories from my parents and from the elders, who liked to tell stories to children whenever we gathered to listen. The stories told to children were usually those that provided some information or knowledge on how to deal with their surrounding environment. The land around my town in those days was communal, and there was a large forest where we could go to fetch firewood, to hunt or to gather wild fruits. I remembered when my parents bought me a slingshot for catching birds, like the other boys. I was told by my mother that the birds are beautiful, and they are here to adorn life with their colors. While most birds were edible, and could be hunted, some others were considered taboo, and there was a prohibition against killing them. For example, one day my mother said: "You must not kill and eat hummingbirds (*tz'unun*), because a child that kills hummingbirds and eats them, his growth will stunt, and he will remain a very small person in life." Her words were enough to scare me off, so from then on, I did not try to shoot hummingbirds, since I wanted to grow as a regular human being and didn't want to stunt my growth for violating this natural law. For a Maya child such as me, this was a very strong teaching, which penetrated not only into my mind, but deep into my soul. These types of teachings were enveloped with a great halo of mystery, which conditioned people to deal with nature in the most appropriate way.

Hummingbirds are considered to be the symbol, or alter ego, of the sun, so they must be protected—although the heart of hummingbirds was used sometimes, for very special purposes. For example, some healers or medicine people use the heart of hummingbirds to cure epilepsy, but this is a rare practice. Similarly, among the Zinacantec Maya of Chiapas, Mexico, Eva Hunt (1977) stated: "What is less known is that hummingbirds are ferocious little creatures, quite fearless and belligerent. Not only do their beaks resemble long sharp weapons; in fact, they are weapons. Even in the wild, hummingbirds are known for their complete fearlessness and disregard for other animals and humans ... Since hummingbirds are such successful warriors, a Zinacantecan man wishing to engage in a fight is believed to gain agility and quick sightedness by eating a hummingbird's heart beforehand" (Hunt 1977:66–67).

For the Jakaltek, then, the hummingbird is protected and admired for the pollinating labor that it provides to ensure the renewal of life in nature. There were many species of hummingbirds to admire in the forest, as we got closer to them and admired their blue-green shining colors. I was fortunate enough that when I grew up, these forms of teaching and passing on the values of the Maya tradition was a common practice in my community. These were not just regular folktales, but myths that were told to children to mold their behavior at an early age. In my case, I did not try to interpret or analyze this story until now that I am writing Mayalogue. The story about not killing hummingbirds was covered by a halo of mystery, mentioned above, which is a Maya method or device for ensuring the persistence of the story in the mind. Certainly, it has had its effect on me, since I still remember this hummingbird story that has controlled my behavior since my childhood. But now that I am bringing Native knowledge to the forefront in Mayalogue, I have made a brief analysis of this story and come up with certain meanings, or the underlying truth hidden under the aura of mystery that overwhelmed me as a child.

The Mayas were great observers and understood the workings of nature and the cycles of life: insemination, growth, and decay of the natural world. The hummingbird (*tz'unun*) is a small bird, but it has a very special mission for the continuity of life and renewal of the ecosystem. We know from the natural sciences that hummingbirds are pollinators of flowers, which then are transformed into fruits that sustain humans and other animals. The seeds from the fruits are also planted for the continuous renewal of forest life, maintaining an ecological balance which is beneficial for humans, plants, and animals. A Maya myth of this type is used as a mechanism to ensure values in the child, and in turn creates ecological knowledge that molds human behavior—a brilliant Maya way of knowing and passing on the wisdom of the ancient Maya up to the present. To kill hummingbirds is to cause problems to the natural process of life renewal. All are interrelated, because the killing a hummingbird will stop pollination and a tree or plant without fruit will not provide food to human beings. So, my mother said to me when I was a child, "If you kill a hummingbird, you will stunt your growth and you will remain small as that bird."

Indigenous People used these ancient ways of teaching to educate their children, as they grew up and maintained a close contact with nature. This is how we learned to listen to the singing of the birds and know if they are just singing or if they are announcing danger to the passerby. This is the case of a yellow bird called *txuyub'*, which is a bird of bad omen. Whenever the bird sings very loudly and intermittently on the side of the road, it is a signal or announcement of an imminent danger ahead for the traveler. Children learn from the adults that it is better to stop at the point where you start hearing the singing of the bird and wait there for a while, so that danger has passed when you arrived at the spot of danger announced by the bird. I know that this kind of story may cause laughter from those who do not understand the messages of birds or do not know how to decode information from nature. As a Maya, I believe in these signs and ways of knowing, as I have experienced it personally, so that I can testify to its accuracy.

On July 2000, I went to see a small piece of land on top of a big mountain (*wiwitz*), because the owner was sick and wanted to sell it and use the profits to cure himself. His messenger told me that there were already coffee trees planted on it, but that the trees were still small and were not producing yet. I have never climbed that mountain, so I asked my wife to accompany me and see the town from that high altitude. When we arrived at the top of the mountain after an hour walk by foot, I saw a small place (500 square meters) cultivated with coffee, but the plants were totally covered with vines and weeds, so it was hard to see if there were any coffee plants. Just as we started to walk through the piece of land, the bird *txuyub'* started to sing, getting closer to us. When the bird sings time after time intermittently, that is a signal of an imminent danger. I wanted to stop there but my guide insisted that we walk at least up to the center of the place and check to see if there were still coffee plants that survived under the vines. I was not prepared with my boots, but at least I had my nickers on, although they were not good enough to protect me from a snake bite. As I walked a few meters more into the land, the bird at the edge of the coffee field came closer and kept singing scandalously. At that point, I got scared and stopped instantly. The guide understood that I was scared and did not wanted to step blindly into the grown weeds, so he stopped too. This man, who was the owner's worker in the field, told me that he would better clean the field with other workers so that I could return and see the place more clearly.

Three days later, the man returned to my home and told me that the place was now cleared. Then he said: "It was good that we didn't enter and walk through the field, since I and other workers who helped me to clean the land killed some twenty big rattlesnakes there. I don't know why there were so many of those snakes concentrated in such a small place." I knew there was a problem, so it was good to act cautiously that day, alerted by the calling of that bird. Fortunately, I acted as my parents told me a long time ago, otherwise I could have placed myself in danger, stepping on one of those poisonous snakes. The *txuyub'* bird truly saved my day.

There are so many stories that I can tell concerning my approach to nature, but I think the stories told and the Maya calendar mentioned above can help us to understand the concept of Mayalogue. There is communication and dialogue with birds, plants, and animals, as well as prayers for each day in which we as humans must celebrate the existence of other beings on earth. For the Mayas, the calendar is the instrument that guides human action, and it is up to us to respond to our mission of being intermediaries or caretakers of nature.

Among Native Americans in the United States and Canada, the vision quest is one of the ways of achieving a vision and obtaining a spiritual guide that teaches you the lessons for life and your future role, be it as a curer, a spiritual leader, or just a regular citizen. These are the most important methods for achieving knowledge and for understanding the workings of nature and the universe. In other words, "becoming open to the natural world with all of one's senses, body, mind, and spirit, is the goal of the practice of Native science" (Cajete 2000:21).

Despite the great contribution of Indigenous People to the world, their knowledge system has not been recognized as knowledge or as science. Starting with the destruction of their knowledge and written histories since the Spanish invasion of their land, the Maya have continued to go through cycles of violence. According to the Truth Commission in Guatemala, the Indigenous People were the most affected by the armed conflict as they were accused of being backward and allies to the guerrillas (Carmack 1988; Montejo 1999). In this context of domination throughout the centuries, Maya people have lost much of their knowledge. There has not been a propitious time for engaging in the production of knowledge as did their ancestors; rather, they struggle day after day for their survival. For this reason, the memories of their connection with their ancient sites and classic Maya culture have faded away.

The stories that I recalled and documented here were not Maya teachings to me when I was a boy. Nobody knew who the Mayas were, since we, the modern descendants, were called *indios*. Supposedly, then, we were not related to the ancient Mayas. This ideological form of domination has had its effect on Native people, since in my case I did not have any idea who the Mayas were when I grew up. My parents called themselves Jakaltek, and I, too, called myself a Jakaltek, so the term *Maya* was only used by anthropologists to refer to the ancient Mayas or to refer to the Indigenous People of the Yucatan. Although, my parents mentioned the *paywinaj*, or the "ancient ones" who lived on these lands in ancient times, we did not know if they were our ancestors, the Mayas.

I remember one day when I followed my father to search for vines to tie our thatched-roof house. We walked through the forest and close to the canyon of the river in La Laguna, then my father entered a cave and not far inside, there were two or three colored vases among some ancient skulls and bones. My father said these were objects of the *paywinaj*, and we should not touch them. My father left the objects inside and we went back home. A few weeks later, we passed through the same place and my father went to see the ancient pottery again, but they were already broken into pieces. Someone entered the cave and smashed them up, since old things were not of any value to people in those days. This is what we thought during the fifties and sixties, when there were no Indigenous scholars or intellectuals fighting for our identity and millennial cultural heritage. Now, most Indigenous children are learning that they are members of their local communities, Jakaltek, Mam, K'iche, Q'anjobal, Chuj, and so on, but they too belong to an ancient culture now called Maya. In other words, the Indigenous People of Guatemala are now calling themselves Maya, as they recognize their share of that ancient Maya culture. This identity process is helping Mayas to develop solidarity among themselves, by creating a unity in diversity, a powerful cultural process now called pan-Mayanism (Warren 1998; Montejo 1997, 2005).

Despite destruction, Native knowledge persists as Native people now value their traditions and give importance to their ancestry and identities. Indigenous knowledge must be considered as a living practice of the respectful relationship between humans, nature, and the cosmos. And this is the function of Mayalogue, to provide us with ideas that we can use to approach nature with respect and to listen to the sounds of nature that are alive. Native knowledge and Maya epistemology must be elevated to the same level of Western scientific knowledge. In this way, Eurocentric practices of doing research—defining, naming, producing, interpreting, and imposing meanings on social actions in Native communities—must stop. The same can be said about anthropological and theoretical proposals that argue for acculturation, assimilation, or de-Indianization (Batalla 2002). We must move forward to a more inclusive, positive, and interactive process that call for syncretic transculturation (Ortiz 1940). The trialogical and interactionist model of communication, reciprocity, and interdependency (human-nature-supernatural) practiced by Indigenous People must continue as a viable way of life.

MAYALOGUE, THE INTERACTIONIST MODEL   EIGHT
Humans, Nature, and the Supernatural World

FOR CENTURIES, the persistence of philosophical dualism—idealism versus materialism, soul versus body, nature versus culture, and so forth—were theoretical frameworks used by social scientists to explain human culture until now, to maintain objectivity in research and academic production. This same pattern has been followed by environmentalists and cultural ecologists who separated nature from society, although considering human action over nature. Again, these theories have been constructed from the etic or outsider's point of view, without considering how Indigenous People or non-Western cultures conceptualize and interact with their natural environments.

The fact that Indigenous People have a strong connection to the land, which for them is sacred, has been recognized by some researchers, but the dimension of that relationship has not been truly understood. That is why Indigenous People have been romanticized, with stereotypical images that present them as noble savages living in perfect harmony with the natural world. Of course, this is a myth, since Indigenous People are not perfect either and have their own problems to solve internally, but they do have different ways of relating to their environment, and this is due to the predicaments of their cosmocentric worldview.

Traditionally, Indigenous People did not see the world as a separate entity from humans and the universe, but as an integrative whole. This holistic understanding of the world and all that lives on it will be explained here by a Native theory (Mayalogue) for synthesizing Maya knowledge and epistemology. There is an ancient mandate to be followed by us, the descendants of the ancient Mayas. We must follow the teachings of the ancestors that have established the norms or rules of *komontat*, sacred relationships with the land and the universe. This is the reciprocal action to be generated from the cosmic trilogy: human—nature—and the supernatural world (ancestors, God, guardian spirits, etc.). In other words, Indigenous People see the world as a cosmic unity in which humans received a responsibility for nourishing the ancestors and the Creator. In this process, they maintain a reciprocal and respectful relationship with the natural world of plants, rivers, mountains, waters, animals and all beings with whom they coexist on earth. That is why in the creation myth of the Mayas, corn plays an important role, because thanks to this plant, human beings were created and sustained.

In other words, corn as a plant is an important contributor to human life and existence. We can argue that for the Mayas, human existence was possible only with the contribution of nature itself. According to the *Popol Vuh*, humans were not created first and were not given the supremacy and domination over other parts of creation, as established in the Christian Bible. The land was considered a sacred gift, which produced the food and sustenance for which humans must be always thankful. "And in this way [humans] were filed with joy, because they had found a beautiful land, full of pleasures, abundant in ears of yellow and ears of white corn, and abundant also in *pataxte* and cacao, and in innumerable *zapotes, anonas, jocotes, nantzes, matasanos*, and honey" (Goetz and Morley 1950:166). In this section, I want to show the importance of the natural world (earth), and other living beings with which humans share their existence. The Maya genesis tells us that it was only through the collaboration between other living creatures that the creation of human beings was possible. For the Mayas, nature has continued to fulfill its role in renewing life and creation, and it is up to humans too to fulfill their mission received since creation to protect mother earth.

According to the *Popol Vuh*, human beings must be thankful for the gift of life and remember to nourish the Creators forever. This is the cosmic relationship and mission that Indigenous People continued to fulfill until now, following the sacred Maya calendar. In the appendixes of most ethnographies, anthropologists have reported the continuous prayers and thankfulness of the Mayas for their life and existence in conjunction with the rest of creation for which they also pray and give thanks with ceremonies. Unfortunately, Indigenous People's spirituality and their reciprocal relationship with the natural world have been diminished because of the constant encroachment on their lands by colonizers who see Indian territories as resources to be exploited for profit. In the *Popol Vuh*, the role of humans is one of stewardship toward nature, and clearly humans are not at the center of creation, but a part of it. Like the Christian Bible, the sequence of creation started with earth, plants, and animals, and then, humans were created last.

But this form of knowledge is difficult to accept, despite the current revisions and arguments in favor of moving away from Cartesian dualism, which separates nature from society, nature from culture, and so on (Descola and Palsson 1996). One of the major reasons is that Westerners have followed a genealogy of culture, science, and knowledge stemming from ancient Mesopotamia, Egypt, Greece, Rome, and Europe. Accordingly, this accumulated knowledge was then passed on to the colonized American continent, and thus, ignoring and destroying in its way Indigenous knowledge systems and distinctive ways of life. In other words,

> Western science today is akin to a world history which discusses only Mediterranean peoples. Indeed, the institutionalization of knowledge in the academic setting has made status more important than accomplishments or ideas when determining the cannon of truth that will give the best explanation of our planet. We are living in a strange kind of dark ages where we have immense capability to bring together information but when we gather this data, we pigeonhole it in the old familiar framework of interpretation, sometimes even torturing the data to make it fit." (Deloria 1997:211)

THE MAYALOGUE MODEL

The cosmic trilogy is based on Maya cosmovision, which integrates nature, humanity, and the supernatural world of spirits, the Creator and the universe. This is an interactionist model, since from the consulted decision and reciprocity between these three universal entities, action and rituals are performed to please God, while maintaining harmony with nature for a productive earth. This respect and reciprocity transcend in time and space as a cosmic consciousness nourished by rituals, songs, prayers, and ceremonies.

Mayalogue is an interactionist model that explains, from the insider's point of view, the appropriate actions to be taken for the maintenance of life on earth. Many calamities, cataclysm, and destruction have occurred in the ancient past, but human beings have survived throughout these cycles of destruction. These cataclysmic cycles have been recorded by ancient civilizations such has the myth of the "Fifth Sun" in Nahua mythology. It is only logical that appropriate action must be taken in relation to earth if we want to maintain a healthy life, happiness, and human productivity. On the other hand, inappropriate action or the avoidance of the sacred norms established for the maintenance of this covenant can produce an imbalance leading to wars, famine, illness, violence, unhappiness, and death.

For this to work, social solidarity must be practiced, while an appropriate action should be taken following the Maya calendar, as explained above. It is important to recognize the appropriate days for giving thanks and praying to the Creator, while petitioning for life, the crops, rains, health, game, good travel, business, agriculture, any activity to be taken on, and so forth. The Mayas believe that by guiding our lives by the Maya calendar, humanity will receive the blessings of heaven for a healthy life or *q'inal* on the face of earth. To understand this Maya philosophy of life, let's discuss each part of the trilogy that integrates Mayalogue.

MAYALOGUE: NATURE AS PART OF THE SYSTEM

The Natural World

If we follow the order of creation established in the *Popol Vuh*, we can consider first the natural world (earth, plants, animals, the waters) as the first part of creation. According to the sacred myth of creation, nothing existed in the darkness, only the immensity of the sea. Only the Creator and the Maker were in the waters surrounded with light. Then, they spoke: "Earth! They said, and instantly it was made. Like the mist, like the cloud, and like a cloud of dust was the creation, when the mountains appeared from the water; and instantly the mountains grew" (Goetz and Morley 1950:83). The Maya men who wrote the Maya genesis said that earth was created first, then, the Creator and Maker "made the small wild animals, the guardian of the woods, the spirits of the mountains, the deer, the birds, pumas, jaguars, serpents, snakes, vipers, guardians of the thickets. And the Forefathers asked: Shall be only silence and calm under the trees, under the vines? It is well that hereafter there be someone to guard them" (Goetz and Morley 1950:84). The animals then, including the birds, were created to guard the forests and to make life more enjoyable for humans, so they must be protected.

In the *Popol Vuh*, Native knowledge is very explicit, as contained and expressed by the language. In the following passage we see this observation, which places Indigenous worldviews at the level of other cultures in terms of scientific observation of nature and the universe. "They were endowed with intelligence, they saw and instantly they could see far, they succeeded in seeing, they succeeded in knowing all that there is in the world. When they looked, instantly they saw all around them, and they contemplated in turn *the arch of heaven and the round face of earth*" (Goetz and Morley 1950:168, my emphasis)

In this quotation, we can read clearly that the first humans created were given "intelligence," and they succeeded in "knowing" about their human condition. The fact that the *Popol Vuh* provides scientific information about the arch of heaven (dome) and the "round face" of earth is an assertion that ancient Mayas and their descendants knew that earth was round. This is a contradiction to the assertions that Indigenous People were not capable of profound observation and analysis of the world around them. In this case, the ancient Maya have reached the same conclusion thousands of years ago, that earth was round, just as the ancient Greeks had concluded with Pythagoras in sixth century BC.

The knowledge of the universe and the observation of stars and the movements of the sun and the moon and other celestial bodies made it possible for the Mayas through millennia to come up with a perfect calendar, which is still with us today. To explain the connection that exists between the heavens and earth, the *Popol Vuh* also mentions the rope or the measuring cord that was tended from the heavens to earth, measuring and connecting the four corners or directions of earth and the universe. Maya cosmology uses the symbolism of the pillar placed at each corner of earth to sustain heaven, and each region of earth is given a color, as we have seen earlier in this work.

The same goes for the ancient Nahuas and Toltecs of Mexico, who recognized and studied the shape and movement of earth and other celestial bodies. In Nahua cosmology the connection between earth and the sky is explained as follows: "The surface of the earth (*tlalticpac*) is a great disk situated in the center of the universe and extending horizontally and vertically. Encircling the earth like a ring is an immense body of water (*teo-atl*), which makes the world *cem-a-nahuac*, 'that–which-is-entirely-surrounded-by-water'... for the universe is divided into four great quadrants of space whose common point of departure is the navel of the earth" (Leon-Portilla 1990:57).

The ancient Mayas, as well as the Nahuas and Toltecs, had a very accurate description of the physical shapes and arrangements of the surface of earth and the heavens. They were also aware of the similar forces in the universe, or the elements such as winds, waters, fire, and movements (earthquakes) that could affect and eventually bring destruction to the world. These powerful elements could produce cataclysms that could cleanse earth, so to begin all over again (world renewal). These different eras are mentioned in the *Popol Vuh* as different creations occurred after each cataclysmic destruction of humans. Similarly, the Toltecs also referred to major destructions of the world and have prophesied that similar events may occur in the future, since our solar system moves with the galaxy into different regions of the universe. For this reason, Maya and Aztec philosophy has established that nothing will survive forever, since there will be always a world building, world dismantling, and world renewal. For the Aztecs, there were previously four eras passed and we are now living under the era of the Fifth Sun, or the Sun of Movement, which will come to an end by earthquakes and hunger (León Portilla 1990).

This is also the concern of Mayas, who are now engaged in a preparation for entering the new era of major changes or the load dropped by the ending of the 13 B'ak'tun. Renewal will start after the world or humanity will pass through that severe weather (k'ayilal, great catastrophe) that will work as the cleansing process, out of which the survivors may emerge to restart life again (world renewal). Many people thought that the historical date chiseled in stone—13 B'ak'tun (December 21, 2012)—was the exact day of destruction, and they worried. But for Mayas, it was the beginning of major changes leading to world destruction in *Oxlanh B'en*, as some elders have suggested. This is a greater and less known cycle that needs to be investigated further.

Hopefully, the Indigenous values and teachings about the respectful relationship between the natural world, humans, and the cosmos will be embraced and learned as an appropriate way for survival, instead of the current wasteful and violent process of destruction and exploitation of the world's resources. We must recognize that planet earth is a special and unique place and that we must change our wasteful habits and protect it. At this juncture in world history (twenty-first century), humanity has accumulated so much knowledge and we can use it for the benefit of all. So, we must also recognize that

> As the horizon of our knowledge extends, we learn that there are limits to the speed and quantity of our economic growth, that natural resources are exhaustible, that the deterioration of our environment has disastrous consequences for the human community as a whole, that the serious loss of genes, species, and ecosystems is endangering the equilibrium of our life-support system, and that a minimum condition for continuous human survival requires the actual practice of sustainable life in highly industrialized society. (Wei-Ming 1997:20)

For Indigenous People, it is refreshing to know that during the past two decades some anthropologists and scientists have advocated for solutions to the ecological problem and worried about the future of planet earth. Some have started to move forward by retaking Indigenous epistemologies and beliefs in the unity of all living beings on earth. For example, Gisli Palsson argues for a paradigm she calls communalism to emphasize unity, rather than the separation between nature and society. "Unlike paternalism, communalism suggests generalized reciprocity, an exchange often metaphorically represented in terms of intimate, personal relationships. The need to develop an ecological theory along such lines, a theory that fully integrates human ecology and social theory, abandoning any radical distinction between nature and society, is often recognized nowadays" (Palsson 1996:72).

As this unified understanding is promoted by modern researchers working within Indigenous politics and epistemology, the result will be partial, since a major component proposed in Mayalogue is missing from this paradigm. There must be respect for the natural world as part of human beings, as well as recognition of an ancient mission taken as a covenant by humans with the Creator to maintain unity and wellness with the universe. The idea of unity between nature and society, avoiding the radical distinction between both as two separate things, will help partially, because, as argued by Philippe Descola (1996), Western privileged epistemology will not allow for major changes.

If nature or the forest is a living entity, then, fortuitous encounters with danger can occur at any time. So, before starting a journey or travel through dangerous places, a person must pray for protection to the Creator and ask for the avoidance of danger on his or her path. It was common to hear mothers praying for their children any time they journeyed to a distant and unknown place, in hopes that the Creator would protect them and clear their way of any danger. If there is danger on the road, the request is that it should happen before or after the individual reaches any spot along the way. For Indigenous People, nature emanates mysterious forces that keep humans alert and in awe. This is the dimension that Roy F. Hellen calls the inner essence of nature, a "vital energy or force outside human control" (Hellen 1996:111).

When I was a boy, I was afraid to travel through the forest, since I did not want to encounter Witz, the guardian of the animals and the forest. While walking in the mountains, you must learn to listen and interpret the singing of the birds for their messages of alarm, or simply of their songs saluting the day and the passerby, as mentioned earlier. We know that mountains have spirit protectors who are good and provide food and resources to the person who asks for it with prayers.

Also, we were told at an early age that corn is a "person," and we must take care of it. If the grains fall from the net where the adults carry it from the cornfield to home, we must pick the grains along the way. Or when the women go to the banks of the river to wash the cooked corn, they too must pick up all the fallen grains. Failure to do so will cause corn to cry as an abandoned baby in the darkness. Corn then, is a sacred plant, and all its parts are useful for human beings and animals for their sustenance. In this respect, corn is the essence of creation, which integrates the three elements of Mayalogue: corn is a plant (nature), corn is a person (human), corn is sacred (divinity, or supernatural realm).

The same rules of respect and reciprocity should be considered when dealing with the animals of the forest. Animals and plants are there to fulfill a mission, but they should be approached with the appropriate respect and gratitude. A hunter must ask permission to the "owner of the animals" for a deer or other animals that will be available for hunting to feed his family. The animals of the forest then, are an integral part of the system and they must be respected and protected, complying with the universal covenant established in the sacred book of the Mayas, the *Popol Vuh*. Referring to this rule for hunting among the Maya of Yucatan, Eric Thompson has said: "A hunter should shoot only what he needs ... The hunter asks the gods of hunting to send him what he needs, and usually points out that he needs food ... The hunter apologizes to the deer he has shot for taking his life and in his prayers, he concludes with the word '*otzilen*,' I had a need" (Thompson 1956:163).

For Indigenous People, animals have their own identities and it is not appropriate to make fun of or ridicule them. This observation has become a strict rule among the Chewong, or traditional inhabitants of Malaysia. For them, the respect for animals is a law that must be observed at an early age by members of the communities. "Openly laughing at or teasing an animal may represent the most blatant kind of human violation of the Chewong's *talaiden* rules protecting other creatures" (Knudson 1991:133). Their traditional law that rules relationship and promotes respect and harmonious relationship with animals and the environment does not even allow having a wild animal as a pet. Children learn about this respectful relationship from an early age; the mistreatment of animals is something punishable according to their traditional norms that control their actions and attitudes toward living beings on earth.

As Indigenous People struggle for their rights, they too understand that the life of other creatures is at humans' hand and their destiny depends on how humans value other forms of life than that of humans. That is why

FIGURE 8.1. Harvest Corn.

some Indigenous People have argued for the right of life of other creatures with whom the share and coexists on earth. Anthropologist Stefano Varese found the same inclination to defend the rights of other creatures and their struggles for maintaining sovereignty over their territorial resources among the Ashaninkas of Peru. The right to live jointly with other living creatures on earth is a major concern for them. For this reason, in their struggle for survival they too respect the rights of the animals to live on the land. So, they pose the question: "It is only the people that need land? Don't the monkeys, the birds, the huanganas and deer also need land to live?" (Varese 1996:122).

With the same tone, the Onondaga Chief Oren Lyons posed the question in the annual forum of the UN Assembly of the Indigenous Working Group in Geneva in 1990. While arguing for the use of Native languages for the defense of human rights, Oren Lyons asked the representatives gathered and seated in the conference auditorium the following: "What of the rights of the natural world? Where is the seat of the buffalo or the eagle? Who is representing them in this forum? Who is speaking for the waters of the earth? Who is speaking for the trees and the forests? Who is speaking for the Fish, for the Whales, for the Beavers, for our children?" (Lyons 1994:26).

For Indigenous People, animals have their own spirit of creation and they have feelings and suffer the pain inflicted on them by humans as they are chased and killed for food. That is why in the Maya dances of the deer performed during the festivities of the patron saints in Maya villages, the presence of animal impersonators is necessary to teach lessons of respect and compassion for the animals. For example, the deer dancer or impersonator presents his complaints, and denounces the hunter's violent action, presenting their pleas to the Lord of the animals, as they call for help in their sufferings. "What is this, mountains and jungles; why are you letting me to be in danger? And you evil hunters, why do you get so tired persecuting me? If you want to kill me, tell the mountains, the jungles, caves, valleys, and ravines what are your reasons for persecuting me. Look at me, I am a tormented deer. Why do unthankful humans want to kill me as the jaguar also does? To whom shall I call and ask for help so that I am freed from this persecution and misfortune?" (Montejo 2018)

This idea of relatedness to other living beings on earth, animals, plants, and the land itself pervades Indigenous spirituality as a central concept of its worldviews. For the Mayas, earth itself has regions of sacredness (sacred geography), because the mountains, volcanoes, and the hills are the personification of the ancestors. In other words, the ancestors have been immortalized as they become the hills and the mountains with historical names that provide identities of the people who live in those regions. The *Popol Vuh* tells us that when the four Fathers or men created became old and were ready to depart from this earth, they bade farewell to their children and wives. "We are going back to our town, there already in his place is Our Lord of the stags to be seen there in the sky. We are going to begin our return, we have completed our mission [here], our days are ended.... In this way they took their leave and immediately they disappeared on the summit of the mountain Hacavitz [Our Lord's Mountain]" (Goetz and Morley 1950:205–6).

In this passage we interpret that the First Fathers became immortalized as they disappeared on the top of the mountain and became mountains themselves. The immortalization of the ancestors in mountains and hills is also mentioned in *El Q'anil* (Montejo 2001). The Q'anil Mountain is the sanctuary of one of the mythical ancestors of the Jakaltek, and it is also the place where the new hero Xhuwan Q'anil stayed after returning from a war in which he acted as the lightning man and defeated the enemy. Having achieved supernatural power, he was not allowed to return to the town (Jacaltenango) as a regular human being, but became a hero and a guardian for the town. Even today, the Jakaltek prayer-makers continue to go to the top of the mountain and pray, requesting his protection over the town and his people.

FIGURE 8.2. The Dance of the Deer, Jacaltenango.

Another important aspect of nature that I want to mention here before focusing on the human part of Mayalogue refers to the ancient knowledge of the Mayas in dealing with major catastrophes such as drought and hunger. We know that the ancient Mayas knew how to deal with their resources, following the cyclical patterns of time established by the Maya calendar. Also, the role of the *ahb'eh*, who is the intermediary between humans and God, or the supernatural realm knew how to pray for rain and good crops for all the people in the communities. The *ahb'eh* knew how to perform ceremonies and pray with eloquence, using flowered words to convince God, so that he provides rain for the crops. But when there were severe droughts, there was a special pre-Hispanic ceremony that still was practiced until recently, which includes now a mixture of Catholic and Maya religious paraphernalia.

In some communities, the patron saints are taken into the streets in procession as part of the ceremonies for petitioning rain, not only for the crops, but for the trees, the animals, and the land that become thirsty. When these ceremonies, prayers, and processions fail, and drought persists in bringing hunger and extreme suffering to the people, the Jakaltek practiced a secret ceremony for bringing down the badly needed rain. I want to clarify that this ceremonial action is only done when everything else has failed and there is extreme suffering for the lack of rain. During the past sixty years, I have seen it only once when I was still a child. I remember my parents being worried for the lack of rain, so the cornfield dried up and there was no food to be harvested that year and the next. The people started to eat all sources of green leaves, roots, and the barks of certain trees that they used in ancient times to survive during these extreme periods of famine.

Then, something unbelievable happened. A few Jakaltek Maya elders knew about a mysterious way to bring down rain from the sky and get life back to earth. The ceremonial action taken, which I partially witnessed as a child, occurred as follows:

A group of prayer-makers (men and women) gathered at the Carrizal River, a small river that crossed many fields where the peasants cultivated their corn and prayed for the rain. Then, a few spiritual leaders went to a specific spot on the shore of that river and prayed to the Creator burning their candles and copal. They complained about their suffering and requested that heaven have pity on them. Meanwhile, other men started to dig and open a channel with picks and shovels, redirecting the flow of the river into a sinkhole or underground cave. They used branches, stones, sand, and mud as a barricade to help stop the flow of the small river, which didn't have much current. This place has been used only for this purpose, and it is kept secret to the public. This small river connects to a larger river, so the section in between the hole and the larger river is the place were action occurred. A couple of days later, the flow of the river stopped on its regular causeway, and a section of about five kilometers started to dry up, exposing the fish that started to struggle in the muddy ponds. I remember that it was easy to pick up fish from the ponds and puddles as the people gathered to collect them in their baskets. On the third day after stopping the flow of the small river, spiritual leaders performed a ceremony asking their followers to join them in their cry to heaven, calling for the winds, the clouds, and the rains to return and bless the land with a formidable thunderstorm. The people looked up desperately into the sky, while asking for solutions to the drought that was decimating the people, the animals, the plants, and even the fish in the dried river.

On the third day after this was done, a storm came down, wetting the dry and thirsty land. The upper current of the river came down furiously, destroying the barricade made by the men, and once again the river started to flow as usual.

This process remains a secret, which indeed it was, and an extraordinary event that is difficult to explain. Usually, three days after the ritual of drying the river takes place, the sky becomes covered with clouds and rain starts wetting the dry fields. This is a secret process, since the expert knows the prayers and knows the specific section of the river where this act of petitioning should be performed, thus obtaining the answer to their requests. I take this as a mystery, because no one tells us how it is done, except the information provided here, which is of general knowledge.

As I have mentioned earlier, this ceremony was practiced only as the last resource. In other words, human interventions in altering nature cannot be done as a first solution. It is only when all the solutions have failed, that humans revert to this cosmic function, making the heavens respond to their petitions. For those who do not understand the workings of the universe of earth and the universe of heaven, this will sound like a ridiculous action taken by desperate villagers. But I, who know the region and have once witnessed this event, still ask myself, how was this possible? Was it a coincidence? We don't need to know or explain this cosmic intervention. It is enough to know that for the Mayas who performed it, it worked when it was needed. Nature responded, enforcing the Indigenous People's concept of "causality." Why did it rain right after they finished their ceremony for petitioning rain? Why did it not rain before the ceremony or much later?

MAYALOGUE: HUMANS AS PART OF THE SYSTEM

Humans must maintain their minds open to the calls of nature, as well as to the needs of their communities. As intermediaries between nature and the supernatural realm, humans must always be ready to dialogue and interact with prayers, songs, and ceremonies, even with complaints and requests to God, the Mighty Power. That is why humans must repay what they take from nature as an act of reciprocity, which is a sacred rule. That is why Indigenous People of the Americas and around the world practice different forms of exchange or communal service and mutuality as a form of social solidarity.

The Jakaltek Maya also practiced in antiquity a form of collective labor they called *wayab'*. In this practice, a person can request the labor of as many people as he requires to help build his house or clean his cornfield, to keep up with the different periods or stages in the growth of corn. In this way, the one who requests help is also required to do the same for those who have helped him when their need arrives. The philosophy of mutuality is valid here: "Today I do it for you, and tomorrow you will do it for me." This is a social contract or reciprocity that must be fulfilled as a communal mandate, which extends to the natural world.

The practice of reciprocity among people, as well as between humans and nature, is considered a sacred mission to be performed in everyday life activities. Among the Quechua of South America, particularly among Indigenous People in Songo, Peru, there is a practice called the *mink'a* for accomplishing a major task, such as building a house or working collectively in the fields. This form of work or reciprocity is a generalized rule, at least before the development of capitalist labor force in the mines and plantations to produce wealth for the colonizers. In South America as in Mesoamerica, "Reciprocity is like a pump at the heart of Andean life. The constant give-and-take of *ayni* and *mink'a* maintains a flow of energy throughout the *ayllu* [community]. This flow extends beyond the human community as well. The obligation extends to domesticated animals and plants, to *pacha* [earth], to the many animated places in the landscape itself, and even to the saints" (Allen 1988:93).

According to the Mayas, human beings are born in this world to fulfill a mission, and the mission is established by the omens and designs at the day of birth. There are special requests or missions to be fulfilled, particularly for those who have been chosen to become rulers, healers, *ahb'eh* or diviners, bone setters, midwives, *ah tz'ib'* or writers, and so forth. The rest of the people have their mission too, to serve God, the community, and to protect the land and all forms of life that exist on it. The major value to be inculcated at an early age is that of "respect." This is the fundamental lesson to be learned and practiced by a child, a youth, and an adult. Indigenous People value these teachings since they come from the ancestors. They gave the norms and rules for behaving and making life sustainable on earth by respecting each other: humans, plants, animals, and the land. For example, among the Jakaltek Maya, their ancestor Balunh Q'ana left a series of teachings or commandments that the Jakaltek must obey if they want to survive and live for the centuries or millennia yet to come. Don Xap Pelnan Santu (RIP), an old storyteller in town, told the following story about the commandments of *B'alunh Q'ana* to his descendants.

> This town will live forever and will survive any calamity or war that will occur in the future. To this people I leave my laws and teachings concerning "respect" for life. There must be respect for the Creator and Former of life, *Komam Yahaw Satkanh* (Our Lord of Heaven); respect to each person or human beings, respect to all the animals, using them rationally for work or for food. Respect to earth which is sacred and to the Lords or Spirits of the Mountains; and to everything that produces, specially the trees and the edible plants; the rivers and waters, because everything that exists on

the face of earth is good and it is at the service of humans. There must be respect for the wind, the clouds, to the Sun Our Father (*Komam Tz'ayik*) and to the Moon Our Mother (*Komi' x-Ahaw*); and respect for the stars; because they guide and help us to predict the coming of the rains and all the natural phenomena on the face of Mother Earth. (personal notes)

The teaching of the Jakaltek ancestor is the continuation of the requests made by the Creator and Former in the *Popol Vuh*. The Creator wanted his creatures to be obedient and respectful human beings. "Let us make him who shall nourish and sustain us! What shall we do to be invoked, in order to be remembered on earth? We have already tried with our first creations, our first creatures; but we could not make them praise and venerate us. So, then, let us try to make obedient, respectful beings who will nourish and sustain us" (Goetz and Morley 1950:86).

This is a sacred covenant made between humans and the Creator, so they must be always remembered and nourished with prayers and ceremonies. This respectful behavior and thankfulness are emphasized by Shas Ko'w, a Maya diviner who has stated briefly: "Because that's the way we live in the world: we exist to honor God" (Colby 1981:122).

The teachings of the ancestors are then the norms to be followed in everyday life activity, and Indigenous People maintain that respect for everything that exists on earth. In this context, each person has the responsibility to do his or her own share in maintaining peace and harmony by reciprocating with nature and the Creator, who provides life that we enjoy. There is also the professional prayer-maker who follows the Maya calendar for his ceremonies of nourishment of the Creator. He uses the sacred discourse or the flowered words, which are poetic orations full of metaphors. This is a special and poetic discourse designed to convince and elicit God's blessings on humans and nature altogether. This petition can be achieved if we act responsible toward earth or nature and maintain the tradition of "clear thinking," according to Chief John Mohawk (RIP). Before and after meetings we must give thanks to the Creator for the life that He has given us.

> This is the talk that our people give at the beginning and at the end of every group gathering, so that we remember our relationships. The point of the talk is to remember that we are related to one another, related to the earth, and related to all the things that support life—and we are related to the universe, too. I've always thought it a very useful thing to remember that relationship requires us to be thankful. (Mohawk 2008:vii)

Unfortunately, the times have changed and the teachings of the ancestors are being forgotten. The road that we now walk is not clear, and there are many problems lurking in our path. We cannot think or concentrate in our traditional and respectful relationships with earth and nature when our relationships with humans are now problematic. In the past, not long ago, the Jakaltek Maya practiced communal ceremonies and had specific responsibilities for earth and life on it. For this purpose, the prayermakers practiced a yearlong ceremony, following the ancient Maya calendar. After La Farge's publication of the *Year Bearer's People* in 1931, this same ancient Maya ceremony went under attack by Catholic missionaries and politicians in town. They argued that the Jakaltek were portraying a bad image to the world by practicing a pre-Hispanic tradition, thus showing that the missionaries' work for conversion have failed.

For the politicians, the argument was that the Jakaltek were still very primitive and Guatemala would not progress if the old traditions remained. For them, this was a problem in the process of creating a homogenous nation-state that is why the Mayas needed to be assimilated. In his ethnography, Oliver La Farge even mentioned that some *ahb'eh*, diviners and calendar experts, were afraid of his presence, since they thought he was a representative of the government who wanted to learn the tradition and destroy it later by denouncing the prayer-makers.

The idea that humans are born to fulfill a mission on earth is still a valid lesson to be learned and practiced today. Human beings must retake their role as caretakers of nature and not destroyers who overexploit it for the accumulation of wealth. The Lacandon Maya have many myths on how human beings have been punished by the Lord of the Forest for their abusive actions against nature. For example, Lacandon men can kill monkeys for food, although they had to follow certain rules, for example, they must not use barbed arrows for hunting monkeys. The monkeys are believed to act and behave very similarly to human beings. So, when a Lacandon hunter does not hit a monkey at a vital organ, this creature can still pull out the arrow from his body and run for his life. But if a Lacandon hunter uses barbed arrows, then the injured monkey will not be able to pull it out, thus not giving the animal a chance to defend its life. This kind of action or offense against life is punished by their law, so they must follow these instructions while hunting in the forest. This is an important lesson learned by children who then interact with nature in the appropriate way. Once in a while a hunter becomes compassionate and would allow the hunted to save its life, if possible.

Another important lesson that human beings must learn and put into practice is the warning that "You must not take more then what you need." Many people overuse resources and do not think of the needs of other human beings. This is the teaching of Native Americans, especially among the Iroquois, who have always emphasized the importance of the "Seventh Generation." In this regard, Oren Lyons, the Onondaga chief, says that whenever people make decisions, they should keep the next seven generations in mind. Whatever decision we make in relation to the natural world it will have an impact on future generations.

Indigenous People, then, should think on the future of their generations as they make their living today. These are the teachings that the elders hope to be continued for the future, since younger people now have already started to forget this teaching of respect for everything that exists. In this context, the teaching of Buddhism is similar here to Maya spirituality: we humans must develop actions that are ecocentric and not homocentric. To develop a caring attitude toward nature or the environment, humans must be willing to go through three major processes. The first step is to be informed of the situation in which you are living. The second is to be aware of the profundity of the problems devastating earth or the environment and have compassion. The third step is to take conspicuous action to fight for changes that must rescue those lives that are in danger (Sponsel 1991). An example is the current struggle to saving the Amazon and other rainforests on earth, in order to maintain biodiversity. There is a reminder that we all are interrelated as a grand family sharing the breath of creation, or that we all are part of a kinship system that extends into the universe. As an example, the Mayas and other Indigenous people call the sun "our Father" and the moon "our Mother." This way of thinking of a universal family with plants, animals, earth, and heaven as kin and members has been also called as "biophilia" by environmental scientists (Wilson 1984).

In present times, there are major problems concerning the environment because of abusive action of humans worldwide. The problem of not considering the well-being of future generations has caused humans to overexploit the environment and the land they call resources. But we know that for human beings to persist on earth, attention must be given to solve these problems that have affected biodiversity, causing great climate changes. As part of the system, humans must act and promote sustainability of life on earth. On this, Thomas Berry has said, "An integral functioning of the entire earth community is a condition for any sustainable mode of human presence upon the planet. This integral functioning must be effective in the existing order of things, not simply a theoretical vision. The human is a subsystem to the earth system. If the earth is not functioning properly, then there is no possibility of the human attaining any proper expression of itself" (Berry 1997:228).

MAYALOGUE: THE SPIRITUAL WORLD AS PART OF THE SYSTEM

For Indigenous People, the spiritual world is the overarching element that creates, produces, moves, and promotes life on earth, be it the sun, the moon, or the cosmic elements (heat, wind, rain, light, etc.) that help to maintain life on earth. In the *Popol Vuh*, as in other ancient traditions, there is always a supernatural being or Creator who designed life on earth and the harmonic movement of the cosmos. Mayas call this great central power or Creator the Heart of Heaven, Heart of Earth—a poetic name given to God. This name given to the Creator in the *Popol Vuh* is a symbolic name that refers to the cosmic connection and unity of Earth and Heaven (Cosmos) as the generators of life. The ancient sacred texts such as the *Popol Vuh* have always stated that this supernatural being, Creator or God, has always existed until He decided to create earth, plants, animals, and human beings. Again, the *Popol Vuh* tells us that human beings were created to carry on a sacred mission to nourish the Creator, while respecting other beings and giving thanks for creation. The Creator and Former said, "The time of dawn has come, let the work be finished, and let those who are to nourish and sustain us appear, the noble sons, the civilized vassals; let man appear, humanity, on the face of earth" (Goetz and Morley 1950:165).

Thus, this is one of the requests of the Creator, that humans, in exchange for their well-being, must always remember and nourish the Heart of Earth, Heart of Heaven. Since time immemorial Indigenous People have maintained and performed their sacred rituals and ceremonies that are fixed within the dates of the Maya calendar. The supernatural or spiritual world has been the center of all attention (cosmocentrism) by the ancient ones, including their descendants who continue to pray, sing, dance, and burn their candles to give thanks and remember their Creator. The parts of the whole are unified by the instrument of great knowledge, the sacred Maya calendar.

As mentioned before, anthropologists who have studied Indigenous People did not refer to the spiritual world as an integral part of Indigenous cultures. In the case of the Mayas and the Aztecs, early scholars have created theories of bizarre religions that promoted massive human sacrifice.

For example, J. Eric Thompson (1970) and Sylvanus G. Morley (1983) wrote about the Maya and their "polytheistic religions," following the wrong interpretations of early missionaries who also condemned the Mayas and Aztecs as devil worshipers. As mentioned earlier, regarding the stages of evolutionism, Indigenous People were considered to be inferior in thinking. That they needed to evolve from magic, to religion, to science to become civilized (Morgan 1877).

But as we know, Indigenous People have responded to the ancient teachings that have emphasized respect and thankfulness to *Hun-Hab'-K'uh* (the Only-One-God). That is why most actions taken by Indigenous People in a Maya community have responded to the dictates of the Maya calendar. In other words, since the first moment when we wake up and throughout the day, up to the moment of going to sleep, Indigenous People have the supernatural world present in every activity. The spirituality of Indigenous People is pervasive in every action that they perform, since for them the mountains, rivers, volcanoes, and earth itself are sacred, and each has a spirit guardian that takes care of it. Indigenous spirituality is not like Western religiosity, in which there are written cannons and designated places (churches) to go at a certain time (scheduled cult) to pray and get in contact with God. For Indigenous People, nature and the whole world is a sanctuary where human beings can get in contact with the Creator, although, there are some important places (sacred geography) that have served historically as centers for pilgrimages, such as the sanctuaries of the Jakaltek Maya ancestors; these are sacred and special places for communicating with the Creator.

For any human activity to be performed, the Creator is to be informed, petitioned, and given an offering in exchange for his blessings. This can be exemplified in the Indigenous agricultural process. When a piece of land is selected for planting, it should be sanctified, as the peasant must burn his or her candle at the four corners of it and place a candle at the center. The agriculturalist will pray to God for forgiveness if he has caused damage to the forest, though for a cause—to make his living and feed his family. There is a mutual understanding and reciprocity between humans, nature, and the supernatural world, as mentioned earlier. This is a continuous dialogue with nature and the Creator, so that humans can maintain their life and existence on earth by practicing mutual respect and thankfulness for what the land provides.

I imagine that in ancient times, the closeness to nature and the lessons to be learned must have been constant throughout a person's life. It is understandable that humans have to make their living and they affect nature in one way or another, but they too are always conscious of their actions and ask permission before affecting the natural world. There are, then, lessons to be learned at an early age on how to interact with the natural world. Here I summarize an essay that I wrote, which was published in *Indigenous Traditions and Ecology* (2001), concerning the relationship between humans, nature, and the spiritual world.

> One afternoon, when I was six years old, I accompanied my mother to the river near our village where she used to wash the cloths. While my mother washed the cloths with other women that afternoon, I played with other children on the sand near her. Since I had taken off my clothes, I decided to enter the water and swim in the shallows, still under the watchful eyes of my mother. While I was standing in the water, which reached up to my knees, I began, unconcerned, to urinate. When my mother saw this, she picked me up and put me back on the shore. Then, she scolded me with these words that I have never forgotten: 'You should never urinate in the river, because whoever does this, when he dies, he will not be able to go directly to heaven. The soul will be sent to the ocean in search of the urine that he has thrown carelessly into the river and remove it from the ocean in order to be accepted into heaven.' (Montejo 2001:189)

As I said in my analysis of this myth, or Maya lesson, I was paralyzed by fear, since I did not have an idea of the greatness of the ocean, and then to find the urine in it would it be an impossible task, so the door of heaven would be then inaccessible to someone who dirties or pollutes the waters. This myth, in which the river is considered a metaphor for the road to heaven, made me understand at an early age that to urinate or to dirty the waters was not acceptable behavior. The halo of mystery surrounding this story was an implacable and an unforgettable lesson given to me by my mother during the first years of my existence.

In the same way, Indigenous children learned the appropriate behavior and relationship with the natural world when the elders told us the stories of Witz, the guardian of the hills and forests. When we children went to fetch firewood in the forests, we were careful not to follow hidden roads in them, because they could be the paths of Witz who lives inside the mountains. Witz was a provider, so a hunter must request that he be provided with an animal for feeding his family. A good hunter understands this reciprocity and he must burn his candle and request that his hunting journey will be safe and without dangers in his path. The good and conscious hunter will also take only what he needs and not to kill animals just for fun or pleasure. If the hunter has fulfilled this request in the appropriate way, he will be granted his wish, so he will hunt an animal that will help him to secure food for his family. For this reason, most hunters are careful and take only what they need and not abuse or waste the species. If the hunter does not follow this norm, he then will be unprotected, and danger may lure in his path.

Among the Q'eqchi' Maya of northern Guatemala, the mountain spirit is called Tzuultaq'a, and for the Indigenous People there, the mountains are considered as living beings and have characteristics of a person. So Tzuultaq'a or Witz, the mountain guardian spirit, has a human form and he has his house and his riches accumulated inside the hills and mountains. According to Richard Wilson (1995), "Q'eqchi' rituals of production can only be analyzed in full of respect to ideas about human reproduction and illnesses, for the mountain deities are vital figures in the well-being and fertility of both maize and humans" (Wilson 1995:52).

This is a Mesoamerican belief system that has persisted until now, with major transformations in some Mayan communities, as well as in South America. In the past, the owner of the hill, also called the "master of the animals," was a friendly spirit in charge of guarding and protecting the animals and the natural world. But with the arrival of the Spaniards and the development of forced labor in the mines and plantations, the owner of the hill was transformed into a different figure, sometimes compared to the devil. In this way, the traditional "use-value" mode of production changed into a capitalist mode or exchange-value system, drastically changing the worldview of Indigenous People in the Americas. In Colombia, there was a common belief that "Male plantation workers sometimes make secret contracts with the devil to increase productivity and increase their wages. Furthermore, it is believed that the individual who makes the contract is likely to die prematurely and in great pain. While alive he is but a puppet in the hands of the devil, and the money obtained from such a contract is barren" (Taussig 1980:94).

In this way, colonial subjugation and exploitation of Indigenous People forced them to rethink their relationships with the land and the supernatural forces, creating these myths of contracts with the devil.

In Mesoamerica, the owner of the hills was not transformed into the devil, but into a Ladino who appears to the proletarian laborers offering them wealth in exchange for their souls. The image then has changed from time and space and this continuous transformation is a response to the violent relationships of humans with the land due to forced labor in the mines and plantations.

Among the Jakaltek Mayas of Western Guatemala, the image of Witz has also been transformed into that of a Ladino person who rides a horse and offers wealth to those who desire it, but in exchange of their soul. Stories of Witz as a Ladino or a foreigner were abundant in the oral tradition of Maya communities up to the 1960s. In the Jakaltek region it is said that Witz sometimes appears as a priest wearing a black robe and mounting a horse. Among the Q'eqchi' Maya, "*Tzuultaq'a* appears in dreams as a tall man, with white skin and blond hair.... The mountain gods resemble priests, it is said, since many appear as bearded Europeans.... *Tzuultaq'a* looks like the Germans" (Wilson 1995:57).

Richard Wilson explains that the resemblance of Tzuultaq'a to the Germans is due to the presence of Germans in Northern Guatemala among the Q'eqchi, where they bought or took the land from the Natives for coffee plantations. A major wave of Germans came to Northern Guatemala after the so-called Liberal reform of Justo Rufino Barrios in 1871. Since then, the Germans have managed the coffee plantations with Indian labor forces that they ill-treated while paying low wages. Therefore, the image of Tzuultaq'a resembles or is compared to that of a Ladino, a gringo, or a German, and is sometimes represented as the devil.

The time is long gone when mothers taught their children in the most natural way possible the appropriate behavior and relationships with Mother Earth. Now, the oral tradition is not much relevant, and the education received by children does not include Native ideas or Indigenous knowledge. There is an intense process of assimilation, because of competition for jobs in cities outside the communities, as well as the flows of migration toward Mexico and the United States. Another major problem is the lack of land, which causes extreme poverty. Finally, I can say that the dismantling of the traditional sociopolitical organization of Maya communities is due to national political parties and fundamentalist churches that have invaded Indigenous communities, separating them from their traditional ways of life and values.

It does not matter now from which church Indigenous People belong, they continue to pray to God for solutions to their problems. It is common to hear Maya evangelical converts praying out loud through radio programs, as they make their request for salvation. In the same way, Catholics also pray to their patron saints about their sufferings on earth. In other words, the problems brought by the Spanish invasion of their lands and territories, as well as the oppression and exploitation suffered throughout the centuries had placed Indigenous People in a precarious condition of poverty and landlessness.

Besides these multiple problems to which Indigenous People were subjected, pandemic diseases, against which they did not have any defenses, also devastated their populations. The old-world diseases brought to this continent such as smallpox, yellow fever, whooping cough, and so forth decimated entire communities to the point of lowering the population close to extinction in some places (Lovell and Lutz, 1995). Having suffered this devastation and not understanding the origin of these lethal diseases, Indigenous People thought they were being punished by God. This painful situation was used by early missionaries to falsely blame Indigenous People for being idolaters and devil worshipers, so that the diseases were God's punishment for not converting to Christianity. This is how the, among the Jakaltek, three killer diseases from the old world—yellow fever, smallpox, and whooping cough (*naj oxwanh hustisya*)—came to be called the "three justices," or punishments by god.

To avoid supernatural punishment, massive conversion of Indigenous People occurred, as they wanted to be saved from the wrath of God. Although conversion to Christianity took place, Indigenous People maintained their own religious beliefs, which they practiced in a syncretic way. I remember my mother going to the church and praying that her sick children be spared from any diseases during childhood.

Among the Jakaltek, where diseases had devastated the population until the early part of the twentieth century, they have considered the early years of a child (from the time of birth to three years old) as the "dangerous age." At this early age, babies or children frequently got sick, and because of the lack of resources such as food and medicine, they were exposed to diseases that often killed them. That is why mothers, including my own, used to go to the churches to request protection for their children, especially on Tuesdays, which is the day dedicated to the soul of children.

When I was about six years of age, my mother took me to the church in Jacaltenango, and in front of the altar she gave thanks to the Virgin for sparing my life, since I reached the age of childhood and passed through the dangerous age without major problems. I remember my mother addressing God and the Virgin with words of thankfulness, while restating her promise to the Virgin that I would "dance" next year during her festivity, as an act of gratitude.

This spiritual compromise or "*promesa*" was very serious, and my mother registered me as a dancer at the house of the captain of the *cofradia* (Brotherhood) who organized the Dance of Conquest for the festivity of the Virgin of Candelaria, the patron saint of my town, Jacaltenango. I danced as a *chichimite* (Chichimec), a little red warrior holding an ax and defending Moctezuma against Cortes. The preparation and training started a few months in advance, so I had to travel twelve kilometers by foot with my oldest sister to come to town and practice every other week. The travel was too tiring at my age, so my sister had to wait for me many times on the path through the forest and mountains, while I lied down to rest before continuing with the trip. This was a sacrifice that I had to endure to comply with the sacred promise made by my mother to God and the Virgin for sparing my life and giving me the blessings for growing up as a normal child.

During the festivity, I had a friend or companion dancer of my own age. We took turns, because it was truly tiring for a boy of my age to dance day after day under the heat of the sun. Another reason for having a companion dancer was because the dancer's colorful custom was rented from an armory at a distant place called Momostenango, in Totonicapán. Renting the costume for a dancer was very expensive for only one family, so our parents had to share the expenses.

Another problem was that until the 1960s there was no transportation in Jacaltenango, so the People who rented the dancers' dresses had to travel by foot some 150 kilometers. This was a kind of pilgrimage, so when those who traveled to bring the dancers' cloth returned a week before the patron saint's festivity, People went to the outskirts of town to wait for them and celebrate their arrival with fireworks and marimba music. At this site, the dancers also tried on the clothing, marking this reception with the beginning of the dance festival in honor of the patron saint that lasted twenty days.

As humans, then, we should nourish these relationships, not only with the natural world but also with the Yahaw Yib'an Q'inal (The-Lord of-Everything that Exists on Earth and in the-Sky). Our lives must be devoted to doing good things, since life is very short and we soon must abandon this beautiful place we call Mother Earth. For the Mayas, as well as for the Nahua and Toltec philosophers, life on earth is said to be like a short visit of a guest. Our life is borrowed from the Creator and we are not the owners of our existence. Life, then, is like a dream; it is short and not perennial. Life on earth is not all happiness—there are problems, misfortunes, and sufferings; that's why the Nahua philosophers questioned the meaning of human life and the dream of eternity, as shown in this fragment.

> Truly, do we live on earth?
> Not forever on earth; only a little while here.

> Although it be jade, it will be broken,
> Although it be gold, it is crushed,
> Although it be quetzal feathers, it is torn asunder.
> Not forever on earth; only a little while here.
> (King Nezahualcoyotl, in Leon Portilla 1990:7)

With the current environmental problems now affecting all latitudes of earth, there should be a conscious return to the original teachings of the ancestors. In this process, Native American belief systems, religion, and the sciences can help us to rethink our mission on earth as established in the *Popol Vuh*, the Sacred Book of the Mayas. And in this process, even the name given to God or Creator—"the Heart of Heaven and the Heart of Earth"—is a unifying concept that links life together in the universe, thus validating this cosmocentric approach to life preached by ancient as well as modern Mayas.

THE TONAL OR SPIRIT BEARER   NINE
Human Nature/Animal Nature
or the Theory of the Self

ONE OF THE BEST EXAMPLES to illustrate the human connection to nature and supernatural beings as explained in Mayalogue is the concept of the *yijomal spixan* (spirit bearer) among the Jakaltek Maya. This is the *tonal* or the *alter ego*, as it is known throughout Mesoamerica by Indigenous People such as Mayas and the Nahuas of Central Mexico. First, let me clarify the term *tonalli*, animal companion or spirit bearer, in relation to the *nahualli*, which refers to the transforming witch. Both terms come from the Nahuatl language and most of the times they are used mistakenly by scholars referring to these Mesoamerican concepts. The *tonalli* or *tonal* is the spiritual animal to which the child is linked at birth, until the person dies. This is the *alter ego* or the other self of the individual, just in a spiritual and animal form. While the *nawal* or *nahual*, refers to a person (a witch) with magic powers to transform into an animal (not necessarily his or her animal companion) for an evil purpose.

My argument here is that these terms have their own counterpart in Mayan languages, but scholars have preferred to use the well-known Nahuatl terms, abandoning the Native ones. Since scholars, considered to be "authorities," wrongly used the term *nahual* for *alter ego* or *tonalli*, the Indigenous People, too, repeated the same mistake, abandoning their own Maya terms. This is sad, because even those who consider themselves *ahq'ij*, or

Maya priests, commit the same mistake and use the wrong term, following this colonial imposition. Fortunately, some Maya linguistic communities maintained their terms, so it is easy to deduce that other Maya people had them, too.

For example, the Jakaltek, Q'anjobal, and Akatek term for the *tonalli* or spirit bearer is "*ijomal pixan*," while the Tzotzil and Tzeltal of Chiapas call it "*ch'ulel*." Obviously, other communities may have lost it because *Nahuatl* terms had supremacy over Mayan terms since the Spanish invasion of 1524, as well as because the Mayas were persecuted by Christian missionaries, who condemned their spiritual beliefs as the teachings of the devil. Under these conditions, the religious leaders and calendar experts abandoned their spiritual knowledge, as they were called witches (*nahual* or *brujo*), a term that has pervaded ethnographic literature since then. "Some researchers such as Foster (1944) and Aguirre Beltrán (1955) have proposed that the early missionaries and friars were, without knowing, those who propagated the *nahual* term far beyond the Nahua territories, and that this phenomena ended up producing a confusion in the usage and meaning of the term not only among the Indigenous People, but also among the observers" (Martínez González 2010:2).

The ethnography of Ruth Bunzel's *Chichicastenango* (1952) is a good example to mention regarding this confusion. She refers correctly to the *tonalli* as "the animal of destiny," but then, she automatically shifts to a definition of the *nahual*, as it can be read in her glossary of terms. "*Nagual or nahual*: Animal of destiny. Spirit or soul that animates a person with whom he is intimately connected. The *nahual* can be a real or fantastic animal. In certain cases the man can take the external aspect of his *nahual*, with the purpose of evading danger or to carry on a deed. From the Mexican *nahualli*" (Bunzel 1952:503).

The first part of her definition is an accurate description of the *tonalli*, but then she used the term *nahual*, mixing both terms with different meanings. It is evident that while doing fieldwork, she had already in mind that the animal spirit is called *nagual* or *nahual*, so like other scholars, she did not asked for the Native term to refer for this concept. The same is true for Oliver La Farge (1931) and the Jakaltek Maya. He defines the *nahual* as follows: "*Nagual, iq-on pican*," literally "Soul Bearer" (La Farge 1931:323). Clearly, he provides the definition for the *tonalli* or the *ijom pixan* (soul or spirit bearer). But he puts the two terms together; "*Nagual, iq-on pican*," literally "soul bearer," though they are two totally different concepts. The same mistake is made by modern scholars who keep mixing the *tonalli* with the *nahualli* as follows: "The most feared sorcerers are those who, in altered states of consciousness, can transform into their animal companion spirit, known as *nahualli* among the Aztec" (Helmke 2009:49).

It is hard to correct the usage of these terms now, just as the term *shaman* or *chiman* was defined indiscriminately by early scholars as a witch or *"brujo."* These terms have become generalized and even Indigenous People (Mayas) started to use them without questioning or without asking their elders for the correct terms in their own languages. Unfortunately, words are lost if they are not used, so here are some terms that may refer to the *tonalli*, animal companion or *alter ego*, in some Maya regions (Martínez González 2010:23).

Jakaltek	Ijom pixan
Tzotzil	Ch'ulel, chanul
Tzutuhil	Ajb'al
Tojolabal	Wayjel
Tzeltal	Yalak
Mam	T'ekelel, kolel

It is a task for the Maya priests or *ajq'ij*, who are experts on the Maya calendar, to search and investigate the forgotten name for the spirit bearer or animal companion (tonal) in the whole Maya region. These are very important terms, which are avoided because of persecution of the Natives, but now it is necessary to correct the mistakes.

The spirit bearer is the most important element that provides humans with the capacity of knowing and producing knowledge from their natural environment, as they are link to nature since the moment of birth. In other words, when a child is born in a community, his or her animal companion (alter ego) is also born in the mountain in a form of a spiritual animal. This is the mystery of life and destiny, since the two—the person and the animal counterpart—are connected to each other throughout their lifetimes. If something happens to the person, the same will happen to the animal companion, because their life and destiny are linked together. This Maya theory of the self provides a framework by which a human (person) is said to have a dual human and animal essence. The belief is that a person with an animal counterpart forms a unity or a totality that is inseparable, and both share the same destiny.

According to the Mayas and other Mesoamerican cultures, the spirit bearer or animal companion is a spiritual counterpart of human beings that is assigned at the moment of birth. This is a very special and secret aspect or identity of the individual that is known only to the *ahb'eh* (Maya priests) who specialize in interpreting and explaining the symbolism of the days through divination. To understand this process, it is necessary to know and interpret the signs and meanings of the days from the Maya calendar. According to the Maya experts (*ahb'eh or* diviners) the twenty day names (or individuals) of the calendar are also interconnected and have a determining influence on the abilities, future, and destiny of an individual.

For the Mayas, life is compared to a candle that is lighted at the moment of birth. The candle may have long life until it is totally burned, or it can be turned off suddenly by the wind. The lighted candle is then a metaphor for the life of an individual who may live a long life or die accidentally. Some people live a long life (a candle that keeps burning), or sometimes the individual dies suddenly because of an accident or illness. The length of life is predetermined from birth, according to the signs from the Maya calendar, which the Jakaltek Maya called (*stz'ayik-yaq'b'al*) or destiny. Some Maya *ahb'eh* or *ajq'ij* use the term *ora*, which comes from the Spanish word *hora*, referring to the concept of "destiny." At the time of birth, the *ahb'eh* performs a divination, consulting the days that are interconnected (past-present-future): the yesterday, today, and tomorrow for establishing the destiny and the animal companion of the individual.

The spirit bearer can be any animal, or a natural phenomenon known to the Mayas, to which the individual will be connected through his or her lifetime. For example, when a child is born, the *ahb'eh* will check the calendar and perform the appropriate divination to tell the parents the name that the child will carry for life. The diviner will also reveal the animal companion of the child to his parents, be it a jaguar, an eagle, a deer, a monkey, and so on. The divination is important because in this way the *ahb'eh* will gather the information or the omens of the days that will mark the child's future or destiny. The most powerful individuals have powerful animal companions, such as the jaguar, the eagle, the snake, and so forth. Also, the power of the day influences the individual, and usually those who are born on a day with a higher value become a well-known individual. A day name from the Maya calendar is repeated from 1 to 13. For example, *1 tox, 2 tox, 3 tox* ... up to *13 tox*. *Tox* from the Jakaltek Maya calendar is "death." So, the individual born on the *13 tox* has more essence or power than the one born on *2 tox* or any other lower number. Of course, the *tonal* information is secret, and it is only revealed to the parents of the child who will also keep it secret until the person grows and can take care of him- or herself.

In the *Popol Vuh* we can recognize the uses of the Maya calendar and the practice of divination in the process of giving the names to individuals. According to the *Popol Vuh*, the first four fathers created appeared after a divination was done and an agreement reached between the Creators and his helpers, Ixmukane and Ixpiyacoc (First Grandmother and First Grandfather). Three of them were given the name jaguar (*b'alam*). There was B'alam Quitze, B'alam Acab', Iqui B'alam, and the fourth father was called Mahucutah (not a *Balam*). These four fathers were very powerful because their alter egos or spirit bearers were also powerful animals: jaguar, eagle, and wasp.

Beside knowing the Maya calendar and explaining the child's possible destiny to the parents, the *ahb'eh* also helps the parents to dispose of the umbilical cord of the newly born child. Among the Jakaltek, there was a practice of burying the umbilical cord close to a water spring or river so that the animal companion of the child would find the appropriate place to make its leaving and not to suffer from hunger and thirst. The parents of the child and the *ahb'eh* used to pray at the place where the placenta was buried. They burn a candle there so that the parents will always remember the place and visit it until the child is old enough to take care of him- or herself. This ceremony of "burying" the placenta is very special, because in this way the child is linked or connected to nature through his or her alter ego (*yijomal spixan*) or animal companion. The prayer-maker asks for blessings and a long life for the child, as well as protection and security for the animal companion, which will live a parallel life with that of the child. If the child gets sick, it is because something may be wrong with the tonal or *yijomal spixan* of the child. Usually, in every community there are people with bad hearts, the *nawal* or *brujo* (witch) who want to do harm to other people who they envy. If the *nawal* gets to know what animal the spirit bearer of a person is, he or she will try to capture it and make it suffer so that the person eventually becomes sick too. That is why the concept of the tonal or *yijomal spixan* is a secret knowledge that only the *ahb'eh* or diviner can know and tell the parents of the child, who must also keep it secret until the person has grown.

The uses of the Maya calendar for naming children and assigning the child's spirit bearer was still a common practice until the early 1960s in some Maya communities of Guatemala and Mexico. Among the Tzotzil-Tzeltal from Chiapas, Mexico, the concept of *ch'ulel*, or animal companion was also important.

> Related to this concept is the belief that individuals have animal soul companions, also given by the sun deity at birth, who share their human counterparts' physical and spiritual destinies. These animals live in two special corrals, one in a sacred mountain and the other in the sky ... They range from jaguars and coyotes for rich and powerful people, the

opossums and squirrels for poor and humble people. Shamans as well as prestigious cargo holders need powerful animal soul companions in order to perform their tasks in the human community. (Gossen 1974:15)

The belief in the spirit bearer or *yijomal spixan* was widely practiced among the Mesoamerican cultures since ancient times. Anthropologists have tried to explain it applying different anthropological theories (Saler 1967), but they have not been able to totally understand this ancient Maya practice of spiritual connection with earth and the environment. The *yijomal spixan* or alter ego and the *nawal* (the transforming witch or *brujo*) are two totally different categories to be discussed below.

THE *YIJOMAL SPIXAN* OR SPIRIT BEARER
(A THEORY OF THE SELF)

As I have mentioned above, the *yijomal spixan* or spirit bearer is an animal companion that is born in the mountain at the same time a human being is born. The *yijomal spixan*, also known as the *tonalli* by the *Nahuatl* speakers of Central Mexico, is a spiritual animal or counterpart of a human being. In other words, humans are not complete if they don't have their animal counterpart with whom they share their destiny. This animal companion is linked to the human person throughout his or her life and whatever happens to the person will happen to his animal companion, or vice versa. This is the sacred knowledge carried out by the *ahb'eh* or Maya diviners, who continued to use the Maya calendar, as was done in antiquity. The naming of the individual and the assignment of his or her appropriate alter ego responds to the power of the day in which the individual was born. "The day of an individual's birth, which is thought to be ruled by a particular day lord, indicates his abilities, fate, companion animal, and personality. The calendar also indicates lucky and unlucky days for each person" (Orellana 1984:103).

The following diagram shows the structure of the alter ego or *yijomal spixan* as a duality of elements: the human/animal nature that integrates or composes the human individual or person.

This model shows us that any person is composed of the two spiritual substances: human spirit and animal spirit, which are joined at the moment of birth of the individual. The idea here is that the individual is not complete without its animal counterpart, who makes the totality of the human being or person. The unity of these two spiritual elements occurs right at birth, thus having human and animal characteristics throughout his life. In other

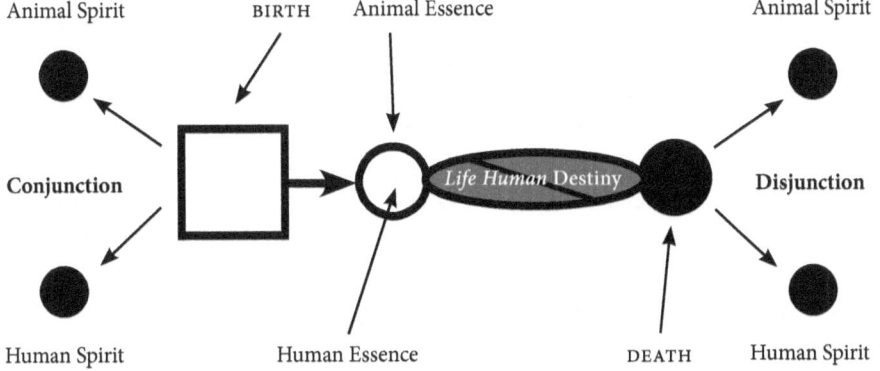

FIGURE 9.1. Structure of the *yijomal spixan* or spirit bearer in a human person.

words, the *yijomal spixan* or spirit bearer is the manifestation of one part of the human being, which is his soul or spirit in a form of an animal that connect him or her to the natural world. The concept of the spirit "bearer" is then important because this is the essence of being human. The animal companion is a spiritual animal that symbolically carries the human spirit, so that the person cannot act without first meditating or thinking on the repercussion that his action will have on his or her spirit bearer and the environment. In other words, humans and nature are intimately connected, so whatever humans do to the natural world, their spirit bearers will suffer the consequence and thus the human being, too. Both are equally important, and one is not complete without the other, since both possess the same breath of life. For this reason, they share the same destiny from the time of birth, up to the time of death.

From the diagram shown above, we can argue that humans are spiritual beings too, and none is superior or in control of the other. According to this Maya model of the self, humans depend on animals to survive and vice versa. During his ethnographic fieldwork among the Jakaltek in 1929, Oliver La Farge mentioned that the Jakaltek continued to practice the ceremonial disposal of the umbilical cord. After the umbilical cord was buried near a water spring, the parents will make sure that their child grows up acting with respect and with the appropriate behavior toward nature, which is part of the child through his or her other self—the child's animal companion. "At the time of the Year Bearer, the Indians go to the springs where they may communicate with their ancestral spirits and pray for the nagual's [*yijomal spixan*] protection" (La Farge 1931:135).

This unity and interrelationship becomes stronger when human beings interact appropriately with their community and the environment from which they extract their living. It is, in this situation that the human-nature relationship becomes charged with a spiritual force that maintains reciprocity and the interspecies dialogue while nourishing the Creator.

Usually, anthropologists and those who study Indigenous cultures can only come to understand and deal with the nature-culture, human-animal dichotomy as separate entities. The common understanding is that humans create cultures and societies separate from nature and unrelated to the domain of nonhuman beings. But as we have seen, Indigenous People maintain this close relationship throughout their lifetimes, to the point that both, human and animal counterparts share the same destiny on earth. It is until death that the animal-human spiritual duality is split and separated, as the human person dies. For Christians, the human spirit is the soul that separates from the body and leaves earth on its way to the place of judgment. If the person was good and managed to avoid capital sins, the soul is received in heaven and enjoys eternal happiness with angels and saints. If the person has committed mortal sins against humans and God, the spirit is condemned to hell where it will suffer for eternity.

For Indigenous People, death is a stage for the human spirit that will continue to live on a different level of heaven, doing the same things that the person did on earth. At the moment of death, the human spirit separates from the animal spirit and the individual's body rests motionless, while the essence of life, which is the *yijomal spixan*, remains and will integrate into another life when the appropriate combination of the time, space, and destiny occurs again in the intermeshing of days, months, and years from the Maya calendar.

The theory of the self-discussed here deals with a dual essence or spirit, one that deals with culture and the other with nature. In other words, humans have animal characteristics, and the *yijomal spixan* is the spiritual element that naturalizes human beings. The duality of human-spirit or body-soul in Western tradition is similar to the human-animal spirit bearer, but with the difference that both are interrelated, and the action or behavior of human beings must be balanced while protecting the animal counterpart. In other words, by having an animal counterpart, humans are tied to nature and they must interact with their other self (animal companion) with care and protection. If you hurt animals or nature, you are hurting yourself, since your life and destiny are tied together from the moment of birth until the moment of death. Human life is then, the mutual coexistence of both animal and human spirits and the actions of people will be focused on how to live in harmony with nature, which represents the other half of his being. We could say that human beings belong equally to their community of human beings as well as to their community of nonhuman beings, or their natural environment. Contrary to the dichotomy nature-culture, person-animal, which are opposites in Western culture, for the Mayas both form and constitute an inseparable unity. The human-animal substance of the "self" does not represent a binomial opposition, but a complementary dualism that makes human beings an integral totality.

By having both human and animal essences, humans are fully equipped to gather and produce knowledge from both human cultures and from the natural world of plants, animals, and other nonhuman beings. So, when people say sympathetically that Indigenous People are "close" to nature, they are not getting the message right, because Indigenous People are not just close to nature, they are part of nature. For this reason, the existence of the spiritual animal companion or alter ego is real, and not a total abstraction, as with the concept of soul in Christian religious belief. The spirit bearer for the Mayas is precisely that, the bearer of life for the individual and the force that makes him or her act with certain abilities, knowledge, and personality.

SPIRIT LOSS, ILLNESS, AND DEATH

According to Maya belief, the individual has a spirit or *pixan*, which is the force that alerts and protects the individual. This spirit bearer or *pixan* can leave the body of the individual at night during his or her dreams or by fright or "*susto*." In other words, the *spixan* can be stolen and leave the body of the individual, who then becomes ill and will die if the spirit bearer is not found and restored to the individual. When this happens, the curer must find the *yijomal spixan*, or the alter ego of the sick individual, because it may be the one who is in trouble, and the reason why the person got sick.

One of the most common sicknesses among children in Mayan communities is fright. The *xiwkilal* or fright is due to the loss of spirit by being frightened by a supernatural being (el sombrerón, la llorona, etc.), a serpent, lightning, near drowning, or frightened by a mountain lion or jaguar. Also, the spirit can get into an imbalance in relation to the natural world because of a transgression of a natural law or norm established by the ancestors as a guide for appropriate human behavior. Some scholars who have focused their attention on *susto*, which is classified as a "folk illness," have argued that *susto* is the product of social stress resulting from the lack of social accommodation of an individual to his or her community. Others argue that this is a psychological problem or expression of schizophrenia. "Some researchers have seen *susto* as simply a way of explaining mental illness for people who lack the education to understand its true significance" (Rubel, O'Nell, and Collado-Ardón 1984:9).

Thus, there are many forms of *susto*, and of course the person who is physically weak and always sick because of the lack of food can be more exposed to other problems. The fact is that *xiwkilal* or *susto*, as related to the loss of spirit, is a pre-Hispanic tradition and a form of knowledge about diseases that has persisted until now. The following is a definition of susto, which can be used to extend our discussion on the concept of the tonal, *yijomal spixan*, or spirit bearer.

> Suffering *susto,* being *asustado*, is based on people's understanding that an individual is composed of a body and an immaterial substance, an essence that may become detached from the body and either wander freely or become a captive of supernatural forces. This essence may leave the body during sleep, particularly when the individual is dreaming, but may also become detached as a consequence of an unsettling or frightening experience. Among Indians, this essence is believed held captive because the patient, wittingly or not, has disturbed the spirit guardians of the earth, river, ponds, forests, or collectivities of animals, birds, or fish. Its release depends upon expiation of the affront. This process dramatically illuminates the relationship that binds humans and suprahumans in these societies. (Rubel, O'Nell, and Collado-Ardón 1984:8–9)

This is common among children, because of their young age, as they are more exposed to this type of natural illness, which is called *xiwkilal* or *susto*. That is why the babies are always carried on the back of the mother, and whenever they enter a dangerous place the mother will bring the baby in front, close to her heart for protection. Also, after resting on an unfamiliar place, when leaving, the mother will call for the spirit bearer of the child by saying: "*Malin, machach kani, txujanach jinhan, paxojonhjtoj jatut*" (María, do not stay behind, follow us, let's go home). Since the animal companion of the human baby is also a young animal, it is normal that these young babies are more playful. So, when the human baby spirit encounters his or her baby animal companion or alter ego, they can leave the body and wander around. That is why there are always dangers around a child, and he or she must be always protected by his or her parents, older sisters, and relatives. "One of the most consistent behavior patterns is a mother's sweeping with her shawl the ground on which she has been sitting to gather up all the parts of the soul of her infant. Parents are expected to treat a small child with utmost care and affection, lest its soul, not yet used to its new receptacle, becomes frightened and leave" (Vogt 1969:370).

The loss of the *yijomal spixan* or spirit bearer occurs very often with children, because they are not yet aware of the dangers around them and their spirit bearer is still a playful spiritual animal, as well as because children are exposed to many diseases and are weak at an early age. There are many problems with their health, so their animal spirit as well as the child him- or herself are taken care of with constant attention if they leave the house or while they play. If a child falls into a river, the loss of spirit will occur immediately, as the child is frightened because of this accident. The imbalance that occurs in the case of a child is not his fault or transgression of moral codes, but an accident from which he or she learns to accommodate within the natural world. In other words, the child as well as his alter ego or animal companion is in the process of learning and experiencing the world. So, the fright that the child gets is in relation to his exploration and understanding of the natural world around, a form of acquiring knowledge. When *xiwkilal* or *susto* occurs, the spirit bearer leaves the body and it is hidden or lost in the place of the accident without returning to the child's body until the appropriate ritual for curing *susto* or fright is performed.

Usually the child does not tell his or her parents that he or she had suffered an accident such as escaping from drowning in a river or a pond. If the child cannot talk yet, a chicken egg will be placed under his or her armpit, and after the ninth day, the parents or the curer will take it and open it to see the sign or image of what has frightened or sickened the child. Generally, the physical appearance of the child changes as his or her face starts to get swollen and the child becomes restless at night and does not want to eat. This is the symptom of fright that is usually diagnosed by the curer in town. The child is asked where the accident took place, or his or her friends will tell the parents of the sick child where that child got into trouble losing his or her soul or spirit bearer. The curer then will go to the place with the parents of the child and at the spot where the near drowning occurred. The child is placed on the edge of the river and a ceremony of cleansing will take place. The curer will start praying calling for the name of the child while sprinkling water or rum on him or her, and requesting that the *yijomal spixan* return to the body of the frightened child. Then, the child is asked to drink the water, and a handful of sand will be taken from the river and be placed under the child's pillow at night while he or she sleeps.

The villagers are also cautioned not to kill animals with strange behavior because they can be the materialization of a lost soul or spirit bearer of someone in town. If a hunter kills an animal that happens to be the animal companion of someone, the person whose alter ego was killed will also die instantly, since their life and destiny are tied together as mentioned earlier. It is believed that the *tonal* or alter ego of a child can wander outside his or her body when the child is asleep, or while sick and restless. The following story was told to Ruth Bunzel when she did fieldwork in Guatemala among the K'iche Maya of Chichicastenango in 1930.

> One day while I was out hunting in the mountains I met a mountain lion. It was standing in front of me in the trail. It did not act like a mountain lion, it was not frightened; it did not charge or run away, it just stood there in the trail, looking at me. I should have known then that it was supernatural, but I did not think. I took my gun and shot it. When I returned to my house they were crying; my son, a little boy had died. He had been sick, but not very sick, just some childish sickness, and he had died quite suddenly at the very moment that I shot the lion. It was the destiny [animal companion] of my child that I had met in the mountains. (Bunzel 1952:274–75)

The spirit loss can also occur with older people, but sometimes they are responsible for their problems and illnesses when they disobey the norms that rule the relationships between humans and nature. According to Evon Vogt: "The concept of the animal spirit companion relates the Zinacantecos in a fundamental way to the world of nature" (Vogt 1969:374). When a man who does not care about nature and overhunts animals for the purpose of selling the meat or just because he has a rifle and can kill more effectively, he provokes the anger of the Earth Lord and guardian of the animals.

The rupture of acceptable behavior of a person in relation to the natural world is punished by Witz, the supernatural being. A punishment is necessary for teaching a lesson to other villagers, so as not to commit the same mistake. The spirit bearer of this abusive hunter will be let out free from the sacred fence where all the alter egos are protected and allowed to materialize as a regular animal, then being exposed to being hunted or killed. That is why the experts are called to pray for the protection of the *yijomal spixan*—to avoid these kinds of dangers. Oliver La Farge documented the following prayer for the protection of the *yijomal spixan* among the Jakaltek Maya of Guatemala. "Hide them for me: guard them for me: do not let them come into the open. If there is any sorcerer, if there is any man who thinks evil against these, our spirits; in you we have hope for these little ones, oh our fathers and mothers, that nothing shall happen to them, that we shall have life and happiness" (La Farge 1931:135).

NAWALISM: SHAPE-SHIFTING AND TRANSFORMATION OF A WITCH

While the tonal or *yijomal spixan* is the focus of my attention in this chapter, I will refer briefly to the *nawal* or witch who transforms into an animal form. As in every human society, there are those who utilize their knowledge and abilities to do wrong things and become transgressors of the community's norms for appropriate behavior.

The *nawal* is usually the term used to name a witch (man or woman) who has the power to transform him- or herself into an animal, not necessarily his or her own animal companion. Contrary to the *yijomal spixan* or soul bearer, which is a companion throughout the individual's lifetime, nawalism is a momentous transformation into an animal for a specific, mostly evil purpose. Once the witch has fulfilled its evil mission, the transformation is reverted, so the person-*nawal* recovers his or her human body again. In other words, *nawalism* is a process of borrowing an animal body-spirit for an evil purpose. The *nawal* was widely known among Indigenous People of Mesoamerica, and this belief persists in some Maya communities today.

The existence of the *nawal* is an affirmation that in any human society there is always the transgressor, and that harmony with nature and community is never total or perfectly functional. Conflicts and problems are part of the functioning of the system that needs to be readjusted constantly through time and space in the search for balance and harmony between humans, nature, and the spiritual world. The following is a model diagram of the *nawal*, or human transformation into an animal (*nawalism*).

The concept of *nawalism* is also evident in the *Popol Vuh*, where Gucumatz is said to have been a marvelous king who could transform himself into different animal forms. "Gucumatz was truly a marvelous king. For seven days he mounted to the skies and for seven days he went down into Xibalba; seven days he changed himself into a snake and really became a serpent; for seven days he changed himself into an eagle; for seven days he became a jaguar; and his appearance was really that of an eagle and a jaguar. Another seven days he changed himself into clotted blood and was only motionless blood" (Goetz and Morley 1950: 219–20).

So King Gucumatz was the prototype of a *nawal* who could transform himself into many different forms of animals. According to the *Popol Vuh*,

THE NAWAL OR WITCH

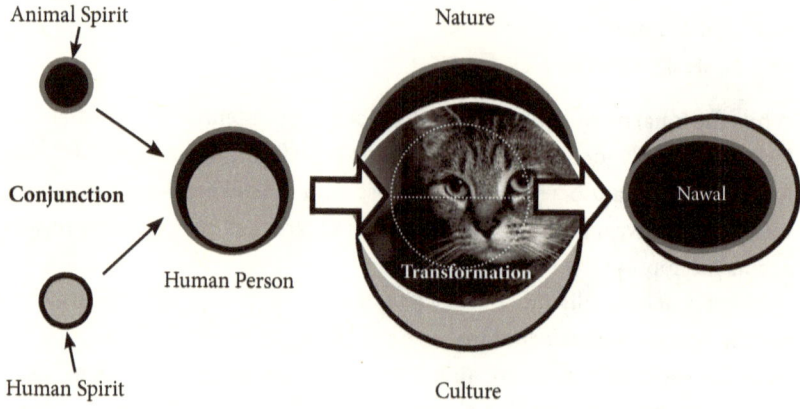

FIGURE 9.2. Structure of *Nawalism*: human-animal transformation.

the nature of this king was marvelous, and he did this transformation to show the other rulers that he was powerful, so when other lords saw him, they were filled with terror.

As I have stated above, the term *nawal* is borrowed from the Nahuatl language from Central Mexico and integrated into Mayan languages. As in the case of the *tonalli*, the term *nahual* was used indiscriminately to refer to both the *nawal* and the *yijomal spixan* (alter ego). The tendency was to use the same term *nawal*, for two separate or different concepts. This confusion is shown in Maud Oakes's ethnographic work among the Mam of Western Guatemala. "I requested Don Pancho to ask Chiman [shaman] Pascual Pablo whether a child has a *nagual* when it is born. The *chiman* answered that this was not true for [the people of] Todos Santos" (Oakes 1951:170). Maud Oakes then presents several stories of human transformation into coyotes, which is what is called *nawalism*. To ask if a child has a *nawal* at birth was the wrong question, because the *nawal* was a totally different concept. She could have asked if a child has an animal companion at birth, in which case she would have received a positive answer. Everybody in a Maya community knows that a *nawal* is an antisocial and evil person, who is feared in the community. Of course everybody would deny being a witch since this personage was fiercely persecuted.

It is important to use the Maya or Native terms to name these spiritual elements to avoid confusion, which was the major problem, not only for anthropologists but for early Christian missionaries. The missionaries who came from Spain to convert the Indians were scandalized when they heard about the practice of *nawalism*. They argued that the devil maintained control over the Indians and it was necessary to free them from paganism and Christianize them by force. Jacinto de la Serna and other missionaries stated that the Natives were controlled by the devil, so they preferred to transform into animals, either a *nawal* or a *tonal*, since for them both were the same. "For this miserable Indians the devil has erased the image of God, in whose image they were made, to the point of being human creation the most beautiful thing that has come from the hands of their Creator, they prefer to be dogs, lions, tigers, caymans, and other dirty animals such as the skunks, and the bats, etc." (De la Serna 1982:204).

Here it becomes evident, that De la Serna was referring to the *nahualli* and not to the *tonal* or *yijomal spixan*, and because of the missionaries' zeal and eagerness to eradicate what they called superstitions and idolatries, they did not understand the deep meaning of the concept of *tonal* or *yijomal spixan*. Instead, they confused *tonalism* with *nawalism* and persecuted the Indigenous People to the point of torture, to force them abandon their ancient cultural and religious beliefs systems.

Despite their persecution for practicing these ancient traditions, *nawalism* continued as a secret cultural belief among Indigenous People throughout Mesoamerica. I remember many stories of the *nawal* told by my mother when I was a child. Even when I was a schoolteacher in Tzisbaj, a Maya village in Western Guatemala, the stories of the *nawal* abounded in this community. It was said that there were many *nawales*, or witches, in this community and people should be careful not to make them angry. An angered witch could cause illness to anyone just by blowing the spell through the air.

The *nawal* or *brujo* is an antisocial man or woman who does not go out during the day and prefers to be hidden from the public. During the night, the *nawal* transforms him- or herself into a dog, or into a nocturnal animal such as a cat, and wanders throughout the village controlling the house of his enemy. It is easier to enter through the roof of a house transformed into a cat, than with a human body. So the *nawal* utilizes the shape-shifting method or transformation for penetrating secret and hidden places, thus discovering the secrets of his or her enemy. Once in control of the information, the *nawal* can cause pain or an illness to an individual who is taken by surprise. Usually, the bewitched person goes to a diviner (*ahb'eh*) who will reveal who is causing the illness. Then the sick person goes to confront the witch, assuring that if he or she does not get well, the *brujo* will be held responsible and will be exterminated. After this threat, generally the person gets well and keeps taking herbal medicine to be cured, and avoids further confrontations with *nawals*. Most of the time, the belief in being cursed or bewitched by a *nawal* is primarily a psychological problem, since the sick person's anxiety increases and little by little he or she is weakened until, finally, the illness takes the life of the person.

The *nawal*, then, is a malevolent person who is consumed by jealousy or envy against his or her neighbor and wants to destroy that successful person. In other words, the concept of the *nawal* does exist among the Indigenous People, but it is often confused with the concept of *yijomal spixan* or the spirit bearer, which is totally a different and positive element. The *tonal* is the counterpart of the individual, and all members of Indigenous societies have an alter ego or animal companion, because as members of a community they have their umbilical cord buried outside, thus making the connection with the natural world. There are some extraordinary individuals, and a very few have natural phenomena such as lightning as their alter ego. These are extremely wise and powerful individuals, who are said to be closer to divinity and act as protectors of the people (*skolomal jet*), also called *komam-komi'* (fathers and mothers), who care for the well-being of their people and community.

During the first half of the twentieth century, Indigenous cultures of Mesoamerica were still very strong, and the concept of the *tonal* (alter ego) was widely spread and practiced in Maya communities. Also, the specialist *ahb'eh* (diviner) continued his or her role as a guide and interpreter of the Maya calendar. Unfortunately, after the 1950s, the cultural beliefs of Indigenous People were once again under attack not only by politicians, but by missionaries such as those of the Protestant religion, and by the so-called Catholic Action. For this reason, the concept of the *tonal* or *yijomal spixan* was continuously confused with the *nawal*, as explained above. It is important to make the differentiation and consider that among Indigenous People, too, there are individuals who are antisocial and who violate the social rules or cultural norms that guide correct behavior in the communities. For a better understanding of Maya belief systems and spirituality, "[i]t is necessary to utilize the native categories for understanding the belief systems and ways of thinking of Indigenous People that are different from Western beliefs. This, of course, at first glance it appears to be incomprehensible and without logic" (Picciotto de Rosembaum 1979:8).

But, of course, the belief systems of Indigenous People concerning the *yijomal spixan* or animal companion, that is, the interrelationship between humans and nature, is truly an extraordinary practice that is logical, or let's say, Mayalogical. Also, it is important to recognize that the Maya calendar (*b'isom tz'ayik*) is an ancient instrument used to order action or to ensure communication between humans, nature and the supernatural world. "The Ixil [Maya] calendar and associated beliefs facilitate communication between people and supernaturals. Although supernaturals are very often punishing beings, they are also seen as beneficial and will sometimes send warnings through dreams and protect or reward people" (Colby 1981:48).

As we can see, the Maya calendar orders human action and behavior throughout the individual's lifetime, fulfilling his or her destiny. For this reason, a good life implies a respectful response to the obligations or missions of the individuals to nourish the Creator and the ancestors. This mission starts when the child becomes aware and participates in community activities or ceremonies with his or her parents. In this way, children learn and achieve knowledge through a direct participation and contact with their surroundings or natural environment.

THE "CARGO SYSTEM" AND WORLD MAINTENANCE

TEN

THE PRECEDING CHAPTERS and the discussion of Native relationships as interactionist models or theories of human action were set off to explain Indigenous belief systems that are enacted in everyday life, as well as in cultural and sociopolitical organizations. In other words, we have explained Indigenous relationships with the natural world and the cosmos at the ideological level. Now we want to see how these abstract ideas are put to work in Indigenous communities by local authorities who must promote social change that is beneficial to humans and the natural world. This community service to which wise men and elders aspire to be elected is called "cargo," which is the metaphor for carrying a load as imitating the role of the four "Year Bearers" or *Ijom Hab'il*. These four titans were placed at the four corners of earth sustaining the heavens and they take turns carrying the year's load, according to Maya cosmology.

To hold public office is then a form of service or "burden" that is carried for a year to serve the people, as well as God, the Creator. The cargo system, or the politico-religious office, is widely found in Mesoamerican cultures and it has a pre-Hispanic origin, as we will see in the following chapter. This system was the expression or the placing in action (community government) of the knowledge acquired not only from the sacred calendar, but from the human relationship with the natural world and the universe. This system has been found by anthropologists in many traditional or Indigenous societies around the world, but our attention will focus on the cargo system among the Indigenous People (Mayas) of Mesoamerica.

The cargo system is the politico-religious institution or communal government that puts into practice the appropriate rules and norms that must govern human actions in relation to their human inhabitants, the natural world, and the Creator. The collective relationship, reciprocity, and kinship system, which includes supernatural beings, is the foundation for this system of government. To understand this complex system of service to God, the ancestors, and the people, it is important to start with the concept of community.

THE MAYA COMMUNITY

Maya communities are settlements that usually were established on sacred sites by the ancestors in ancient times. Others were settlements where Indigenous People were relocated during the Spanish conquest and early colonization known as *reducciones* and *encomiendas* named *"pueblo de indios"* (Indian townships) as separate from the new settlements of the Spaniards. The important thing to remember is that Indigenous communities were already established with their sociopolitical organization long before they were disrupted by wars of conquest and colonization. Their sociopolitical and religious organizations were under attack by early missionaries, so they created different forms of resistance, which later produced a syncretic form of religion and worldviews. Let me illustrate this process by using the Jakaltek form of sociopolitical and religious organization called *alkal txah*, or sacred authority (La Farge 1931, Casaverde 1976).

The township of Jacaltenango is located at the back slope of the Cuchumatan highland, close to the Guatemala-Mexico border. Since pre-Hispanic times, the name Jacaltenango was imposed by the Nahuatl (Toltecs) speakers who had their colonies in the Cuchumatan highlands, mainly (Petatlan and Buena Vista). The name Jacaltenango or Xacal-tenan-go means (*xacal* = hut, *tenam* = stones, *go* = place of [the place of huts surrounded by a fence of stones]). While the name in Spanish was known as Jacaltenango, the Maya people of the town and the surrounding villages used the term *Xajla'* (the Place-of-Water and Limestone). And since *Xajla* was a main town in the region in ancient times, it was also called *Niman Konhob'* or "Great Town."

According to the ancient myths of origin, the Jakaltek Maya were descendants of B'alunh Q'ana', which could mean (9 Yellow water) or Q'anab'al

(9 Serpents). The First Father B'alunh Q'ana' is said to be of divine origin (lightning). The Jakaltek, like any other Maya community of Mesoamerica or any other Indigenous culture of the Americas, have their own histories of origin, which are sometimes ethnocentric. The Jakaltek believe that creation occurred in their own territories and that they have been specially blessed as the "chosen ones," since their origin is said to be linked to the heavens. While other cultures and communities argue that they are placed on the navel or earth (*mixik banamil*) like the Tzotzil Maya of Chiapas, the Jakaltek argue that they were placed at the navel of the sky or heaven (*smuxuk kanh*) because of their divine origin. They are descendants of mythical ancestors named

FIGURE 10.1. Divine Origin of the Jakaltek.

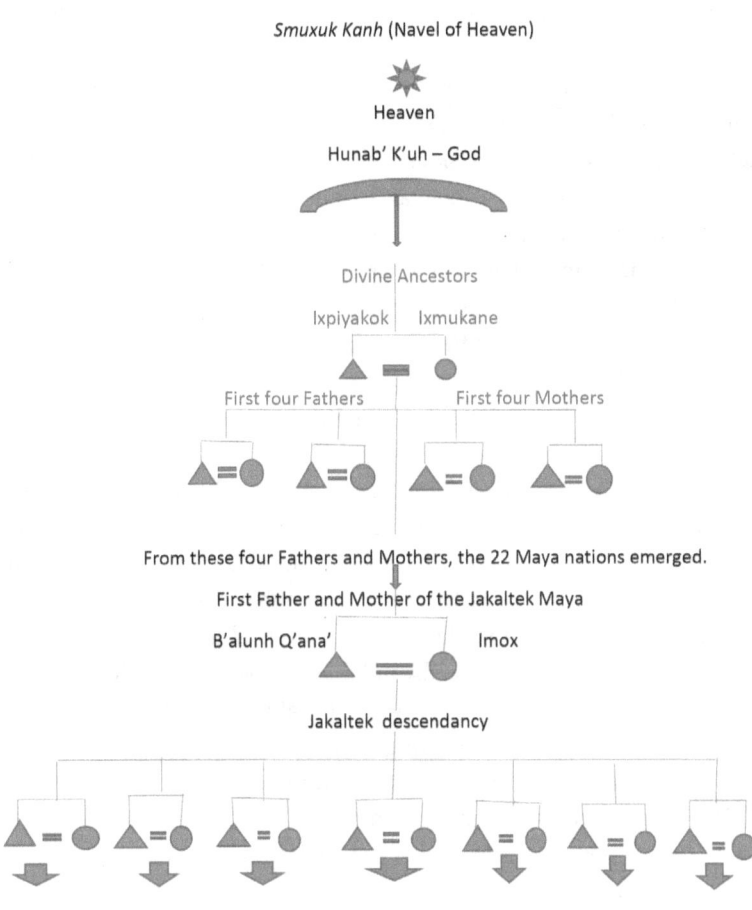

THE "CARGO SYSTEM" AND WORLD MAINTENANCE 165

B'alunh Q'ana', the First Father, and Imox, the First Mother, whose origin is divine and both are among the twenty day names of the Maya calendar.

According to the Jakaltek myths of origin, B'alunh Q'ana', the divine ancestor, provided the land and the seeds to the Jakaltek so that they could cultivate the land and produce their food for a healthy life, taking care of earth, which was also the gift of God. The Jakaltek territory surrounded by stone markers, separating them from other nearby Indigenous communities around. For this reason, during the Year Bearer ceremony the prayer-makers and *alkal txah*, sacred authorities, travel to the landmarks or borders of the territory, placing candles for the ancestors in every region marked with stones or crosses. This is how they maintained their unity with the land, remembering and practicing the teachings of the ancestor. In this way, the community recognized the sacredness of the land and used the resources to feed the people and the ancestors (God) in a collective or communal way called *komontat*.

The *komontat* is the community's way by which the sacred authorities provide guidance for using the cultivated land in a communal and rational way, so that it is not overused and abused. The ancestors had given the rules or norms to follow. The land was to be used communally, so that it was collectively protected against outsiders' invasions. One of these sacred communal lands is the mountain known as Aq'oma' (giver of water) located at the eastern part of Jacaltenango.

This is a virgin mountain, where the authorities, with the help of the community, bring the logs and wood to build communal houses and schools, and for repairing the roof of the Catholic Church. Then, four pieces of land located in each section of the cardinal points was selected as the community's sacred land, to be used only for sustaining the elected authorities (*alkal txah*) or sacred alcalde and the Principales. This is a council of elders who act as advisers to the elected rulers or authorities. The name of the land is also called *komontat*, and these pieces of land are cultivated communally with corn. The product is used first, to sustain the sacred authorities and feed the people during the festivities related to the Year Bearers. Then, corn and other products from the land are used to feed the poor, the orphans, widows, people with special needs, and those who have been sick and could not cultivate their own crops. This was the real meaning of the *komontat*, a land communally owned for making one's own living.

On the northern part of the town, from the cliff down to the Blue River (Río Azul), there was another communal land planted with fruit trees. When I was a boy, I used to go there to fetch firewood and check to see if there were fallen fruits on the ground. These were big and old fruit trees,

FIGURE 10.2. The Aq'oma' Mountain (Giver of Water) and Yula', the shire of B'alun Q'ana', the Jakaltek ancestor.

the kind known as *zapotes* and *koyew* (a type of avocado), that grow only at this template climate of Jacaltenango. In the past, there were strict rules to be followed concerning these communal fruit trees. No able person was allowed to climb the trees and bring down the fruits, but they could collect those ripe fruits that had fallen to ground by the wind. The reason is that these fruit trees were planted in olden times as a resource for the widows and elderly women who could count on them for their survival. I remember that early in the morning the widows and elderly women went down to the cliff at the banks of the Río Azul (Blue River) to collect the fruits to sell at the market to earn some income. Again, this was the most expressive way of taking care of the elderly women who were given the opportunity to make their living from natural resources destined to them by the local authorities since ancient times.

The Jakaltek community is said to be protected by the ancestors, and there are twenty lightning guardian angels located around the community (Montejo 1999, 2001). The most important one is Q'anil, which is the name of the mountain located toward the south of Jacaltenango. On top of this mountain is the sanctuary of Xhuwan Q'anil, the Jakaltek hero who was immortalized after defeating the enemy and saving the people from war and destruction.

The second important place, which is more distant from Jacaltenango, is the sanctuary or the tomb of the legendary First Father, B'alunh Q'ana', and that of the First Mother, Imox. This sacred site is located at a place with cliffs called Yula', where the Rio Azul is borne at the foot of the Cuchumatan Mountain. In this place, the different ethnic communities of the Cuchumatan highlands—Jakaltek, Mam, Q'anjob'al, Chuj, Akatek—continue to visit the ancestor's sanctuary every year in a form of a pilgrimage. For the people of this region, this is the place of origin where, according to the *Popol Vuh*, the other tribes came together and then were dispersed. Anthropologist Oliver La Farge heard about the site of Yula', and he said that the Mam Indians confused it with Tula, the mythical place of Toltec origin.

The Jakaltek, like the rest of the Maya linguistic communities of Guatemala, have maintained their histories of origin and migration since ancient times, as mentioned in the *Popol Vuh* and other ethnohistorical documents. In this way, the communities maintain their relationship with the sacred places and geography, which are sometimes marked with crosses. According to Jakaltek Maya tradition, the people are protected while they are within the borders of the town, which is surrounded with lightning bolts that act as guardian angels. When people move away from the community, they become exposed to danger in their paths. For this reason, there are crosses at the entrance or exit roads of the town, so each day when a peasant or traveler exits the town, he must take his hat off and talk to the Maya cross by saying: "I am a son of the town and I am now leaving my home because I need to go to work or travel far away from the community. Do not forget that I am a member of the community, who is now leaving because of a need. Do not allow any danger to threaten my life, so I request that you clear my path from accidents and misfortunes." The peasant, man or woman talks to the cross as if it were a person or guardian taking note or making a list of those who enter or exit the town. This is a system of relationship in which each inhabitant is counted as a member of the human community, as well as a part of the natural world protected by the power of the cross or supernatural being.

THE CARGO SYSTEM

For the Jakaltek Maya, as for any other cultures of Mesoamerica, human beings are born to fulfill a mission on earth. When the baby is born the *ahb'eh* or calendar expert prays and asks God for the baby's health and a long life. He insists on the baby's human destiny and mission by saying, "You will grow up and become a man or a woman (depending on the sex of the newborn child), so that you will serve God, your community; while protecting the natural world where you will make your living."

FIGURE 10.3. The Maya cross at the outskirt of Concepcion Huista, Jakaltek region.

Everyone knows that a human being has come to life to fulfill that mission, which was given to the individual even when he or she was still in his or her mother's womb. This period is called *sk'ejal yaq'b'al* or the "darkness of his nights," referring to the nine-month gestation of the individuals. No one escapes from his or her destiny. It is up to human beings to find out or to discover what will be their futures and how to best perform and be prepared for those futures. As mentioned earlier, at the moment of birth the parents are told about the *tonal* or *yijomal spixan* of the newborn. With the help of the *ahb'eh* (diviner), each individual will know about his or her future and destiny, in order to understand that we humans live to serve the Creator and to enjoy the beauty of the world of which he or she is a part.

There are many ways to serve God and the community, but the most prestigious one is to become the head prayer-maker (*alkal-txah*) or sacred alcalde. The day before the Maya New Year, the ceremony of change of authorities occurred and it is called *helilal*, change or transfer of power. This transfer of power is called *scha sbara*, or to "receive the scepter of power." The *bara* (from the Spanish *vara* or rod) is a symbol of power that refers to the fact that a *bara* or scepter is straight and strong—just like the way justice should be administered: rigidly and straight without bending toward favoritism. But the idea of ascending to power for Indigenous People is not for the purpose of feeling powerful as a person, but to become a "servant" to the people. For example, just as the Year Bearer carries the year on his back with all its baggage, so, too, the human authority will carry the pleas of his people and seek solutions to the problems. The sacred authority will stay in office for a whole year.

To become an authority is like carrying a load of corn with a tumpline on your back, which can be heavy and difficult to carry. Evon Vogt describes the cargo system as follows: "The cargo system in Zinacantan is enormously complicated, both in its structural and economic aspects as well as in its ritual, for no day passes in the ceremonial center without some ritual's being performed by the cargoholders for the benefit of the community" (Vogt 1969:246).

The cargo system among the Jakaltek and Q'anjob'al was different from that of the Zinacantecos described by Evon Vogt, in the sense that the whole community supported those who are elected to the cargo office. The communal land *"komontat"* was used to produce the food and other resources needed by the sacred authorities, as well as for the celebration of patron saint's festivities and other saints under the control of *cofradías*. The *alkal txah*, or sacred *alcalde*, and his council are elected by the whole community in a process they call *lah-ti'*. This is the community's gathering that takes place a few times in December in order to find the appropriate leaders who will be elected on the last day of the year to become *alkal txah* or "sacred authority." The *lah-ti'*, then, is the community's assembly, in which all of those who want to voice their concern can do it, in favor or against the nominated individual for the cargo office. The term *lah-ti'* means to voice your thoughts and compare and balance discourses to come to a consensus; literally, it means to compare, discern, and balance the ideas or words coming from the mouth for reaching an agreement.

During the early 1900s the *alkal txah* (Maya traditional authority system) functioned parallel to the Spanish-imposed system of *alcaldes* or Meyers who governed regional municipalities, which are the smallest unit of political government in the modern country of Guatemala. Oliver La Farge provides the following list of elected traditional authorities.

> The Prayer makers, *txahlom*, "one who prays," known in Spanish as *Rezadores*, are elected annually by the village as a whole, and take office, like the civil authorities, at the Christian New Year. There is a head *alcalde*, Prayer maker, *sat alkal txah*, called here the Head Chief Prayer Maker, a "second

FIGURE 10.4. Prayer-makers in front of the Catholic Church, Jacaltenango.

alcalde Prayer Maker," *skab' alkal txah*, four Regidores, *lextol txah*, and two judges, *xuwes txah*. They are attended by *mayores*, who serve exactly as for the civil administration. Four auxiliary officials are known by the Spanish name of *mayordomos*, whose business is to provide turkeys for sacrifice, candles, etc. (La Farge 1931:144)

The elected individuals are generally those who have spent more time serving the community in any of its needs. This is a person who is always ready to help in any event in the town as a volunteer, be it to collect money for the saints' festivity, for the family of a dead person, for clearing the roads toward the cornfields, or for building a school, a church, a bridge, and so on. The *cargo* is one of the most important ways for serving the Creator and the community. All services in the cargo system are important for any individual to fulfill the mission or destiny established at the time of birth according to the Maya calendar. That is why, "Regardless of the status of a cargo position, however, it should be performed with religious commitment, for it is a genuine service to the community" (Gossen 1974:14).

The cargo is so sacred, so when an individual is called to fulfill this service, the person called must accept immediately. To reject the calling is to expose yourself to pain, suffering, and even premature death as a supernatural punishment. Craziness is a disease that is caused by the supernatural power for not fulfilling one's promise or destiny established since the moment of birth. Oliver La Farge said: "that it is believed that, whatever the nature of one's gifts, to refuse to use them is to incur God's wrath and lay one's self open to punishment, possibly to death, from *naj justicia*" (La Farge 1931:140). The cargo system, then, was the traditional form of authority and community government that ensured the appropriate relationships with humans, nature, and the supernatural world.

The nature of the "cargo service" is sacred, so the *alkal txah* and his wife become sacred and must observe sexual abstinence for the year that they are in office. If they do not comply with the rules, the ceremonies that they perform will not be successful or effective because they will be deceiving the Creator. In other words, since their prayers are directed to the heavens to please Hunab' K'uh (the-Only-One-God) or Creator, their actions and behavior must be totally clear and truthful, or else they would place the community in danger by neglecting the sacred rules of office. For this reason, the sacred authorities must be spiritually clean with penitence before addressing God, for example, when praying and petitioning for rain (*q'anb'al nhab'*), self-sacrifice by the sacred authorities. and prayers starts twenty days before the offerings are presented to God for soliciting the rain. If rain does not come at the appropriate time, or if there is rain in excess that becomes destructive, then it is because the petition was not well done, or that the *alkal txah* committed a sin secretly, such as sleeping with his wife, thus breaking the rule of sexual abstinence. That is why an *ahb'eh* (diviner) is always at the side of the *alkal txah*, guiding him through his civil and religious functions, so that the offerings are presented at the precise moment following the dictates of the Maya calendar. The *ahb'eh* is the wise and knowledgeable person who advises the rulers during their period of service in office. "The fundamental power of the soothsayer is an inborn ability to know things that are out of sight in space or time or both and which know things which seems to involve the faculty of communication with the crosses" (La Farge 1947:160).

When something goes wrong, the *ahb'eh* is questioned, and he must explain the reasons for his failure. Usually, it is the *alkal txah* or someone close to him in office that is to be blamed for not observing the norms of sexual abstinence. Or perhaps it was a fight or an action of abuse against the natural world that has placed humans in a predicament or imbalance. The person who is found guilty (who has accepted his sin) is punished by the council of elders (Principales) and placed in the communal jail for a little while. An interesting case among the Q'anjob'al Maya of Western Guatemala is referred to by anthropologist Oliver La Farge as the "ceremonial conflict" in his ethnography, *Santa Eulalia: The Religion of a Cuchumatan Indian Town* (1947).

Oliver La Farge was a victim of this situation when he usurped the function of a diviner and said that he too was an *ahb'eh* and prayer-maker among his people in the United States. He said that he was visiting the Mayas of Guatemala to see if they practiced the Year Bearer ceremony as it was observed among his people. This was the method he used to elicit secret information from the *ahb'eh* and prayer-makers in Jacaltenango while learning about the Year Bearer ceremony. He did the same among the Q'anjob'al of Santa Eulalia where he was accused of stealing an idol and causing problems to the community.

It was during the end of May (1932) and rain had not come yet despite the prayers of the prayer-makers. While staying in Santa Eulalia, La Farge and his assistant had a short trip to Huehuetenango to pick up his wife. La Farge explained: "During our absence the prayermakers found themselves in real danger of being put in jail for their failure to produce the necessary weather. It will be remembered that such a failure is commonly attributed to some misbehavior on the part of the ceremonial group" (La Farge 1947:185).

So, when La Farge returned to the town in mid-May, he was blamed for stealing an idol from a sacred site at the outskirts of the village. Then, he was asked to perform a "rain petitioning ceremony," which he obviously refused to do, despite having said that he was an *ahb'eh* or diviner who had done these ceremonies among his people in the US. Because of La Farge's refusal and because of the stolen idol he had photographed a few weeks earlier, he was almost burned in the town and had to escape at night, armed with his rifle.

As I have mentioned above, the cargo system called *alkal txah* (sacred authority) was the continuation of the pre-Hispanic system of government among the Jakaltek Maya. The fundamental function of these authorities is to make sure that the sacred days of the Maya calendar are observed, as a form of maintaining harmony and securing the cyclical passage of time without major disasters that could affect the community. Every day of the year, the prayer-maker will pray and receive the advice of the *ahb'eh*, a person who foresees the future and tells the prayer-maker what to do to nourish the Creator. The Cargo or sacred service was very special, so in the case of the Jakaltek, the head of the prayer-makers (*sat alkal txah*) kept in his house the sacred coffer where the seeds, books, and ancient clothing of the ancestor or First Father (*Jich Mam*) was guarded. When someone was elected or named sacred authority, his house automatically becomes the sacred house or *popb'al nha*. At the same time, the wife of the prayer-maker also becomes the sacred mother who will attend women's issues and serve during her husband's time in office.

With the attacks against the traditional cargo system, or politico-religious system of community government, the Indigenous leaders adopted the Christian *cofradías* (*coplal*) to keep up with the maintenance of the natural world, including the celebration of the patron saints' festivities. In other words, the cargo system was a pre-Hispanic tradition that focused on the celebration of the Maya New Year and the so-called games or carnival. At present, these celebrations and festivities have continued in a syncretic manner throughout the Christian *cofradías*, in which the role of women is very relevant. Richard Wilson has documented the same process of syncretic religion expressed in the *cofradías* among the Q'eqchi' Maya of northern Guatemala. "Single man cannot hold an office in the *cofradías*. Female participation in the civil-religious hierarchy has, in my view, been underemphasized in ethnographies of Mesoamerica. Because the *chinam* (head of *cofradia*) must host a feast, and women control consumption, no *cofradía* event can be organized without their collaboration" (Wilson 1995:164).

The cargo system was the most prestigious office to be held by a Maya religious and political leader. To achieve this honor, the Maya man must work hard so that one day he may be elected to such office and become the sacred authority (*alkal txah*). Until the 1950s, the Maya religious ceremonies such as the Year Bearer among the Jakaltek went under attack by religious and civilian authorities. With the democratic government of Juan José Arévalo, elected president of Guatemala in 1944, the political parties were formed, and local authorities wanted to modernize the political/municipal systems, getting rid of the ancient Maya cargo system. In the same way, the Catholic Church continued its attack against the *alkal txah*, or politico-religious system, mainly through the abusive attacks by Catholic Action during the 1970s. The rule of the elders through the *alkal txah* system and traditional Maya culture was ridiculed and condemned as paganism.

According to anthropologist Kay Warren, "gerontocracy" or the rule of the elders or Principales and *cofradías* went under attack and was dismantled during the new wave of church conversion by evangelical proselytizing and by young leadership in Maya communities guided by Catholic Action. Kay Warren explains that:

> A politicized younger generation successfully challenged the legality of obligatory unpaid community service and the right of saint societies to hold communal lands for their own benefit. These actions echoed fears expressed by the *k'amol b'ey* that youths would refuse to follow traditionalist constructions of authority. On the one hand, local evangelizing groups, including Catholic Action and several protestant denominations, had eroded the monopoly of the *cofradías* by converting traditionalists, who were no longer permitted by their new congregations to participate in activities of *costumbre*. (Warren 1998:170–71)

The decline in the power and authority of the elders and the practice of tradition or *costumbre* was also evident among the Indigenous People of highland Chiapas. Among the Tzeltal Mayas of Zinacantan there was an enormous desire to serve the community and God as a cargo holder. Anthropologist Gary Gossen (1974) wrote that there was a long waiting list for those who wanted to become *mayordomo* or Maya religious officers. The list of those men waiting to serve was so long, sometimes extending to ten years in advance (Vogt 1969, Gossen 1974). The reason for staying on the waiting list was because there was prestige in having served as a cargo holder. "A Zinacanteco may define himself as a person of a certain category simply by having his name on the waiting list for a certain cargo" (Vogt 1969:262). Unfortunately, now, some of the men refuse to serve because of the heavy load that it implies, serving the community without pay. They must spend their own resources and end up very poor after serving the community, while those who do not serve may have more economic means than those who do.

Currently, many traditional festivities and ceremonies related to the land as provider and sustainer of life are not practiced anymore. For example, in Jacaltenango there was a ritual called *poh xuhew* (breaking of little ceramic bird flutes) and the sharing of bean tamales made from the first product harvested in September. Each family made their bean tamales and they shared or exchanged them with their relatives and neighbors (La Farge 1931).

The ceremonies of gratitude for land production are now forgotten in almost all Indigenous communities, particularly with the current generations that have internalized the workings of the materialist and capitalist market system. These days, nobody shares as in the old days when the Mayas were still largely an agriculturalist society. Now, there is not much knowledge about land production, since most young people can only go to the market and buy the products without even knowing where, how, and by whom they are produced. Little by little we are getting out of touch with nature, forgetting the ancient teachings of respect, stewardship, and reciprocity.

Another important reason why people are not following the traditions of sacred service is because of the great suffering and poverty in which they are living as a result of Spanish colonialism. This domination continued in the postindependence period when Indigenous People were kept under servitude as labor forces in the plantations by the new elites in control of the newly created Guatemalan nation-state. When I grew up in Western Guatemala, I still saw truckloads of Maya peasants being carried to the southern coast to work in the sugar, cotton, and coffee plantations. This practice continued up to the 1980s, until Indigenous People were dispersed and became internal and external refugees because of the armed conflict in the 1980s. The guerrilla movement persecuted the landowners and with this, the labor force also stopped going down to the *finca* plantations where they have been exploited for centuries. At the same time, the army persecuted the poor peasants, accusing them of being guerrilla supporters. Thousands of them were massacred, thus enforcing the pattern of unequal and exploitative relationships between patrons and laborers.

At that period of time (1970s and 1980s), the youth also started to value education and have become more assimilated into the Western way of life. Currently, no one wants to offer his or her service freely to the community as in the past. Community service and traditions are now considered unproductive and a waste of time, practiced only by backward or ignorant people.

In modern times, political parties, and civilian authorities that are controlled by the national government are the ones who rule the communities, so that the power of the elders has been eroded. The modern *alcaldes* or Meyers now respond to the national authorities and to the political parties to which they belong and not to the communities. Obviously, the destruction of traditional and moral authorities has now immersed the communities into modern problems of disrespect, abuse of power, and corruption.

When the *alkal txah* or cargo system was in place, those who served as *alkal txah* (sacred alcaldes) after finishing their terms in office, passed on to form part of the council of elders or Principales. The Principales or *watx' winaj* (righteous men) played an important role as they guided and counseled the newly elected authorities on how to best exercise their power in this politico-religious office. To serve the people and God as a cargo holder was a great satisfaction, since it was done with humility, dedication, transparency, and accountability. The cargo system then, was a politico-religious office that was based on the ancient Maya tradition of interpreting, practicing, and living the mandates of the Creator established in the *Popol Vuh*. It was a system that worked for maintaining equity and harmony in the community and nature, as well as for nourishing God. The day-keepers or *ahb'eh*, diviners, worked side by side with the sacred authorities and were guided by the instrument of "great knowledge" or the Maya calendar. In this way, they could understand and interpret the past, present, and future, observing the world in its cyclical patterns of movement into the Sb'elen Chew (Road of Frost) or Milky Way galaxy.

MAYALOGUE AS A COSMOCENTRIC PARADIGM   ELEVEN

AS I HAVE NOTED IN THIS WORK, early anthropologists and sociologists made reference to the complexities of Indigenous ideas and their relationships with other living beings on earth. Based on this information, they created sociological and anthropological concepts that referred to this universal awareness. The French sociologist Emile Durkheim talked about the "conscience collective" or collective consciousness, which made his philosophical approach to the study of cultures as universal—although, his definition of culture as "the totality of beliefs and sentiments common to average citizens of the same society" (Langness 1985:110) does not reflect his total observation. But in his *Elementary Forms of Religious Life* (1912), he argued that for Indigenous People, totemic religion united people with their natural world. From this, they created a common consciousness that moved to collective action and reciprocity he called "mechanical solidarity" (Durkheim 1893, 1964).

This ancient idea can be retaken and used once again for explaining Indigenous beliefs systems in relation to the great connection or trilogy—human-nature-supernatural—as the *conciencia cósmica* developed in Mayalogue. In other words, for Indigenous People there is a consciousness of belonging to the totality of creation: humans, plants, animals, rivers, mountains, the moon the sun, the galaxies, and the spiritual word. This interconnectedness is constantly nourished, despite the assimilating forces of colonialism and the modern capitalist world system that threatens Indigenous People's collective survival for the future.

Stemming from the works of Durkheim and his concepts of organic and mechanic solidarity, Radcliffe Brown came out with his social structure while referring to the concept of "moral universe." In the same way Bronislaw Malinowski extended those concepts of social relationship to the concepts of structure and function, while describing the ceremonial exchange among the Trobriand Islanders. Although, Malinowski spent a whole year among the Natives of these islands observing and writing about their cultural traditions, he chose, as any Westerner of the time might, to provide his own explanations to the ritualistic connections practiced by these people in relation to their islands, waters, and territories. Bronislaw Malinowski did pay attention to the economic exchange of resources practiced by these communities in the most ceremonially organized way, which he referred to as the "kula ring." From the ritual exchange and reciprocity practiced by the islanders, Malinowski came out with his functionalist theory illuminated by the concepts of exchange and reciprocity practiced among the people of the Pacific Islands.

In his major ethnographic work, *Argonauts of the Western Pacific* (1922), he also referred to spiritual beings from the sea, mountains, and rivers as being "exotic" and bizarre" (Barrett 1984). In other words, Malinowski observed the ritual behavior of the Natives, and from his Western point of view, to him their culture and behavior was exotic and bizarre. There was no true understanding of their rituals as the expression of a cosmic solidarity between humans, nature, and the supernatural in response to their adaptation to a harsh environment. The social action of exchange and reciprocity among the Natives was taken as a mechanical process and not as a solid and organic way of life.

Nevertheless, certain Indigenous practices observed by these functionalist scholars motivated them to come out with ideas such as the "equilibrium model." This is the idea that humans are related to their environments to fulfill basic needs. It is not to say that Western Europe at the time did not know about human relationships with nature or the environment, but the concept of "equilibrium" of course came from anthropologists' observation of Indigenous People's relationship with nature. In other words, researchers observed Indigenous People making conscious use of their resources by applying their precapitalist mode of production (use-value), which imposes taboos, myths, and norms on individuals. The basic norm for action was to use only what you need, or else you will face supernatural punishment by the guardian of the mountains, rivers, and so on. This type of reciprocity with nature gives meaning to the concept of "equilibrium" or balance, which has been always the concern of Indigenous People. This is why the functionalists' model of "equilibrium" was criticized, because it just focused on social or cultural action (human-to-human relationship) and not to the reciprocal relationship between the trilogies: human-nature, and the spiritual world.

It is my argument that early scholars came across major ideas and actions practiced by Indigenous People, and they tried to describe them, but within their own usual Western settled mind, molded by philosophical dualism. In other words, ethnographic works described Native cultures, dividing the Native world in binomial oppositions, such as nature versus. society (Descola and Palson 1996). For this reason, an interactionist model is appropriate for explaining Indigenous cultures as a totality of beliefs and actions, responding to the collective consciousness of belonging to this cosmic unity: humans, nature, and the spiritual world. The interactionist concept used here is taken in a wider context and not as it has been used by behaviorists and sociologists who call attention to small-scale levels of interaction between individuals and small groups.

Here we use interactionism in a macro level form of communication and interaction between human societies and cultures, human to nature as persons, and human to supernatural beings. This is similar to the Lakota concept of *wakan* or the creative power of the universe that exist in all things. "When Lakota speak of the Great Mystery, they speak of Wakan Tanka, which is more of an abstract force of creation and spirituality that is to be honored and given thanks. It is not a reference to a personified or singular deity, but rather an encompassing life force and energy existing in all things" (Lee: September 29, 2015).

This trialogical connection and reciprocity is of a great scale that extends to the cosmic dimension for which rituals and ceremonies are necessary for pleasing the Creator. For human beings, to live on earth they must think of themselves in relation to other living beings with whom they interact for their survival. This is a dynamic interaction or reciprocity in which all aspects of the trilogy (human-nature-supernatural) are considered to be influencing each other. The appropriate way for addressing each part of the whole results in peace and harmony, while the opposite brings illness, suffering, and imbalance. Interactionism here can be labeled with the Maya word *salap*, the cross-weaving of threads to produce multicolored patterns of weaving, a metaphor for the diversity of cultures.

It is important to explain this interrelationship and move away from the Eurocentric and dominant capitalist mode of production, which focus on nature as material goods to be exploited for economic purposes. For Indigenous People, earth is a living entity that requires reciprocal action for ensuring production and sharing. Once again, the concept of *salap* (weaving vivid patterns) refers to the weaving of relationships between communities and the land, their territories and the sacred landscape or topos, including forests, caves, and the upper- and the underworld.

> This indigenous axiological and epistemological approximation to the relationships between individuals, society and nature (cosmos) use what Elizabeth Cook-Lynn calls "the language of place." A language interwoven with the locality and in the concrete space where the culture has its roots; and where it is constantly reproduced in a familiar landscape in which the names of objects, spaces, plants, animals, living people and the dead, the subterranean world and the celestial infinity evoke the total cosmic network in the mysterious and feared divine construction. (Varese 2006:337)

To explain what Varese sees and understands concerning Indigenous epistemologies, I have provided some of my empirical views on Indigenous cultures as a Maya individual, and as a US trained anthropologist. In other words, I have emphasized the insider's or "emic" perspective, an aspect that has been given less importance in anthropological research. Only by presenting this point of view as the missing aspect (Native epistemologies) in anthropological theories, we will move forward to a more integrated concept of culture that is superorganic and cosmocentric. This responds to what we have called *conciencia cósmica*, extending Durkheim's proposed concept of "collective consciousness." In other words, culture as explained by Indigenous People is the learned experience and respectful action of members of the human society in relationship to the environment and all living beings on earth. This is not much the web of significance proposed by Clifford Geertz in his semiotic explanation of culture: "that, man is an animal suspended in a web of significance he himself has spun" (Geertz 1973:5). I tend to follow Chief Seattle's concern for the continuity of life on earth and the connectedness of all things that exist. He said, "Earth does not belong to man, man belongs to earth and that we are merely a strand in the web of life" (Chief Seattle [1854] 1993). Thus, Clifford Geertz's metaphoric explanation pertains only to human action (culture and society), and can be extended to the web of significance that envelops the cosmic trilogy: humans, nature, and the cosmos. In this model, humans and their cultures, then, are just one part of the whole, according to this Mayalogical approach.

That is why Indigenous traditional cultures believe that nonhuman entities—trees, animals, rivers, mountains, and so forth—are persons (not humans) and that they have a parallel world and are organized into families and communities like human beings. These nonhuman social organizations are ethical statements that help us approach the world of other beings with respect and appreciation, and not to think of them just as "resources." We know that the natural world of plants, animals, waters, mountains, and so on provides a service to humans for their survival, and for this we must always be thankful. For example, when collecting medicinal plants for a curing ritual, the Lakota medicine person offers his or her deepest reverence for the mystery of life and the essence or curative power of the plant. "During the collection, Cheengwun addressed the plants as sentient beings, petitioning them to confer their healing powers upon the sick, and asking their pardon from removing them from the land and from their hold upon life" (Johnston 1990:14).

This act of compassion and gratitude teaches us that we must not think only of our immediate needs but also of the needs of future generations. This is a teaching that emphasizes the conscious use of resources and avoids the devastation of the natural environment as a result of human greed.

It does not matter what field of research or discipline is being undertaken, we must pay attention to the philosophy of unity, respect, and reciprocity observed by Indigenous People in relation to their environment. In other words, the Native philosophy of relativity or kinship with everything that exists must be the guiding principle in our everyday-life activities.

In terms of the economics, we know that people and communities must make their own living and extract resources from their environments, but this action must be taken with an attitude of respect and thankfulness toward the world around us. Respect is the human value that defines and ordains Indigenous activities within the larger community that integrates earth, the heavens, or the supernatural world. The understanding of this global/cosmic community is difficult, as we tend to think only on the basic needs of human beings or those of our local communities. But for Native Americans, the concept of community is cosmocentric and extends to all living beings on earth and in the universe. This concept of community is well explained by Ronald T. Trosper who has stated that "Men and women are members of a community that includes all beings. Each has its proper role, and each has obligations to others. The sacred aspect of this assumption is that all beings have spirit. The political aspect of this assumption is that human-to-human relationships are similar to human-to-animal and human-to-plant relationships. The economic aspect is that reciprocity in exchange must exist" (Trosper 1999:140).

To consider nature or earth as a living being is something that can be hard to grasp, because Western science has established the dichotomy of animate and inanimate beings. For this reason, scientists and scholars are more comfortable segmenting the world into multiple parts or "problems" that they try to solve, and not interested in the living totally and its interdependency. Or as stated by David Suzuki and Peter Knudson, "Science's basic strategy for making sense of the natural world is to break it up into conceptual fragments. Faced with the almost overwhelming complexity and size of nature, it prudently opts to engage it not all at once in its fearsome totality but in piecemeal fashion, one digestible morsel at a time" (Suzuki and Knudson 1992:77).

This is how scientists have dissected the world, a practice also followed by social scientists who claim to be scientific by applying the hard science rules and laws to cultures and traditions they study with their supposed objectivity. Although, more recently, some scientists have changed their approach to nature as they are engaged on issues concerning climate change, ecological failure, and environmental ethics, and so forth. They have started to propose theories that challenge their own scientific community, as they argue now for the rights and moral standing of other organisms as well as on ecological justice (Boylan 2001; Callicot 1999; Baxter 2005; and others). Not all scientists believe on this, of course, but at least it is becoming a concern or perhaps a moral or spiritual feeling among some scholars who now argue for the proper place of humans in relation to other living beings. For some, "It suddenly became crystal clear how much human moral thought, from all traditions, had simply ignored a whole vital dimension. For the first time it was becoming possible to reorient much that was valuable within these traditions into a perspective in which the human found its proper place—prominent, but not isolated" (Baxter 2005:193).

As I have mentioned above, the immense majority does not agree, believe, or even think on these pressing issues concerning land ethics (Leopold 1949), and the moral universe (Varese 2006). The key issue for humans now, of course, is the economy: resources, capital, investments, economic development, market, and profit. It will be hard to change our behavior if the persistent and powerful Western worldview continues to revolve around money and profit (greed). The unnatural form of Western capitalist worldview according to Michael Tausig is the reification of the economy in which money (capital) takes a life for itself and becomes a fetish or an animate thing. Money or the currency becomes itself a fetish, as it is said "to grow" if you put it to work. "Capital, for instance is often compared to a tree that bears fruit; the thing itself is the source of its own increase. Hence, reification leads to fetishism" (Tausig 1980:36).

For Indigenous People, capitalism seems to be contradictory; not only is money reified, but it has also an exploitative force and contagious greed. This unnaturalness also attracts and moves people to search, fight, and kill for it. One way to mask the problems of capitalism is to bless its major symbol (the currency) with religious or spiritual approval such as with the name of God written in it. The US currency in which we can read "In God We Trust," is a good example of the religious blessing hoped for by capitalism.

As we can see, even in the most powerful capitalist country of the world, the United States, the idea of God and the connection of the economy to the supernatural being is present, as shown in the US currency. This is of course a very distant comparison with the real sense of connectedness that Indigenous People maintain with the supernatural world in an effort to maintain unity and harmony with the universe.

FIGURE 11.1. In God We Trust.

Another important human activity in which Indigenous spirituality and concern for the cosmos is ever present is in architecture or in the human affair of building houses. The representation of earth as a living being and the importance of the sacred center or earth's umbilical cord can be explained in terms of ancient Native architecture such as that of the Mayas, Toltecs, and Aztecs. It has been a tradition among Indigenous People to sanctify earth or the place where a house or a building will be constructed. Some scholars (Paul Weathley 1971) have started to focus on this important aspect of human knowledge of building and taking a space as "home" or dwelling on earth, under the universe. They argue that traditional cities of the ancient Maya, such as the Templo Major in Tikal are models of how ancient cities were organized replicating symbolically the cosmic order.

> More specifically, the ancient ideal type city was a sacred space oriented around a quintessentially sacred center in the form of a temple or temple pyramid. This pivot of the community partook of the "symbolism of the center," meaning that it was believed to be the center of the world, the point of intersection of all the world's paths, both terrestrial and celestial. The central structure was an *axis mundis*, regarded as the meeting point of heaven, earth, and hell. (Carrasco 1984:129)

The symbolism of the temple as a marker for the sacred center of the universe is not only an ancient idea but a belief that was still practiced up to the 1950s among the Mayas of Western Guatemala. Among the Jakaltek Maya, Oliver La Farge mentioned that houses in the town were built with community help. "But first the Soothsayer is consulted as to whether the chosen site for the house is propitious" (La Farge 1931:40). Unfortunately, La Farge did not interview the elders and *ahb'eh* or diviners whom he called soothsayers. Otherwise, he could have had more information on the ceremonial construction of houses.

But this practice slightly continued in Jacaltenango until the 1980s. The site selected by the owner was sanctified by the prayer-maker as candles were placed and burned at the four corners of the square, and one candle at the center. In this way, the prayer-maker requests the blessings of the Creator on the family who will live in the house to be built. These traditional thatched-roof houses had four corners, which were the living replica of the universe.

As a young man, I witnessed the communal work carried out by community members as they built a house. The wife and other women prayed along the prayer-maker saying, "I ask permission to our Lord to build my house on this spot. Our Lord knows that we need to raise our children and family in a place, and we selected this one. We don't know how many other people have walked on this spot or have lived on this place that we are now taking as our home, but we ask patience to the spirits and that the Hearth of Heaven and Hearth of Earth protects us from evil spirits, winds, and hurricanes that may threaten our lives and communities" (from my notes).

After the prayers, the four posts are planted at the four corners of the square, replicating the mythological four pillars that sustain the heavens. The four pillars are said to be selected specifically to take the job of supporting the house that will give shelter to the family, just as the heavens give shelter and protection to humanity and all life on earth. The four posts become then "living beings" and will always protect the family if the ceremonies of cleansing were done properly. This is how the ancient Maya architects built their temples and cities, petitioning for the protection of heaven on the inhabitants of their towns and communities. Presently, there is a belief among the Jakaltek and other Mayan communities that a house has a heart, or a spirit, and it will always stand from the ground sheltering those who inhabit it. Even if the house is very old and at the point of collapse, it will not fall on top of the family, until it is left inhabited or abandoned completely. In other words, once an old house is abandoned, then its heart or spirit leaves and it would eventually fall to the ground without anyone getting injured.

The house as the replica of the cosmos on earth is an important metaphor, which maintains knowledge about construction and about the cosmos itself, thus perpetuating the ancient Maya worldview that is cosmocentric. That is, human life and nature's life as integral parts of the global unity with the cosmos should be maintained and honored with acts of respect, compassion, and reciprocity. Indigenous People's knowledge is created and nurtured by this human-nature interrelationship and it takes a spiritual dimension when connecting these ancient teachings to the ancestors. In other words, "Traditional knowledge systems tend to have a large moral and ethical context; there is no separation between nature and culture. In many traditional cultures, nature is imbued with sacredness ... This is 'sacred ecology' in the most expansive, rather in the scientifically restrictive, sense of the word 'ecology' " (Berkes 2008:11).

The Indigenous cosmocentric approach to nature, culture, and society is also expressed in their spirituality, religion, and philosophy. In Christian terms, salvation of the individual and his or her soul is the central activity of religion and everything else is separate, but for Indigenous People religion or spirituality is not separate from the rest of life. Any human activity such as art, history, economics, politics, education, agriculture, hunting, or fishing has a religious or spiritual significance. For Indigenous People, actions such as planting corn must start with the request of a blessing by the "Great Mystery" as we deal with the natural world. Native Americans know that "Wisdom comes by paying attention to the living world, discerning the spiritual dimension within it, and debating its significance with others in the community. For people holding this perspective, everyday realities can carry extraordinary significance" (Martin 2001:5).

And, of course, living in a community where the surroundings are known, such as sacred mountains carrying names of ancestors and harboring spirits, is to live in communion with the natural world or the living earth.

Some Native and non-Native scholars have criticized Western religion, which is dogmatic and ritualized with predisposed patterns of beliefs coming from ancient Hebrew tradition (Deloria 1999; Martin 2001). The most criticized aspect of Christianity is on its teaching based on the Sacred Bible concerning creation from Genesis. "Then God said, 'Let us make man in our image, after our likeness; and let them have dominion over the fish of the sea, and over the birds of the air, and over the cattle, and over all the earth and over every creeping thing that creeps upon the earth'" (Genesis 1:26).

This Biblical passage is considered as God's approval for humans' supremacy and abusive behavior against the natural world and other living beings. This is contrary to the myths of creation in the *Popol Vuh*, which documents that animals found corn (a plant), from which the body and blood of human begins was created. This shows us that humans were created because of the collective action of other beings, so that man has not supremacy over creation, as I have mentioned earlier. Christianity has focused more on the salvation of the individual that is totally differentiated or separated from other creatures and from earth itself, although some of these ancient connections to earth are still mentioned by the Catholic Church, as priests draw small crosses on the forehead of Catholics on Ash Wednesday while repeating: "Remember that you are dust, and to dust you shall return."

Religion then has separated humans from the world and focused on certain sacred sites (church building, sites of Christian pilgrimages, etc.) in the same way social scientists have focused on cultures as separated from nature. But as we have insisted, Native Americans and Indigenous People everywhere take the land as the focal point of their spirituality, so nature, culture, and religion are intimately connected. This respectful or *quasi*-religious way in which Native Americans relate themselves to the natural world was reported by Jesuit missionaries to their superiors during the colonial period. "They believe that Native Americans had knowledge of God through the natural law. According to Catholic doctrine, the natural law is God's law written on creation and on the consciences of all people. Even non-Christians, Catholics believed, could gain some knowledge of God through studying nature and through examining their own consciences" (Enoch 1977:200).

In terms of religion or spirituality as shown in Mayalogue, the Maya had specific methods of passing on to the younger generations the most important lessons and moral behavior to be observed for maintaining a respectful relationship with the natural and supernatural world.

In chapter 8, I referred to a powerful teaching that I learned from my mother (not to urinate in the river), a story wrapped in mystery, and which has left a permanent imprint in my mind as an unforgettable lesson. This was an ancient way of knowing and teaching that she used to make sure that I learned once and for all that to urinate in a river was not an appropriate behavior. This story teaches us that pollution or ecological destruction in a long run will have its frightening consequences for the individual involved in such an unacceptable behavior. This story also reflects the cosmic unity and reciprocity that must exist between humans, nature, and the spiritual world. We must remind ourselves that Indigenous People have always struggled for their lands and sacred sites, as places of origin and connection with their ancestors.

I insist, along with other scholars, that: "Traditional Native ways of knowing may not distinguish between the economic, religious, political, educational, social, and personal spheres, as mainstream American culture does" (Jorgensen 1997:130). This wholeness or unity in conceptualizing life and human action, namely, cultural behavior as practiced by Native Americans, responds to their holistic view of nature as inherently sacred. That is, the universe and all that exists, such as earth and all living beings, share the same breath or spirit of creation.

This is what Mayalogue tries to establish for other sciences to take into consideration—that Indigenous People consider themselves to be part of the living earth, nature, and the cosmos, a cosmocentric paradigm. In other words, "Native wisdom tends to assign human beings enormous responsibility for sustaining harmonious relations within the whole natural world rather than granting them unbridled license to follow personal or economic whim" (Sukuki and Knudson 1993:17).

Just as we exemplified the tri-dimensional approach taken by Mayalogue in terms of the economy, architecture, religion, agriculture, the environment, and so on, these ideas extend to all the social and hard sciences since we all live in relation to our natural world. The ideas of stewardship and connectedness preached by Indigenous leaders such as Chief Seattle are important messages for today's ecological problems. Unfortunately, for others these messages are only a part of a folkloric past of those who are now remembered with nostalgia as the "noble savages." We all know that the attitudes of today concerning nature are often that of control, domination by force, and wars for securing resources elsewhere in the world.

At this point, we need to speak to the world about these dramatic changes that will affect the whole world. We must return to or convert to a way of life that is compassionate and respectful to all living beings with which we share earth and the universe. We are not saying that Indigenous People do not use the resources around them, but that they follow their traditional rules based on respect and reciprocity. Obviously, Indigenous People need to live, and they take and use rationally what they need for their daily subsistence. This is what anthropologist Stefano Varese observed among the Ashaninka of Peru, as he described their subsistence economy as a "moral economy." According to Varese: "Our analytical proposition sustains that for indigenous people the principles of *diversity (bio-cultural), reciprocity (social and cosmical)* and *complementarity* have constituted for millennia the axiological, moral and epistemological structure of their civilizational project. Their cosmocentrical conception of societal land and bio-physical life is sustained by and expressed in the principles of diversity, reciprocity and complementarity" (Varese 2006:338–41).

The idea of humans as part of a greater circle of life is shown in almost all Native or Indigenous traditional belief systems, including in Africa, Asia, the Pacific Islands, the Americas, and so forth. This belief system was practiced by the Ainu of Japan, who personified all organisms and classified them according to religious categories, developing a social solidarity between humans and nature. "The Ainu world was full of divine visitors: all that natural resources exploited by them were *kamui*-spirits in temporary guises. In consequence all their gathering activities implied social intercourse with *kamui*. Moreover, each *kamui* had its own function in relation to the economic and social activities of the Ainu. Thus, there was a close interdependence between Ainu and *kamui*, and their rituals and taboos were an expression of this relationship" (Watanabe 1973:78).

We can argue that all traditional communities have a consciousness of a pulsing cosmic time, and they explain their existence within this mysterious whole or power that involves the past, present, and future—the superficial world, the underworld, the sky, and the universe. These cycles of time appear in the Navajo universe as well, and their concept of beauty and health responds to the conscious relationships and reciprocities carried out through ceremonies. It is only in this way that harmony is maintained while receiving blessings from the ancestors and the spiritual world. This unity is expressed in the prayer by a Yokust Indian of California, while asking for blessings and support from the spiritual beings. "See me, Echepat! See me, Pitsuriut! See me, 'Tsukit! See me, Ukat! Do you all help me! My words are tied in one with the great mountain, with the great rocks, with the great trees, in one with my body and my heart. Do you help me with supernatural power? And you, day, and you night! All of you see me, one with this world!" (Bierhorst 1994:118–19).

The extended relationship or kinship with other living beings has been an idea used by ecologists as a banner for their struggles against wasteful institutions all over the world. Through the years, conscious ecologists have followed the Indian model of social and natural relationships and have developed concerns for a nonviolent ecology. "Nonviolent ecology refers to a society which is economically and socially just, ecologically sustainable, and non-killing and compassionate in relating to its environment" (Sponsel 1991:139).

In other words, the search for a better approach to nature, one that promotes the rights of all living beings is being developed. Perhaps the Buddhist philosophy of life is a good teaching to follow, in which a person identifies him- or herself with all living beings. To understand the dimension of life and its beauty, the Buddhist have developed their three principles of action for a conscious human being. In other words, the biocentric approach proposed by these philosophers "focuses on the interaction of mind and nature through the three practices of direct knowing, discriminating awareness, and deep compassion" (Sponsel 1991:140). It is important to be informed and to know about the rights and suffering of other beings; once we achieve that transformation of heart, then we can move to a positive action and fulfill our mission of stewardship emphasized by Native Americans.

Once again, this moral universe in which Indigenous life moves is in a continuous struggle for maintaining itself within the current weaves of globalization. For this reason, it is important to revise original texts by major scholars who have identified the power of Native beliefs. For example, the cosmic appreciation and the reverence for life on the vastness of Mother Earth is also explained by Mircea Eliade as follows: "The cosmos as a whole is an organism at once real, living, and sacred; it simultaneously reveals the modalities of being and sanctity. Ortophany and hierophany meet" (Eliade 1959:117).

In other words, Western scholars who have spent time searching for the connections of ancient and modern times in terms of continuities of religion and spirituality have demonstrated that Indigenous People have a solid cosmocentric view of life and nature.

Unfortunately, the intensity of this respectful relationship with the land among the Mayas has diminished, starting with the second half of the twentieth century. The reason was that their religious practices and their connectedness with the land and the natural world were seen as a form of paganism by the Catholic Church. As I have mentioned earlier, during the 1930s and 1940s, the prayer-makers were forced to abandon their spirituality under severe punishment, even jail and slashing by the priests and civilian authorities (La Farge 1931). More recently, with the armed conflict, the Mayas who continued with community service were also forced to build roads and churches as a way of maintaining their unity. That is why it was easy for the Guatemalan army to create civil patrols since Indigenous People were well organized as a result of their traditional practice of service to the community.

Unfortunately, major changes have occurred among Indigenous in terms of religion and spirituality. Among the Jakaltek, we now realize that this traditionalist view of human relationship with nature as practiced in the past is now weakened. In any case, this is due to the influence of Western technology and globalization. Also, Christian proselytism or religious conversion by Protestants, as well as massive transnational migration, has ruptured traditional Maya worldviews. It is not the same as some eighty or fifty years ago, when anthropologists could document the stories, myths, and taboos concerning human relationship to the sacred and the natural world. For example, in 1965 when Evon Z. Vogt initiated the Harvard Project of ethnographic documentation among the Indigenous People of Chiapas, Mexico, he stated that "Zinacantecos have developed a model for their social structure, their ritual behavior and their conceptualization of the natural and cultural world which generates rules of appropriate behavior" (Vogt 1969:571). The same could be observed among all Maya linguistic communities at that time, when Indigenous People of Mesoamerica guided their action and prayers to the cosmic forces following the sacred Maya calendar.

The understanding of the cosmic alliance between earth, the sun, the moon, and the *sb'elen chew* (Milky Way) was to be learned at an early age, so that this knowledge becomes the guidance and the path for the search of one's mission on earth as a human being. This is the cosmic vision received by the Lakota Chief Black Elk on top of the sacred mountain. The Black Hills, where he received his mission to become one of the sixth grandfathers or guardians who takes care of the gates of the sixth directions (North, South, East, West, Down, and the Above). But first, he was instructed by "The fifth grandfather who represented the Great Spirit above. He said: 'Boy, I sent for you and you came. Behold me, my power you shall see.' He stretched his hands out and turned into a spotted eagle" (DeMallie 1984:119). This cosmocentric way of achieving knowledge and Native epistemologies is now weakened by the lack of opportunities for Indigenous People to practice and promote their visions and knowledge systems. Ultimately, the hegemonic imposition of Euro-American theories and methods of knowing and learning has prevailed.

This is changing slowly since some social scientists, mainly from the anthropological discipline, are now shifting from their Eurocentric approach to the acceptance of Indigenous ideas and worldviews, as they argue for a more balanced history and ethnographical research and production. Of course, we cannot mystify or idealize Indigenous People's relationship to the land as a perfect and harmonious one. Indigenous People are human beings who have basic needs and problems that they struggle to solve, as any other humans elsewhere. They too, need and have used the land as a mean of production and subsistence for millennia. "But the usufruct of the land as individually or collectively practiced by Indigenous People [h]as been the base for the development of a culture of moral ecology, which considers the environment, the territory in its most ample and integrated sense, as a 'good' to be used with regulations and limitations, not only by human decision, but by a cosmic pact which integrates all the living universe" (Varese 2006:341).

There is then, a need for a shift in paradigm, considering the global or cosmic attention brought to the world because of the 13 B'ak'tun or closing of the Maya fifth millennia (the *baktunian* paradigm, Montejo 2005). The paradigm needed is one that responds to the ethical questions posed by Indigenous People as they have always constructed their world and made their subsistence based on the concepts of respect, compassion, and reciprocity. This is a universal Native expression or practice that leads toward a moral economy and ecology that can sustain the now, up to the seventh generations, as a continuous cycle.

WORLD BUILDING, WORLD MAINTENANCE, AND WORLD DISMANTLING

TWELVE

SINCE THE SIGNING OF THE PEACE ACCORDS IN 1996, which put an end to the armed conflict in Guatemala, Maya spirituality has emerged with full force. Now, the Maya priests no longer practice their ceremonies in secrecy, but in full view of the public as it was done in pre-Hispanic times. Most importantly, spiritual leaders are now promoting the uses of the Maya calendar, as they have struggled for centuries against the systematic persecution and dismantling of their belief systems and sacred knowledge.

The calendar is the sacred instrument that directs human activity, since it is the source of knowledge that guides human life. Attention must be paid to each day, and any activity to be performed must be done within the appropriate moment (*naj ora*) or time marked by the sacred calendar, for obtaining the best result. If a job, travel, meeting, or event is performed during the wrong day, there can be bad results. For this reason, consultation must be done with the *ahb'eh* or calendar expert and diviner if a major task has to be done for the benefit of the community. It is very important that any human activity be planned and ordered within the power of the particular day ruling from the twenty day names of the Maya calendar.

To understand Native American worldviews and the insistence on nourishing human relationships with the natural and supernatural world, we must start with appropriate respect and thankfulness to the Creator. The mission received by Indigenous People since creation (according to the *Popol Vuh*) is to nourish God and be thankful for creation. For this reason, the creation stories are not just myths that serve to frighten individuals (such as the concept of hell and the devil preached by Christianity), but as daily teachings and practices that contribute to the maintenance of a harmonious relationship between nature, humans, and the universe.

> An examination of various Native creation stories, for example, reveals a set of beliefs in which human beings are but one integral part of the natural order. They are not assumed to be superior or to exercise dominion, nor are they assumed to be the sole proprietors of spirituality. Stories from the land and the landscape bring forth a constant reconnection between people (human people, animal people, plant people, rock people, etc.) and spiritual powers and generates stronger ties between the past, the present and the future. (Harvard Project 2007:285)

For Indigenous People, then, time and space are important, and Maya metaphysics are pervasive in the everyday life of ancient and modern Mayas. It is obvious that, by creating the most perfect calendar, the Mayas understood time and space very deeply, because of their timeless observations until they reached their scientific conclusions. When the calendar was fixed with the omens and predictions, as well as the rituals and ceremonies to take place in relation to the life cycle, time then became a burden for human beings who needed to constantly pray, self-sacrifice, and pay their dues for ensuring existence on earth. In other words, the processes of world building, world maintenance, and eras of destruction and world renewal have kept Indigenous People worried and busy, as they are aware of their collective role for maintaining the world moving in a healthy direction and being healthy for future generations.

To better understand this Indigenous theory of cosmic alliance or the interrelated web of life in danger, we can always meditate on the words of Chief Seattle mentioned earlier—on how he envisioned the fate of his people and the land, or the destruction of the web of life that connected humans, nature, and the Great Spirit. This is truly a deep philosophical thinking and a genuine human concern for the fate of the natural world. This is an ancient teaching preached everywhere by Indigenous spiritual leaders all over the world. From the *Popol Vuh* we can learn that this philosophy of unity and peaceful coexistence with all that exists was a way of life, and it is as ancient as humanity itself. Native Americans know that this teaching of cosmic unity is not the product of a "delirious imagination, but a cult to something that really exist" (Pritchard 1987:57).

In every religious tradition of the world there exists sacred texts and prophecies that mention the end of the world and life, not because God wants it, but because of humans' attitude and behavior in forgetting and abandoning the ancient teachings of the ancestors. For Indigenous people, the origin of life and creation was a happy thought of the Creator, so that all creatures must be responsive to the gift of life given to them. As we have seen, there are rules for sharing life in a greater community of beings on earth and the universe, because all share a common origin. For this reason, the sacred places such as mountains, volcanoes, rivers, lakes, and so on become the major sources of human spirituality as they keep the memory of the ancestors who were personified in those hills and mountains, thus keeping an eternal presence on earth.

But we also know that human beings, from time to time, have failed to nourish the Creator and have precipitated punishment to themselves for their nonmeditated actions. From a Native interpretation of the *Popol Vuh* we will see these patterns of creation, nourishment, and failure, the cyclical destruction of life and eras of human existence on earth. In other words, by interpreting and understanding the lessons provided in this sacred text of ancient events—calamities and worldwide catastrophes—we can learn and react to the present problems that the whole world is now facing. These are global warming, acid rain, atomic testing, nuclear waste, water pollution, pandemic diseases, and so forth that may bring apocalyptic consequences to our blue-green world that we all know as earth.

We must correct our actions and change our attitudes toward human life and nature, as Indigenous People have shown the way since antiquity. That earth, human life, plants, animals, and the universe are linked together, and all breathe the breath of creation or *Wakan*, which is the unifying power that maintains the balance with all that exist on earth and in the universe. This cosmic whole has passed and continues to pass through cyclical processes of world building, world maintenance, world dismantling, and world renewal. In this context, I want to focus on the role of scholars and activists in this process of world building, maintenance, and renewal of the Maya world. This prophetic process can be detected from the *Popol Vuh*, the *Chilam Balam*, and other sources such as the oral tradition among Native Americans and Indigenous People all over the world.

WORLD BUILDING

Following Peter L. Berger's argument that world religions have followed a necessary process of world building and world maintenance, I want to show that the same ideas can be applied to the Maya world. However, I want to extend it to the processes of world dismantling and renewal of ancient and modern Maya worlds, following a diachronic perspective. According to Peter Berger, human beings at birth are not complete and as they grow they maintain a process of building a world for themselves. "Man does not have a given relationship to the world. He must ongoingly establish a relationship with it ... Human existence is an ongoing 'balancing act' between man and his body, man and his world" (Berger 1967:5).

In this balancing act or process, religion becomes and ideological world-building process in which humans establish and explain themselves within a sacred cosmos. Religion becomes a dominant institution that can control the will of an individual through the fear of punishment from God, who may eventually dismantle the world (Apocalypse) if this great power is not nourished properly.

The person, as part of a society learns from his or her own culture as member of a world constructed by his or her ancestors, which in turn continues to be built and expanded by the individuals in society. This world-building is a continuous process carried out through socialization, since the meanings and values from one generation are passed on to the next, and so on. For example, Creationism, which was the paradigm or a world built during the Middle Ages, was passed on forcibly and even imposed violently with what was called "sacred wars." For example, in Peru: "When Pizarro killed Atahualpa, he began the destruction of a world of which the Inca was not only the representative but the essential mainstay. By his act, he shattered a world, redefined reality, and consequently redefined the existence of those who have been 'inhabitants' of this world" (Berger 1967:46).

For centuries, the world built by Western religious men became the only "one" world that every human community on earth must live in or accept as the absolute truth. This Eurocentric worldview that has persisted until now was imposed on Indigenous People by wars of conquest, forced labor, and colonization. In other words, a prefabricated world of religious ideas was transported from Europe and imposed on the multiple worldviews or cultures in the American continent. Despite the violent imposition of Christianity that condemned Native religions and spirituality, sacred cosmologies have persisted as Indigenous People revitalize their cultures. But the focus of my attention here is not the conflict of religions or the clash of worldviews, but the process of world building among Indigenous People such as the Maya, ancient and modern.

Early scholars of the Maya have provided us with conflicting accounts on the pre-Classic and Classic Maya history, particularly in terms of religion; but we can argue that as an empire, it must have had a state religion. Obviously, some Mayanists, mostly archaeologist, have come out with horrifying descriptions of fierce rulers and Maya priests who promoted a bloody religion, while the despotic rulers pushed the commoners to harsh work as slaves in the construction of temples and palaces. Evidently, these scholars assume that, since this was the practice by ancient civilizations in the old world, the Mayas automatically did the same. On the contrary, the continuity of Maya religion in the post-Classic period documented by missionaries who interviewed the elders (e.g., Las Casas, Landa, Sahagún) tell us that Indigenous People had a respectful relationship with the universe, the land, and the people.

Maya spirituality and knowledge of the cosmos was condensed in myths of creation and became dogma to live by, as human beings must always remember and give thanks to the Creator. Thus, cosmogenesis occurs after the struggle inside the earth, as symbolized by the ball game between the hero twins and the Lords of Xibalba. Earth and heavens were illuminated when Hunajpu became the sun and Ixbalanke became the moon. Mayas call them father and mother, respectively, as they were the originators of life and builders of order and harmony on earth. In classic Maya times, the concepts of the Year Bearers became necessary, as they were symbolically placed at the four corners of earth (directions) sustaining the heavens. Their importance in world building became essential as they have been canonized or immortalized in the Maya calendar. They are the four *bakab'* according to Diego de Landas's report on Maya beliefs, or the *Ijom Hab'il*, among the Jakaltek Maya, as reported by Oliver La Farge (1931). This ancient world-building or civilizational project was enforced by *Quetzalcoatl* or *Q'uq'ulkan* (QuetzalPlumed Serpent) who lived among the Toltecs and Mayas of Chichen Itza. From these places he extended his philosophy throughout Mesoamerica with the help of his disciples.

The classic example of world building can be found in the *Popol Vuh, Sacred Book of the Maya*. With the power of the word, the Creator and Former created earth and gave life to plants, animals, and everything else that exists.

In this world-building process or creation, Hunab' K'uh (the Only One God), provided the habitat to each species of animals, so that they could continue to live as part of a created world.

> "You deer will sleep along the courses of the rivers and in the canyons. Here you will be in the meadows and in the orchards. In the forests you shall multiply. You will walk on all fours, and thus you will be able to stand," they were told. Then they established the home of the birds, both small and great. "You birds, you will make your homes and your houses in the tops of the trees, and in the top of the bushes. There you will multiply and increase in numbers in the branches of the trees and the bushes," the deer and the birds were told. When this had been done, all of them received their places to sleep and their places to rest. Homes were provided for the animals on the earth. (Christenson 2003:74–75)

As it has been established in this passage of the *Popol Vuh*, the Creator and Former, or "World builder," provided homes and places for the animals, so that they are protected as they multiply in numbers. This is a good example of Mesoamerican philosophy in terms of world building, and the norms provided by the Creator are still followed as Mayas continue to construct and build their multiple worlds as a replica of the cosmos that must be sustained continuously.

WORLD MAINTENANCE

Once the world was built and things were named by the Creator, the act of sustaining and maintaining the world through religion was needed. In the context of world maintenance, Peter Berger argues that there are many forces that threaten to dismantle a socially constructed world, so there is a need to socialize the reasons for construction, using social control to mitigate the threats. According to Berger, the most important ideological tool that helps to maintain the cosmic order placed by religion is the process of legitimation. "By legitimation is meant socially objectivized 'knowledge' that served to explain and justify the social order" (Berger 1967:29).

World religions legitimate and justify the social order by creating norms, canons, and rituals that sanctify the world; a way of controlling human behavior and action for maintaining world order against chaos. In this process, the role of myths of creation is important as sacred information that reveals the origin of life, and the work of the Creator which must be recognized

FIGURE 12.1. Communal work. The maintenance of the Catholic Church, Jacaltenango.

with prayers, songs, rituals, dances, ceremonies, and so forth. In this way the cosmos is organized and ordered by the Great Spirit, and it is the duty or "mission" of humanity of all times and places to nourish God for the maintenance of a harmonious life within the great cycles of time in the universe. Of course, harmony or balance is the most difficult aspect to achieve, if ever achieved, since life is constantly building itself in new forms through different cultures and languages.

In ancient times, the Maya instituted the sacred games and festivals to honor the guardians of the hills (Witz-ak'al) a mythical figure who plays an important role in the maintenance of the natural world. This personage gets a different Maya name in the thirty-one Maya linguistic communities, but all of these names signify the same: "the guardian of the hills and valleys." According to Maya beliefs, this guardian angel of nature (plants, animals, mountains, rivers, etc.) was placed by God to protect the animals and the forests (sacred geography). There are as many guardians as the number of big mountains, hills, and volcanoes that exist. Humans must recognize them as natural authorities to whom they should ask permission before making use of those finite resources for agriculture, hunting, or building. Witz-ak'al is the immediate figure or intermediary between Hunab' K'uh and human beings, who possesses the authority for rewarding respectful men, or for punishing the transgressors.

The figure of Witz-ak'al, then, is the representation of a benevolent protector of animals, plants, and the natural world. The festivals of the game, such as the ball game and the dances of the rags, presented by the hero twins in Xibalba, were ancient celebrations that Mayas continued until very recently, for example, among the Chamulas in Chiapas, Mexico, as described by anthropologist Gary H. Gossen (1974), and among the Jakaltek, as documented by Oliver La Farge in his *Year Bearer's People* (1931). During this festival called *"sajach"* (games) Witz, the lords of the hills are freed from their duties and they play and run free in the forests, hills, mountains, and canyons. For this reason, humans may be careful and stay home to observe their own games, which are replica of the game festival carried out in Xibalba, or the underworld. At this time, people are called to pray and celebrate *sajach*, "the sacred game," of which the hero twins from the *Popol Vuh* emerged triumphant against the Lords of Death. I remember that in the village of La Laguna, the young adults and the youth would dress as animals, using masks or deer pelts, and dance with the drum, or simulating other instruments. Others dressed as beggars or in rugs (*xilwej*), such as the dance performed by Hunajpu and Xbalanke in the underworld.

And the following day, two poor men presented themselves with very old looking faces and of miserable appearance, and ragged cloths, whose countenances did not commend them. So they were seen by those of Xibalba. And what they did was very little. They only performed the dance of the *puhuy* (owl), the dance of the (*cux*) weasel, and the dance of the *iboy* (armadillo), and they also danced the *ixtul* (centipede), and the *chit-ic* (that walks on stilts). Furthermore, they worked many miracles. They burned houses as though they really were burning and instantly they were as they had been before. Many of those of *Xibalba* watched them in wonder. (Goetz and Morley 1983:156)

This pre-Hispanic festivity coincides with the Christian celebration of "carnival" and Lenten before the Holy Week, so, it was easy to continue with this ancient Maya tradition. "In theory, carnival takes place during the five unholy days with which the Indian year ends, the *Ch'aik'in*. Carnival is said to be a portrayal of older times, with men dressed and painted taking the parts of mythical and historical figures" (Guiteras-Holmes 1961:101).

As mentioned above, when I was eight years old, I danced as a deer in my community of La Laguna during carnival. The *sajach* was a simulacrum in which animals had the freedom to come out and play and interact with human beings, as they were protected by Witz-ak'al on these special days. The continuity of this ancient dance of the rags was due to the existence of brotherhoods (*koplal*) in the communities in charge of celebrating carnival. This Maya and Christian tradition ended with the sharing of food and the sacred meat of the deer (later a bull) called "*yet wich*," which possible meant "*yet witz*" (what belongs to Witz-ak'al or the Lord of the hills and valleys).

Once again, we realize that community service practiced since pre-Hispanic times among Indigenous People of the Americas is the extension of the ancient practice of serving God and the community—a "mission or destiny" to be fulfilled by human beings. For this reason, the spiritual commitment to serve God, the community, and the people is taken seriously, because in this way the continuity of life and human existence is ensured. The "cargo system" mentioned in chapter 10 is precisely a "service" to the people, the community, and God for the maintenance and continuity of the world that is our home. That is why the metaphor of the umbilical cord, *kusansum*, serves as symbolic representation of this continuous nourishment between the universe and earth, between the spiritual world and the natural world, and between the Creator and his creatures—humans, plants, animals, and all living beings, including forests and rivers.

There are then norms and rules for maintaining appropriate behavior in relation to the natural world and the cosmos, so that the world is maintained with all its beauty and generative life force. World maintenance, then, has to do with belonging to the web of life and maintaining this unity through reciprocity and respect, because the land is the source and focus of Indigenous spirituality. If creation occurred here, land is sacred; so you must nourish the patron saints or guardians, and ultimately please God as a way to avoid the destruction of this planet we call Mother Earth.

WORLD DISMANTLING (K'AYILAL)

Ancient civilizations have left myths and accounts of major cataclysms and world destruction such as that of the universal flood mentioned in the oral tradition of Indigenous People all over the world. It is obvious, as shown by the disappearance of the dinosaurs, mammoths, and other species of large animals, that a major catastrophe had occurred, exterminating part of the existing species in ancient times. Obviously, humanity has gone through many of these world dismantlings such as that of the destruction of previous worlds or suns, according to Nahua and Toltec mythology. In the same way, the *Popol Vuh* refers to the various destructions of the world, sometimes as the result of natural causes or cataclysms, other times as the result of the carelessness and abuses committed by humanity against the natural world.

This was the case of the "wooden men," according to the *Popol Vuh* who lost their heart and mind. They were senseless and abusive to their objects, animals, and the forest. These human beings totally forgot their Creator and did not think about their own destiny, or about future generations. That is why their dogs and objects attacked them and made them suffer the torments they themselves had inflicted on other creatures. This is how the world of the wooden men was destroyed and dismantled: "This was to punish them because they had not thought of their mother, nor their father, the hearth of Heaven, called *Hurakan*. And for this reason, the face of the earth was darkened and a black rain began to fall, by day and by night" (Goetz and Morley 1991:90).

As I have mentioned above, the same process or cycles of world building and world destruction have been mentioned by the Nahuas and Toltecs and according to the myth of the "Fifth Sun." Four previous worlds or eras have existed, and the present one is the Sun of Movement (*4-Ollin*) which according to their prophecy will end with earthquakes and famine (Diaz 2002). In terms of previous worlds, we can also refer to the creation stories of the

FIGURE 12.2.
The Flood
(Dresden Codex).

Pueblo Indians and that of the Navajos, who refer to the emergence into the fourth world after surviving in the previous worlds or eras.

It is evident that when civilizations grow excessively, surpassing the carrying capacity of their environments and worlds, the effects of human's action on their natural environments can be catastrophic, producing the collapse and destruction of those ancient worlds. This is the situation blamed on the Classic Maya, who supposedly overused their resources and caused the decline of the empire (Diamond 2005). There have been many theories trying to explain the reasons for the "collapse" of Maya civilization, after reaching the most spectacular achievements in science, art, agriculture, mathematics, astronomy, and so on. Some modern anthropologists exaggerated the amount of warfare and violence from within Classic Maya culture, which caused its own demise (Freidel and Schele 1992). This explanation, emphasizing the savage behavior of the Mayas as cruel human sacrificers, has become the story line by filmmakers who have revived bloody worlds for the ancient Mayas, as shown in the film *Apocalypto* by Mel Gibson (2006).

The destructive and abusive behavior of the Classic Maya is what we learn from archaeologist's "reading" of the past, but Indigenous People have their own oral histories that repeat the same teachings of their ancestors, mainly to approach nature with respect and acts of reciprocity. Perhaps they have witnessed in the past or they have suffered the consequences of extreme deprivation of food, so that they have created myths that are repeated constantly for molding behavior of children in their communities. Thus, to maintain a harmonious life in relation to earth and the universe, human action must be directed following the cycles of the sacred Maya calendar. In this way we can comply with the ceremonies and prayers that are necessary before starting any kind of enterprise in order to be successful.

> Such attitudes towards nature are common among indigenous peoples around the world, but in the case of the Maya, they may have been reinforced as a consequence of the environmental collapse that doomed the Classic Mayan world in the ninth century. The extended drought that decimated the civilization during that period arose from the population's over-consumption of trees. It seems likely that the Mayan veneration for the natural world was powerfully shaped by this devastating experience. (Sittler 2010:76)

There is a common concern for survival, and not only from Indigenous People. At the present, there are many problems threatening the very existence of human beings on earth. Some of these current problems are

FIGURE 12.3. The Maya Calendar in front of the Catholic Church, San Rafael La Independencia, Huehuetenango.

earthquakes, famines, wars, ethnocide, pandemic diseases, migration, and many other malaises that are signaling the end of a dominant era. World destruction has been seen and experienced before, such as the great Maya droughts (Richardson 2000), but as in previous catastrophes there were always survivors who will start the cyclical process of world renewal and the regeneration of life all over again.

PROPHETIC CYCLES AND WORLD RENEWAL   THIRTEEN

THE PRESENT WORK, Mayalogue, is intended to show that the Mayas have placed life at the center of any human action. Stemming from this philosophy of unity and interdependency of all forms of life on earth, Indigenous People have insisted on ancient norms or teachings (sacred myths)—that we pay respect and admiration to this cosmic unity, which is the basis for Indigenous spirituality. But as we have seen from the works of previous scholars, the spiritual world of Indigenous People has been misinterpreted or little understood, while Western scholars have followed their own classificatory systems and values. In other words, a great deal of knowledge accumulated by Indigenous People has been lost through centuries of colonization. Unfortunately, what is left continues to erode and is not given the recognition by dominant societies that it deserves.

This is how colonialism has been largely successful in weakening traditional belief systems around the world. If at the present we cannot totally explain or understand Native American philosophy and metaphysics, it is obvious that early Western thinkers could not interpret Indigenous ideas and worldviews either. One of these early scholars criticized by Evans-Pritchard was Ernest Crowley (1909), who stated: "Primitive man's whole mental habit is religious or superstitious, and magic is therefore not to be distinguished from religion. In his ignorance he lives in a world of mystery in which he does not distinguish between subjective and objective reality" (Pritchard 1987:36).

As mentioned earlier, Indigenous beliefs and spirituality were considered expressions of their childish behavior, as the Natives were thought to live in an animistic world of fear and confusion. But in spite of centuries of neglect, the global belief in the spiritual unity that exists between humans and the natural world persists. This is a common understanding based on reciprocity and thankfulness for life, as discussed earlier. This belief system, previously misunderstood, is becoming a universal doctrine that the world is starting to embrace in its current struggle to save the earth from human-caused catastrophes.

Currently, there is exaggerated greed, which leads to abuses and disrespect for the natural and spiritual world. Meanwhile, the world is starting to suffer major global problems such as wars, pandemic diseases, global warming, and so on, so that some religious sects believe that the end of the world is coming soon. The world has gone through all of these problems before, so an apocalyptic event will occur, but we do not know when. What we have are the lessons from previous world destructions recorded by ancient civilizations. In this context, we know that great civilizations were born, came to their highest expressions, and then collapsed, splitting in to smaller communities, thus giving space to new developments.

The ancient Mayas have left many prophecies and stories that were documented in the prophetic texts *Chilam Balam* of Yucatan, Mexico. One of these stories refers metaphorically to the end of the present era because of drought. "The 'old lady' at the cave of Mani will demand a boy for every cup of water. When she has taken all the boys, no more water will be available.... The earth will be transformed again and a new generation of people will come to inhabit this world, and the next cycle will begin again" (Burns 1983:34).

WORLD RENEWAL (*CH'AK'B'I SATYIB'AN Q'INAL*)

Apparently, the *Chilam Balam* of Mani refers to major catastrophes or cycles of change and destruction suffered by the Mayas in ancient times. World destruction is inevitable, so the prophecies warned the people to be prepared for the painful days of famine and drought that will affect their world. Once the catastrophe has passed, leaving behind a devastated world of pain and suffering, a process of world renewal starts all over again.

For example, the Christian Bible tells us the story of the universal flood, and that Noah took care of all the animal species, following the guidance of

God. For Indigenous People this is the Creator's command that they keep in mind, by giving thanks for their collective life and existence. They take care of all other forms of life, a lesson already forgotten by the West as a result of industrialization and market-oriented capitalist economy.

There are many stories among Indigenous People of the Americas that explain the current ecological problems we are now facing. Some argue that the ancestors are angry because Native people are forgetting the way of earth, as established by the ancient teachings. There are wasteful practices and disobedience to the traditional norms established for maintaining balance and reciprocity between humans, earth, and the spiritual beings.

Among the Jakaltek, the elders tell stories or dreams of ancestors threatening to retrieve the seeds of corn and other traditional cultigens because there is disrespect for what is native to the land. This is the case of corn, which is being replaced by coffee as a foreign product that is cultivated for export to international markets. Since the 1980s, coffee has taken the place of corn among the Jakaltek, and this mono-cultivation has destroyed the ecosystem's biodiversity, eliminating other native plants (Montejo 2006).

That is why it is not sufficient to pray and chant, asking for changes of heart for a more respectful approach to life on earth. We know that action and "respect for the parts of nature on which humans rely is necessary if there is to be any possibility of sustaining yields and of renewing resources that have become endangered" (Bierhorst 1994:246).

World renewal has been reenacted in rituals and ceremonies among Indigenous People in the Americas. For example, the new fire celebration among the Incas in Peru, the *inti-raymi* (sun feast), was a yearly ceremony to reignite the fire, which was totally extinguished in all households and then rekindled with the new fire to be distributed to all the inhabitants. The same occurred among the Aztecs who practiced the New Fire ceremony every fifty-two-year period, a prophetic cycle that refers to the coming of the fifth sun. This is the era of humans made of corn, who have renewed the world and are now populating earth, according to the Maya. These are ceremonies of symbolic renewal of the sun, earth, time, and life itself after major catastrophes. The Jakaltek Maya refer to this world renewal and radical changes with the term *ch'ak'b'i sat yib'anh q'inal*, meaning, the renewal of the world, or life is made anew on earth again.

Modern ecologists and environmentalist scientists are moving forward by letting people know more about the workings of nature. Very often we now hear about ecological sanctuaries, land ethics, the moral universe, and so forth, terms used to push forward the same ideas proposed by Indigenous

People, for the purpose of making people think about their roles in this process of world renewal. The violent attitude toward nature and the environment must stop. We should learn and give credit to Native Americans who have treated nature with respect, while avoiding conflicts and sufferings that are intrinsically part of human existence. In all this process, Indigenous People are still suffering the dispossession and neglect in which they have been living within the modern nation-states. How can you maintain your traditions if you are separated from your place of origin, displaced, and kept isolated in reservations?

This was the painful experience of Native Americans when they were forcibly relocated from their homelands or places of origin. The sorrow of abandoning the Native homeland and the familiar landscape was unbearable for the displaced, as shown in the following statement by Peter Nabokov: "As one Choctaw community was about to move from its ancestral Mississippi forest and start the westward trek to Indian Territory, the women made a formal procession through the trees surrounding their abandoned cabins, stroking the leaves and trunks of the oak and elm trees in silent farewell" (Nabokov 1991:151).

There has been too much pain and suffering for Indigenous People since the invasion of their lands by early colonizers. Sometimes the problems of wars, diseases, hunger, and dislocation suffered by Native Americans were so unbearable that they developed multiple forms of resistance for their own survival. The "Ghost Dance" among the Plain Indians is a good example of this nativistic and millenarian resistance that was geared toward a world renewal or the regeneration of earth. According to its believers, this would occur at the end of a great cycle, as a messiah or prophet would guide his people to a new beginning. The Ghost doctrine preached that earth was becoming old and sick and that life needed to be renewed. This renewal would occur right after destruction by a flood of water and mud, according to Wovoka, the Paiute prophet and originator of the Ghost Dance movement (Mooney 1965).

Throughout the Americas we know that Indigenous resistance and uprisings were met with brutal repression, thus truncating their hopes and efforts for liberating themselves from colonial domination. Despite these sufferings and massacres against Indigenous People, they continued to practice their ceremonies of thanksgiving for life, while maintaining their beliefs and faith in the wisdom of the elders and ancestors. This implies keeping the world in balance and productive for future generations. Obviously, to maintain a healthy world is not a mission confined only to Native Americans, but to all people and human communities that live and inhabit the world.

From the religious point of view, we need a change of heart and a change in our attitude toward the natural world, as shown by traditional religions and spirituality all over the world. For example, Buddhist monks have been preaching the change of heart for centuries, as they have emphasized awareness through knowledge and human compassion in our relationships with all that exists on earth. In his speech delivered in Oslo when receiving the Nobel Peace Prize, the Dalai Lama said the following:

As a Buddhist monk, my concern extends to all members of the human family and, indeed, to all sentient beings who suffer. I believe all suffering is caused by ignorance. People inflict pain on others in the selfish pursuit of their happiness or satisfaction. Yet true happiness comes from a sense of inner peace and contentment, which in turn must be achieved through the cultivation of altruism, of love and compassion and elimination of ignorance, selfishness and greed. The problems we face today, violent conflicts, destruction of nature, poverty, hunger, and so on, are human-created problems which can be resolved through human effort, understanding and the development of a sense of brotherhood and sisterhood. We need to cultivate a universal responsibility for one another and the planet we share. Although I have found my own Buddhist religion helpful in generating love and compassion, even for those we consider our enemies, I am convinced that everyone can develop a good heart and a sense of universal responsibility with or without religion. (Dalai Lama 1989)

The profound and genuine understanding and basic truths preached by the Dalai Lama resonates with the teachings and admonitions given by early Indigenous leaders and prophets in the Americas. This is the case of Ce-Acatl or Quetzalcoatl of Mesoamerica and Deganawidah of the Six Nations (Iroquois Confederacy) in precolonial North America. Deganawidah urged the Indian Nations to stop fighting among themselves and to bury their hatchets under the roots of the tree of peace. Then, he preached his gospels of peace, unity, and democracy, so that humans must always have the seventh generation in mind when dealing with the natural world and its resources. This teaching is still followed and preached by Native American chiefs and leaders today (Barreiro 1992).

In the same way, the Catholic Church is now preaching for a more humanistic solution to the natural problems and not to stay idle, waiting for a supernatural solution. The maintenance of life on earth and the ability to survive in an uncertain future requires human responsibility, not placing all responsibilities on God, waiting for Him to solve the problems that we have created. In other words, human respect for earth as preached by Indigenous People is not something optional for humans, but a necessity. Obviously, non-Indigenous People must be ready to change their hearts and attitudes in order to understand and practice this Native way of life.

It is important to note that some churches now are calling for a new form of "conversion" to be carried out all around the world—a conversion to the way of the earth. "Without a change of heart, the world faced a number of doomsday scenarios including the ultimate tragedy of humanity gradually choked, drowned, or starved by its own stupidity" (William 2009).

The renewal of the world is in our hands and it should be done following the ancient wisdom that "all things are related." Native Americans have followed these ancient teachings for centuries, and they are still passing on the torch of ancient knowledge to younger generations. One way Indigenous People renew the world is through their service to the community and their respectful relationship with Mother Earth. In terms of the natural resources that are necessary for survival, the norm is clear: take only what you need. Obviously, this ancient teaching has become a difficult task to follow, since greed and the accumulation of wealth is the current goal of people in modern societies. The capitalist market economy has removed people from their traditionalist ways of life. In our days, success is measured according to the ability to exploit the land, the waters, and minerals from earth to accumulate wealth. This rupture of Indigenous worldviews occurred early during the colonial time, when Indigenous People in different regions of the Americas were sent into the mines under harsh conditions to search for gold and silver. This lust for gold was a fever that spread among the Spaniards as they searched for El Dorado, a legendary place never found.

Another example of massive destruction and the overuse of resources was the fur trade in North America, where the buffalo was almost made extinct by hunters who just wanted the pelt and left the whole body of the animal to rot (Weatherford 1988).

Among the modern Mayas, the renewal of the world is also reenacted in ceremonies and festivities to the patron saints, a syncretic way that maintains the ancient cults to the lords or guardians of nature, now represented by the saints, Jesus, and the Virgin Mary. The connection between humans, nature, and the supernatural world is still maintained, despite influence by Catholic religion, which emphasizes the struggle between good and evil. This ancient struggle is represented in the *Popol Vuh*, where the hero twins were successful in defeating the Lords of Xibalba in a ball-game competition. As the Maya hero twins traveled to the underworld, they defeated the lords of

FIGURE 13.1. Rath and Wright's Company yard with buffalo hides, Dodge City, Kansas, 1878.

sickness and death and then emerged triumphant. Then, they raised to the sky where Hunajpu became the sun (Christ) and Ixbalanke became the moon (Virgin Mary), thus renewing the world.

Cycles of creation, destruction, and renewal have occurred throughout the millennia in Maya history, and we are, once again, entering into one of those cosmic changes as marked by the prophetic cycle 13 B'ak'tun, which ended on December 21, 2012. This is an important cycle and date for the Maya of Mesoamerica, since it marks important changes yet to come. The ancient prophecies mention that the renewal of life will occur when ancient heroes come to life and empower their Maya descendants. This is the period of Oxlanh B'en, according to Antun Luk, the old man who narrated part of the epic myth of *El Q'anil: The Man of Lightning* (Montejo 2001). Oxlanh B'en is a larger Maya cycle of time in the Maya calendar, which is equal to thirteen times the 13 B'ak'tun. B'en is a day-name in the calendar of the Maya lowlands such as Yucatan.

Indigenous leaders and intellectuals must continue to redefine the appropriate image of their own people in their literary and academic production and get rid of the colonial images. Hopefully, their knowledge systems and the hidden truths of Indigenous cultures will become relevant once again. We could argue that with the uses of the Maya calendar, known as the sacred instrument that contains the "great knowledge," the cosmocentric paradigm that unifies humans, nature, and the supernatural world presented in Mayalogue will be better understood.

On the other hand, the hidden messages in the *Popol Vuh* are now becoming evident in the eyes of the thinkers, Mayas and non-Mayas, alike. A new interpretation of the Maya Bible *Popol Vuh*, brings to world attention the messages hidden in the text, or passages that were there, that no one had interpreted in the most appropriate way. One passage from this sacred book is key to our understanding of world dismantling and world renewal through the creation of human beings out of "corn." In other words, the *Popol Vuh* mentions a cataclysm by "flood" that dismantled or destroyed the world, but previous humans were intelligent and were prepared to survive and re-create the world after the deluge.

As we know, cultures all around the world have stories about a universal flood similar to that recounted in the Christian Bible. In fact, most critics believe that those flood stories are borrowed by all those cultures from ancient biblical stories, but truly, those are ancient stories retold in the oral tradition of those other cultures.

For example, among the Jakaltek there is a story of the flood in which *usmij*, the vulture, is said to get its mission of cleaning the world, as it was condemned to eat rotten meat of dead animals because of its disobedience.

> After a little time more, they sent usmij, the buzzard, to find out how much the water was receding. The messenger, circling through the air, left the house. After a while he flew toward one of the newly uncovered hills and landed with great hunger. There he found a large number of dead and rotting animals. Forgetting his mission, he began to devour chunks of the meat until he satisfied his appetite. When he returned to make his report, the other animals would not let him in among them because his smell was unbearable. And to punish him for his disobedience, Usmij was condemned to eat only dead animals and to clean the world of stench and rottenness. From that time on the buzzard has been called "The Bird Who Cleans the World" because his duty is to carry off in his beak all that might contaminate the land. (Montejo 1991: 29–30)

Stories of the universal deluge exist in all cultures all over the world. In the case of the Maya of Guatemala, this cataclysmic event recorded in the *Popol Vuh* establishes a starting point for the renewal of life on earth. After the deluge, a long period of time passed before the sun showed up again from the darkened sky. In the darkness, the first fathers of the K'iche Maya and all other tribes were waiting on the top of a mountain for the appearance of the sun. There, they suffered under the rain and cold as they were left without fire. The *Popol Vuh* tells the story that earth was cold and muddy, so they had nothing to eat while they waited for the sun to shine again. "But, then, the sun came up. The small and large animals were happy; and arose from the banks of the river, in the ravines, and on the tops of the mountains, and all turned their eyes to where the sun was rising" (Goetz and Morley 1983:187).

This passage shows that after the deluge that pushed people and animals to protect themselves on the top of mountains, there was a very long period of turbulence, fog, and rain that kept earth under darkness. That is why all the tribes were there, constantly waiting for the sun to appear in the sky as they lived in darkness and with cold. This was a drastic world change that they survived in order to regenerate life and their cultures once again on earth.

But the major point that I want to present here is that the Indigenous People of Mesoamerica in ancient times had already domesticated corn, beans, squash, cacao, and so on, which was their major sustenance. With the ending of the previous great cycle 13 *B'ak'tun*, the ancient people were ready and prepared, so they hid their seeds in caves at high altitudes, hoping to rescue the seeds after the flood. With the regeneration of life or world building in which surviving cultures were engaged, the seeds were important. As we have already discussed, in the process of telescoping of time, ancient stories of creation were used to explain the new event of re-creation or world renewal. This time, the symbolism of creation or re-creation was based on the major crop, "corn," which has sustained life in Mesoamerica and the entire continent.

My interpretation of the Maya Bible or *Popol Vuh* concerning the passage on creation is that this ethnohistorical document states that corn was found at the places called Paxil (Place of Return) and K'ayal-ha' (Bitter Water).

"From Paxil, from Cayala" as they were called, came the yellow ears of corn and the white ears of corn. These are the names of the animals that brought the food: *yac* (the mountain cat), *utiu* (the coyote), *quel* (the small parrot), and *hoh* (the crow). These four animals gave tidings of the yellow ears of corn and the white ears of corn, they told them that they should go to Paxil and they showed them the road to Paxil. And thus, they found the food, and this was what went into the flesh of created man; this was his blood; of this, the blood of man was made. So, they entered [into the formation of man] by the works of the Forefathers [Creators]. (Goetz and Morley 1983:165–66)

This passage shows us that the varieties of corn already existed, which was also the food for these four animals mentioned in the story. In other words, corn was already domesticated and the ancient ones had already created

FIGURE 13.2. *Komi' Ixim*, Mother Corn.

varieties of it that could be cultivated at various latitudes. Obviously, the story reveals that the corn was hidden, so these animals found it and showed the way to Paxil and K'ayala'.

In other Maya stories of the flood and the origin of corn it is stated that corn was found inside a stone hill with other seeds such as beans, squash, cacao, and so forth, and it was the big ant that found corn first. The Jakaltek myth of how corn was found after the flood is specific in this case. Corn was found by the ant inside a hole in a stone cave called *k'unah-ch'en* (the stone crib) in the Kuchumatan highlands. This place is between Xajla', Jacaltenango and Iwila', San Antonio Huista, in Western Guatemala.

According to this Jakaltek myth, after the flood the people went hungry, while they searched for the food that they knew was hidden before the flood. The storytellers say: Jich Mam, the ancient father of the Jakaltek found an ant carrying a grain of corn. He requested that the ant tell him where it found the corn, but the ant did not want to reveal the place where corn was hidden. Jich Mam commanded the ant to answer; still, it did not reveal the place of the hidden corn. Then, Jich Mam tied a thread at the waist of the ant, which he pulled, little by little putting pressure on the ant to reveal the secret. The ant did not respond, but when it found its waist reduced and its body ready to split in two, the ant finally agreed to show humans where to find the corn inside the mountain rock or k'unha-ch'en (stone crib). Here they noticed that corn and all kinds of seeds were hidden there, but it was difficult to reach them inside the crevices of the rock. For this reason, Jich Mam called the lightning man to help. It was with lightning that they split the rock and uncovered the seeds that were hidden there (Montejo 2021).

This story is interesting, since it mentions all varieties of corn and other seeds of domesticated plants accumulated in a place. It seems to me that the Mayas were prepared when the flood came, just as some people worried and prepared themselves for the recent ending of the great cycle 13 B'ak'tun. The Mayas have used their calendar for millennia, so by knowing the cycles they predicted the events that took place at the end of every great cycle. The *Popol Vuh* makes reference to three different creation stories, or cycles of destruction and creation—the story of the men made of mud, the disrespectful men made of wood, and the respectful ones made of corn (present humanity).

The same stories exist among the ancient Nahuas and Toltecs, who maintained the myth of previous eras, up to the Fifth Sun, which is the present era. In other words, the ancient cultures of Mesoamerica knew through their oral and written histories about the ending of previous great cycles and the related events that ended each world. From this world dismantling, the survivors emerged from previous cataclysms and managed to save their seeds in order to restart life again, making possible the continuity of human existence on earth.

The concern for an eventual apocalypse, either by natural or cataclysmic warfare, has kept people worried all around the world. We know that some scientists in many parts of the world are building bunkers and seed banks inside the mountains to secure food and crop seeds for the future, in case of a megadisaster or cataclysm. The hopes are that those humans who will survive any eventual worldwide catastrophe be able to restart life again with the food and seeds hidden deep inside the mountains. An example is the so-called doomsday vault, which is designed to hold 2 million varieties of seeds. This seed bank is being built on the island of Spitsbergen, near the North

Pole, by the government of Norway. "The facility preserves a wide variety of plant seeds in an underground cavern. The seeds are duplicate samples, or 'spare' copies, of seeds held in gene banks worldwide. The seed vault is an attempt to provide insurance against the loss of seeds in gene banks, as well as a refuge for seeds in the case of large-scale regional or global crises" (http://en.wikipedia.org/wiki/Svalbard-global-Seed-Vault).

Just as the ancient Maya prepared themselves for a global crises or cataclysm and survived with corn, current scientists and governments are now preparing themselves for the future in case of a major catastrophe. The seed banks mentioned above are sophisticated and in extremely secure places, compared to that of the *k'unha ch'en* (the stone crib), a natural seed bank of the ancient Maya. We can only think that, if in the future there will be a major cataclysm, the survivors will be able to find the new places of Paxil and K'ayala that now are being built in many parts of the world. From these protected places, corn will be brought again to nourish humans who will eventually restart another cycle of creation or world building and maintenance, as has occurred many times in the distant past.

All these cycles recorded by mythical events continued among the Mayas, such as the ceremony of the New Fire celebrated every fifty-two-year period. A profound understanding of the calendar will show us that the Mayas did know and still practice a true relationship with what exists, tangible and intangible. In modern times, we still need a deeper understanding of the Maya calendar as a sacred instrument that has linked time and space; past, present, and future. Once we understand the Maya calendar and practice it, a true reading of the Maya hieroglyphs may develop as another form of renewing the largely misinterpreted Maya world. This is a project within the pan-Maya movement, in which the intention is not to glorify only the past, but to celebrate the present by passing on the torch of knowledge to those who admire Maya civilization, past and present.

We must help the Maya to do their internal research and speak for themselves. One thing we have learned with the closing of the 13 *B'ak'tun* (December 21, 2012) is that the world did not end, as pseudoprophets had suggested would happen. But has we have clarified earlier, these were stories created by outsiders who claimed to be Maya prophets. At that time, some Maya scholars (Montejo 2012) and other Maya priests, or ajq'ij, argued that this was a change of time, and the beginning of a *b'ak'tun* of major changes and suffering. It was not the end of the world in the Christian sense, with the coming of the anti-Christ and the end of days of suffering called the apocalypse. Instead, the Mayas were concerned about the future of earth as a result of new forces operating worldwide, that is, the globalization of the world as a new form of world dismantling. This new world disorder will use up resources, search for new ones, and invade other territories and nations by consuming, wasting, and creating new needs in societies. These crises added to the problems of drug trafficking and consumption, as well as corruption and organized crime, are now the major burden of modern societies all around the world.

These issues or problems were the focus of the world conference of Indigenous People that took place in Bolivia—mainly on climate change and the rights of Mother Earth documented in the People's Accord, undersigned by Indigenous leaders and participating organizations. "That humanity is facing a new disjunctive; to continue with capitalist exploitation, depredation and death or to take the road of harmony with nature and the respect for life" (the People's Accord, 2010). The Accord contemplated the needs for establishing harmony with nature, and the needs for strengthening Native knowledge, so that we understand that earth is a living being with which we must maintain an interdependent and spiritual relationship.

PROPHETIC CYCLES, 2013, AND BEYOND

I want to briefly refer to the recent events that took place at the closing of the fifth millennia Maya, the 13 *B'ak'tun*, or the great prophetic cycle that ended on December 21, 2012. It was amazing to see how worldwide interest was centered on the ancient Mayas and the year 2012, as the media created scary stories about the apocalypse and the end of the world. Certainly the ancient and modern Maya spiritual guides have prophesized major and dramatic changes that must occur within the new cycle that has started. In other words, the ending of an era is the beginning of another in which, hopefully, Indigenous beliefs and knowledge systems will be better understood and embraced as a way of life.

Obviously, people all around the world started to fear the possibility of a major catastrophe or an apocalyptic ending of the present world. The series of talk shows and programs broadcasted on TV about the end of the world bombarded the public with stories ranging from interpretations of Christian documents, such as the Book of Revelation, to the prophecies of Nostradamus and the breaking of the De Vinci Code. Others predicted the end of the world as a result of dramatic changes coming from outer space, such as the possibility of an asteroid hitting earth, while others expected the return of the ancient astronauts or aliens who in the ancient past were supposed to be the creators of major civilizations on earth, such the Maya and Egyptian ancient cultures (von Daniken 1968; Arguelles 1987).

Of course, we should pay attention to this prophetic time cycle marked in the Maya calendar. The 13 B'ak'tun was the closing of a great cycle of the calendar (13 times 400). The end of a cycle marks the beginning of another new great cycle of 13 b'ak'tuns into the future. Then, the cycles of 13 B'ak'tun are counted into a greater cycle of 1 to 13 B'en (13 times 5,200), a larger period of time, meaning going back and forth from a point in time and space. So, there is no 14 B'ak'tun, as some experts think. The question is to find out how many b'ak'tuns we still have to go through to conclude the 13 B'en (67,600 years), a greater Maya cycle—the cycle of the "great return" of heroes and knowledge, combined with major wars and conflicts that will dismantle the world (Antun Luk, personal communication).

Historically, the 13 B'ak'tun was the reference point used for the beginning of a turbulent era ahead that will lead to great suffering and transformations up to a new beginning or world renewal. It will be a time for recognizing our failures, and a time for developing unity and solidarity among people in the search of a new global society within the Indigenous cosmocentric paradigm.

Part of this universal change is also the prophecy of the Eagle and the Condor, in which the people of this continent will come together and support each other, but with respect for each other's laws and cultures. The power of the Eagle of the North and the subdued Condor from the South will finally meet under the blue-and-green feather of the Quetzal of Central America. This brotherhood will be achieved by uniting the land and reclaiming ancient teachings of respect, unity, solidarity, and a collective action needed to deal with the uncertain future that we are facing.

While the prophecies and their explanations belong to the *ajq'ij*, or Maya priests and diviners, we Native scholars should continue with our efforts and agenda for rectifying the record while producing knowledge with our creativity in literature, art, ceremonies, and research, as we propose new ideas that may become useful in the process of renewing our world. What, then, are the roles of scholars and activists in the renewal of the Maya world? I understand these cycles of time as "eras"—periods of growth and improvement (orthogenesis), with the achievement of great knowledge, and then, the consequent decline because of excessive greed and disrespect for life. This process is expressed in the myths of Indigenous People as a continuous process of world building, world maintenance, world dismantling, and world renewal. In other words, humanity has lived on the face of earth longer than is told by scientists and religious accounts.

Finally, and after centuries of neglect, Native belief systems manifested in the tri-focal philosophy of connectedness between humans, nature, and the supernatural world are now becoming a universal doctrine that the world is starting to embrace. There is now a wider concern for the fate of earth and the future of life itself, so there is an outcry for action to save earth and humans from major catastrophes that will bring the world to its cyclical dismantling. A current example is the pandemic disease coronavirus or COVID-19, now ravaging the world, thus showing that major worldwide catastrophes can occur and dismantle the world if not controlled.

By interpreting and understanding the lessons provided in the sacred Maya texts of calamities in antiquity such as wars, pandemic diseases, hunger and drought, deluges, and other worldwide catastrophes, we should reflect on human action past, present, and future. We hope to find some solutions to the present problems that may bring apocalyptic consequences to life on earth. Some spiritual leaders ask that we correct our actions and change our attitudes toward human life and nature and follow the ways shown by our ancestors, since the ancient teachings are still valid and necessary today.

The elders in Maya villages were aware of the major changes occurring in their communities as local and national authorities have allowed massive destruction of the forest for economic development. At the same time, Indigenous People, too, were forgetting the ancient teachings of respect and unity with the natural world. Victor Perera wrote in 1982 that "Chan K'in knows full well what is going around him as the bulldozers and the tractors move ever closer to Naha'. Chan K'in himself led me to the formula that governs their life: 'Without its mahogany a forest dies into jungle, where only the snakes can live; without traditions, the *hach winik* turn into drunken ladinos, no different from those who burn and destroy the forest'" (Perera and Bruce 1982:301).

For this reason, the ending of the 13 *B'aktun*, or the fifth Maya millennia is still of much concern for Mayas and non-Mayas who are interested in knowing more about the messages coming from the ancestors. These are the words of hope, repeated by the Maya guides and *ajq'ij* of today. The wisdom of our ancestors continue to be valid at these time of hardships for human beings and the massive destruction of the natural world, such as the Amazon rainforest. Certainly, there are reasons to be worried. On this, Robert Sittler said,

> The dire ecological and societal circumstances we have created now oblige us to act thoughtfully to avoid further irreparable damage to our home planet. We can and must transform ourselves and our societies; and the ideals of Mayan culture provide an experientially proven framework for beginning this radical renovation. The invaluable lessons from the living Maya are not esoteric messages from the stars or complex prophecies hidden in hieroglyphic texts that we must struggle to interpret. On the contrary, they are gems of wisdom drawn from thousands of years of human experience. (Sittler 2010:121)

In fact, it has been very difficult to have Mayan voices heard, as they are still involved in cultural activism to promote the invaluable lessons achieved through the centuries. The fact that we have to respond and accommodate within the norms and theoretical frameworks approved by imperialist academic research institutions such as universities limits the creativity of the individual or Indigenous researchers. In the same way, the problems of oppression and the fact that Indigenous People have been always struggling for survival, have limited their abilities to create new Indigenous agendas for community research. Indigenous People need the freedom and the time to engage in creative work, and thus come out of this intellectual colonialism that has caused opacity of the mind. It is for this purpose that Mayalogue tries to identify traditional or Indigenous methodologies and theories that need to be developed further to privilege Indigenous epistemologies. These are viable frameworks for research in all the disciplines traditionally taught at colleges and universities.

Ultimately, the Mayas and other cultures around the world are paying attention to the Maya calendar and the previous prophecies of the ancient Maya. There are many interpretations of the prophecies that now are being discussed and interpreted by scholars and New Age believers. It is difficult to lie down and wait idly what the post-13 *B'ak'tun* period will bring us. According to the *Chilam Balam of Tizimin*, "When the original 13 *bak'tuns* were created, a war was waged which caused the country to cease to exist" (Makemson 1951:29). But the events that caused the major changes were preceded by major droughts and famine, so that the *Chilam Balam* also mentioned that people will be eating the barks of trees, and there will be war. This occurred when the recently ended 13 *B'ak'tun* was created, according to the *Chilam Balam* prophet: "Presently, Baktun 13 shall come sailing, figuratively speaking; bringing the ornaments, of which I have spoken, from your ancestors. Then the God will come to visit his little ones. Perhaps 'After Death' will be the subject of his discourse" (Makemson 1951:189).

As the fifth Maya millennium and the 13 B'ak'tun has ended, we must listen and pay attention to the teachings and prophecies of the ancient Mayas. In the above quote, the *Chilam Balam* states that problems occurred at the "beginning" or creation of the "original" 13 B'ak'tun. According to the Mayas, humanity has lived for many previous cycles or *b'ak'tuns*. The year 2013, was the beginning of another set of thirteen *b'ak'tuns* (13 × 400) to be ended roughly on December 21, 7212. So, we are now the living ancestors of those who will live and worry during that other major cycle of thirteen *b'ak'tuns* into the future. Unfortunately, the real Chilam are now gone, and we don't know the future that will await us as human beings. In the past, when Maya culture was strong and fully alive, there lived the true Chilam (those who foresee the future). He knew how to read and interpret the sacred Maya calendar, as he carried in his pouch, symbolically, the lottery of life.

Currently, the business of life is becoming more difficult, as there now are many problems facing humanity as a result of its own mistake. As human beings, we cannot avoid the cosmic cycles through which earth must go as it follows its path through the universe. For this reason, we must rethink and correct our actions in relation to the natural world, and the unknown

FIGURE 13.3. Imagining our place in the Milky Way.

powers and mysteries of the universe. Earth is our homeland and we must take care of it with all other living beings with which we share the breath of life. As inhabitants of earth, we imagine ourselves as pilgrims or travelers surviving in one of the branches of the Milky Way, which keeps moving and expanding toward infinity.

BIBLIOGRAPHY

Adorno, Rolena. 1988. *Guamán Poma: Writing and Resistance in Colonial Peru.* Austin: University of Texas Press.

Allen, Catherine J. 1988. *The Hold Life Has: Coca and Cultural Identity in an Andean Community.* Washington, DC: Smithsonian Institution Press.

Andía Chávez, Juan. 2002. *El Cronista Felipe Guamán Poma de Ayala: Un Precursor de los Derechos Humanos.* Lima, Perú: Gráfica Industrial Davi Cub.

Arias, Arturo. 2017. *Recovering Lost Footprints: Contemporary Maya Narratives,* vol. 1. Albany: State University of New York Press.

———. 2018. *Recovering Lost Footprints: Contemporary Maya Narratives,* vol. 2. Albany: State University of New York Press.

Arias, Jacinto. 1975. *El Mundo Numinoso de los Mayas: estructura y cambios contemporáneos.* México, Secretaría de Educación Pública, Dirección General de Divulgación.

Arguelles, José. 1987. *The Maya Factor: Path beyond Technology.* Santa Fe, NM: Bear & Company Publishers.

Asad, Talal. 1988. *Anthropology & the Colonial Encounter.* Highlands, NJ: Humanities Press.

Barreiro, José (ed.). 1992. *Indian Roots of American Democracy.* Ithaca, NY: Cornell University Press.

——— (ed.). 2011. *Thinking in Indian: A John Mohawk Reader.* Phoenix, AZ: Indian Country Today.

Barrett, Stanley R. 1984. *The Rebirth of Anthropological Theory*. Toronto, ON: University of Toronto Press.

Batalla, Guillermo Bonfil. 2002. *México Profundo: Reclaiming a Civilization*. Austin: University of Texas Press.

Baxter, Brian. 2005. *A Theory of Ecological Justice*. London and New York: Routledge.

Berger, Peter L. 1967. *The Sacred Canopy: Elements of a Theory of Religion*. New York: Doubleday.

Berkes, Fikret. 2008. *Sacred Ecology*. New York, London: Routledge.

Berlin, Brenty, and Paul Kay. 1969. *Basic Color Terms: Their Universality and Evolution*. Berkeley: University of California Press.

Berry, Thomas. 1997. "Ecological Geography." In *Worldviews and Ecology: Religion, Philosophy, and the Environment*, edited by Mary Evelyn Tucker and John A. Grim. New York: Orbis Books.

Bierhorst, John. 1994. *The Way of the Earth: Native America and the Environment*. New York: William Morrow.

Blue Cloud, Peter. 1987. "Talking with the Past." In *Survival this Way: Interviews with American Indian Poets*, edited by Joseph Bruchac. Tucson: University of Arizona Press.

Boas, Franz. [1896] 1940. "The Limitations of the Comparative Method of Anthropology."*Race, Language and Culture*. New York: Macmillan.

Boremanse, Didier. 1998. *Hach Winik: The Lacandon Maya of Chiapas, Southern Mexico*. Institute for Mesoamerican Studies. Monograph 11, State University of New York at Albany.

Boylan, Michael. 2001. *Environmental Ethics*. Upper Saddle River, NJ: Prentice Hall.

Bricker, Victoria R. 1981. *The Indian Christ, the Indian King: The Historical Substrate of Maya Myth and Ritual*. Austin: University of Texas Press.

Bunzel, Ruth. 1952. *Chichicastenango: A Guatemalan Village*. (Publication of the American Ethnological Society, vol. 22. Locust Valley, NY: J. J. Augustin.

Burns, Allan F. 1983. *An Epoch of Miracles: Oral Literature of the Yucatec Maya*. Austin: University of Texas Press.

Cajete, Gregory. 2000. Native *Science: Natural Laws of Interdependence*. Santa Fe, NM: Clear Light Publishers.

Callicott, J. Baird. 1999. *Beyond the Land Ethic: More Essays in Environmental Philosophy*. Albany: State University of New York Press.

Carmack, Robert M. 1988. *Harvest of Violence: The Maya Indians and the Guatemalan Crisis*, Norman: University of Oklahoma Press.

Carmack, Robert M., Janine Gasco, and Gary H. Gossen. 1996. *The Legacy of Mesoamerica: History and Culture of a Native American Civilization*. Upper Saddle River: NJ: Prentice Hall.

Carrasco, David. 1984. *Quetzalcoatl and the Irony of Empire: Myths and Prophecies in the Aztec*. Chicago, IL: University of Chicago Press.

Casaverde, Juvenal. 1976. *Jacaltec Social and Political Structure*. Ann Arbor, MI: University Microfilms International.

Cavender, W. Angela. 1997. "Power of the Spoken Word: Native Oral Traditions in American Indian History." In *Rethinking American Indian History*, edited by Donald L. Fixico. Albuquerque: University of New Mexico Press.

Chacón, Gloria E. 2018. *Indigenous Cosmoletics: Kab'awil and the Making of Maya and Zapotec Literatures*. Durham: University of North Carolina Press.

Chief Seattle. [1854] 1993. *No Quiet Place: A Speech of Chief Seattle, an American Indian, to the President of the United States, 1854*. East Sussex, UK: Pickpocket Books.

Christenson, Allen J. (trans.). 2003. *Popol Vuh: The Sacred Book of the Maya: The Great Classic of Central American Spirituality*, Translated from the Original Maya Text. Norman: University of Oklahom Press.

Clifford, James. 1988. *The Predicament of Culture: Twentieth-Century Ethnography, Literature, and Art*. Cambridge, MA: Harvard University Press.

Clifford, James, and George E. Marcus, eds. 1986. *Writing Culture: The Poetics and Politics of Ethnography*. Berkeley: University of California Press.

Colby, Benjamin N. 1981. *The Daykeeper: The Life and Discourse of and Ixil Diviner*. Cambridge, MA: Harvard University Press.

Dalai Lama. 1989. "The 14th Dalai Lama: Acceptance Speech." Nobelprize.org. http://nobelprize.org/nobel_prizes/peace/laureates/1989/lama-^laccep tance.html.

Darío, Rubén. 1985. *Los motivos del Lobo*. Guatemala City, Editorial Universitaria Centroamericana, EDUCA.

De la Serna, Jacinto. [1953] 2014. Tratado de las idolatrías, supersticiones y costumbres. Barcelona, Spain: Linkgua.

Deloria, Vine Jr. 1997. *Red Earth, White Lies: Native Americans and the Myth of Scientific Fact*. Golden, CO: Fulcrum.

———. 1999. Spirit and Reason: *The Vine Deloria Reader*. Golden, CO: Fulcrum.

Del Valle Escalante, Emilio. 2008. *Nacionalismos Mayas y desafíos postcoloniales en Guatemala: Colonialidad, modernidad y políticas de la identidad cultural*. Colección de lecturas de ciencias sociales, tomo IV. Ciudad de Guatemala: Editorial de Ciencias Sociales.

DeMallie, Raymond J. Editor, 1984. *The Sixth Grandfather: Black Elk's Teachings Given to John G. Neihardt*. Lincoln: University of Nebraska Press.

Descola, Philippe, and Gisli Palsson. 1996. *Nature and Culture: Anthropological Perspectives*. New York: Routledge.

Diamond, Jared. 2005. *Collapse: How Societies Choose to Fail or Succeed*. London: Penguin.

Diaz, Frank. 2002. *The Gospel of the Toltec: The Life and Teachings of Quetzalcoatl*. Rochester, VT: Bear & Company.

Documentos Inéditos. 1898. *Colección de Documentos Inéditos de Ultramar*, tomo 11, Relaciones de Yucatán I. Madrid, Spain: Impresos de la Real Casa.

Durkheim, Emile, and Marcel Mauss. 1963. *Primitive Classification*. Chicago, IL: University of Chicago Press.

Durkheim, Emile. [1893] 1964. *The Division of Labor in Society*. New York: Free Press.

———. [1912] 1961. *Elementary Forms of Religious Life*. Translated by J. S. Swain. New York: Collier.

Eliade, Mircea. 1959. *The Sacred and the Profane: The Nature of Religion*. New York: Houghton Mifflin Harcourt.

Evans-Pritchard, E. E. 1987. *Theories of Primitive Religion*. New York: Oxford University Press.

Fabian, Johannes. 1983. *Time and the Other: How Anthropology Makes Its Object*. New York: Columbia University Press.

Faris, James, 1988. "Pax Britannica and the Sudan: S.F. Nadel." In *Anthropology & the Colonial Encounter*, edited by Talal Asad. Highlands, NJ: Humanities Press.

———. 1990. *The Nightway: A History and a History of Documentation of a Navajo Ceremonial*. Albuquerque: University of New Mexico Press.

Farriss, Nancy M. 1984. *Maya Society under Colonial Rule: The Collective Enterprise for Survival*. Princeton, NJ: Princeton University Press.

Fahsen, Federico, and Daniel Matul. 2007. *Los Códices. Códice de Madrid, Tz'ib' rech Madrid*. Reproducción comentada por Federico Fahsen y Daniel Matul, Ciudad de Guatemala, Publicación de Liga Maya Guatemala.

First, T. Peter, dir. 1969. *To Find Our Life: The Peyote Hunt of the Huichols of Mexico*. Ethnographic film. Department of Anthropology, State University of New York at Albany. Film.

Fischer, Edward F. 2001. *Cultural Logics and Global Economics: Maya Identity in Thought and Practice*. Austin: University of Texas Press.

Fischer, Edward F., and Robert M. Brown. 1996. *Maya Cultural Activism in Guatemala*. Austin: University of Texas Press.

Freidel, David, and Linda Schele. 1992. *A Forest of Kings: The Untold Story of the Ancient Maya*. New York: Harper Collins.

Geertz, Clifford. 1973. *The Interpretation of Cultures*. New York: Basic Books.

———. 1983. *Local Knowledge: Further Essays in Interpretive Anthropology*. New York: Basic Books.

Gibson, Mel, dir. 2008. *Apocalypto*. Touchstone Pictures Movies. USA. Film. https://en.wikipedia.org/wiki/Apocalypto.

Gill, Richardson B. 2000. *The Great Maya Droughts: Water, Life and Death*. Albuquerque: University of New Mexico Press.

Goetz Delia, and Sylvanus G. Morley. 1950. *Popol Vuh: The Sacred Book of the Ancient Quiche Maya*. Norman and London: University of Oklahoma Press.

González Martin, and Juan de Dios. 2001. *La Cosmovisión Indígena Guatemalteca, Ayer y Hoy*. Instituto de Investigaciones Económicas y Sociales. Guatemala City: Universidad Rafael Landívar.

Gossen, Gary H. 1974. *Chamulas in the World of the Sun: Time and Space in Maya Oral Tradition*. Cambridge, MA: Harvard University Press.

———. 1999. *Telling Maya Tales: Tzotzil Identities in Modern Mexico*. New York: Routledge Press.

Gould, Stephen Jay. 1981. *The Mismeasure of Man*. New York: W. W. Norton.

Grim, John, and Mary Evelyn Tucker. 2014. *Ecology and Religion*. Washington, DC: Island Press.

Grinde, Donald, and Bruce E. Johansen. 1995. *Ecocide of Native America: Environmental Destruction of Indian Lands and Peoples*. Santa Fe, NM: Clear Light Publishers.

Guiteras-Holmes, Calixta. 1961. *Perils of the Soul: The World View of a Tzotzil Indian*. Glencoe, IL: Free Press.

Harris, Marvin, 1968. *The Rise of Anthropological Theory*. New York: Thomas Y. Crowell.

Hellen, Roy F. 1996. "The Cognitive Geometry of Nature: A Contextual Approach." In *Nature and Culture: Anthropological Perspectives*, edited by Philippe Descola and Gisli Palsson. New York: Routledge.

Helmke, Christophe. 2009. "Hidden Identity & Power in Ancient Mesoamerica: Supernatural Alter Egos as Personified Diseases." *Acta Americana* 17, no. 2: 49–98.

Holthaus, Gary. 2008. *Learning Native Wisdom: What Traditional Cultures Teach Us about Subsistence, Sustainability and Spirituality?* Lexington: University of Kentucky Press.

Hunt, Eva. 1977. *The Transformation of the Hummingbird: Cultural Roots of a Zinacantecan Mythical Poem*. Ithaca, NY: Cornell University Press.

Johnston, Basil. 1990. *Ojibway Ceremonies*. Lincoln: University of Nebraska Press.

Kaiser, Rudolf. 1991. *The Voice of the Great Spirit: Prophecies of the Hopi Indians*. Boston, MA: Shambala Press.

Knudson, Peter. 1991. *A Mirror to Nature: Reflections on Science, Scientists and Society*. Toronto, ON: Stoddart Publishing.

Kovach, Margaret. 2009. *Indigenous Methodologies: Characteristics, Conversations, and Contexts*. Toronto, ON: University of Toronto Press.

Kuhn, S. Thomas. 1962. *The Structure of Scientific Revolution*. Chicago, IL: University of Chicago Press.

La Farge, Oliver, and Douglas Byers. 1931. *The Year Bearers People*. Middle American Research Series, Publication No. 3, New Orleans, LA: Tulane University.

———. 1947. *Santa Eulalia: The Religion of a Cuchumatan Indian Town*. Chicago, IL: University of Chicago Press.

Landa, Diego de. 1983. *Relaciones de las Cosas de Yucatán*. Yucatán, México: Ediciones Dante.

Langness, Luis L. 1985. *The Study of Culture*. Novato, California, Chandler & Sharp Publishers.

Las Casas, Bartolome. [1552] 1974. *In Defense of the Indians*, translated by Stafford Poole. DeKalb: Northern Illinois University Press.

Lee, Murray. September 29, 2015. "Native American Beliefs: The Great Mystery." http://blog.nativepartnership.org/native-american-beliefs-the-great-mystery/.

Lee Woodward, Ralph. 2002. *Rafael Carrera and the Emergence of the Republic of Guatemala*. Translated by Jorge Skinner-Klee. South Woodstock, VT: Plumsock Mesoamerican Studies.

Leon-Portilla, Miguel. 1990. *Aztec Thought and Culture*. Rev. ed. Norman: University of Oklahoma Press.

———. 1999. *Bernardino de Sahagun: First Anthropologist*. Norman: University of Oklahoma Press.

Leopold, Aldo. 1949. *A Sand Country Almanac*. USA, Oxford, UK: University of Oxford Press.

Lévi-Strauss, Claude. 1966. *The Savage Mind*. Chicago, IL: University of Chicago Press.

———. 1978. *Myth and Meaning*. London and New York: Routledge.López, Carlos M. 1999. *Los Popol Wuj y sus epistemologías: Las diferencias, el conocimiento y los ciclos del infinito*. Quito, Ecuador: Ediciones Abya-Yala.

Lévy-Bruhl, Lucien. 1979. *How Natives Think*. London: Ravenio Books Publication.

Lovell, George W., and Christopher Lutz. 1995. *Demography and Empire: A Guide to the Population History of Spanish Central America, 1500–1821*. Boulder, CO: West View Press.

Lutz Christopher H., and Karen Dakin. 1996. *Nuestro Pesar, Nuestra Aflicción*. Mexico City: Universidad Nacional Autónoma de México.

Lyons, Oren. 1994. *Native People Address the United Nations*, edited by Alexander Ewen. Santa Fe, NM: Clear Light Publishers.

———. 2008. *Looking toward the Seventh Generation*. Indigenous Governance Database, Native Nations Institute, University of Arizona.

Makemson, Maud Worcester. 1951. *The Book of the Jaguar Priest: A Translation of the Book of Chilam Balam of Tizimin*. New York: Henry Schuman.

Malinowski, Bronislaw. 1922. *Argonauts of the Western Pacific*. New York: Dutton.

———. 1944. *A Scientific Theory of Culture*. Chapel Hill: University of North Carolina Press.

Mallon, Florencia E. 2012. *Decolonizing Native Histories: Collaboration, Knowledge and Language in the Americas*. Durham, NC: Duke University Press.

Manz, Beatriz. 1995. "Reflexions on an Anthropologia Comprometida: Conversations with Ricardo Falla." In *Fieldwork under Fire: Contemporary Studies of Violence and Survival*, edited by Carolyn Nordstrom and Antonius C. G. M. Robben. Berkeley: University of California Press.

Marcus, George E., and Michael M. J. Fischer. 1986. *Anthropology as Cultural Critique: An Experimental Moment in the Human Sciences*. Chicago, IL: University of Chicago Press.

Martínez González, Roberto. 2010. El-nahual-y-otras-coesencias-entre-los-mayas-una-primera-síntesis, Instituto de Investigaciones Históricas, UNAM. Edición digital. https://es.scribd.com/doc/31930533/.

Maybury-Lewis, David. 1972. *Cultural Survival*. Cambridge, MA: Harvard University and David Rockefeller Center for Latin American Studies.

Menchú, Rigoberta. 1984. *I Rigoberta Menchú: An Indian Woman in Guatemala*. New York: Verso.

Mignolo, Walter D. 2011. *The Darker Side of Western Modernity: Global Futures, Decolonial Options*. Durham, NC: Duke University Press.

Mohawk, John. 2011. *Thinking in Indian: A John Mohawk Reader*, by Ray Cook, *Indian Country Today*. March 23, 2011.

Momaday, Scott. 1987. "The Magic of Words." In *Survival this Way: Interviews with American Indian Poets*, edited by Joseph Bruchac. Tucson: University of Arizona Press.

Montejo, Victor D. 1997. "Pan Mayanismo: La pluriformidad de la cultura maya y el proceso de autorrepresentación de los mayas." *Mesoamérica* 18, no. 33: 93–123.

———. 1991. "*The Bird Who Cleans the World and Other Mayan Fables*," Willimantic, CT: Curbstone Press.

———. 1993. "In the Name of the Pot, the Sun, the Rock, the Spear … Ad Infinitum & Ad Nauseum: An Expose of Anglo Anthropologists Obsessions with and Invention of Maya Gods." *Wicaso SA, Review* 9, no. 1: 12–16. Minneapolis: University of Minnesota Press.

———. 1993. *Voices from Exile: Violence and Survival in Modern Maya History*. Norman: University of Oklahoma Press.

———. 2001. "The Road to Heaven: Jakaltek Maya Beliefs, Religion and the Ecology." In *Indigenous Traditions and Ecology: The Interbeing of Cosmology and Community*. Cambridge, MA: Harvard University Press.

———. 2001. *El Q'anil: Man of Lightning*. Tucson: University of Arizona Press.

———. 2005. *Maya Intellectual Renaissance: Identity, Representation and Leadership*. Austin: University of Texas Press.

———. 2006. Relaciones interétnicas en Jacaltenango, Huehuetenango, Guatemala, de 1944 a 2000 (una historia local), edited by Richard Adams and Santiago Bastos. Antigua, Guatemala: CIRMA.

———. 2018. Field Notes on the "Dance of the Deer," performed during the patron saint's festivity. Jacaltenango, Guatemala.

———. 2020. *Secuestro a ultratumba*. California: Windmills International Editions, Inc.
———. 2021. *Entre dos Mundos: Una Memoria*. Ciudad de Guatemala: Editorial Piedra Santa.
———. 2021. *Ixim: La leyenda del descubrimiento del maíz*. Quetzaltenango, Guatemala: Pequeña Ostuncalco Editorial (POE)
Mooney, James. 1965. *The Ghost Religion and the Sioux Outbreak of 1890*. Chicago, IL: University of Chicago Press.
Morgan, Lewis H. 1877. *Ancient Society*. London, Macmillan.
Morley, Sylvanus G. 1983. *La Civilización Maya*. Mexico City: Fondo de Cultura Económica.
Nabokov, Peter. 1991. *Native American Testimony: A Chronicle of Indian-White Relations from Prophecy to the Present*. New York: Penguin Books.
Nash, June. 1979. *We Eat the Mines and the Mines Eat Us: Dependency and Exploitation in Bolivian Tin Mines*. New York: Columbia University Press.
Niatum, Duane. 1987. "Closing the Circle." In *Survival this Way: Interviews with American Indian Poets*, edited by Joseph Bruchac. Tucson: University of Arizona Press.
Oakes, Maud. 1951. *The Two Crosses of Todos Santos: Survivals of Mayan Religious Ritual*. New York: Pantheon Books.
Orellana, Sandra. 1984. *The Tzutujil Mayas: Continuity and Change, 1250–1630*. Norman: University of Oklahoma Press.
Ortíz, Fernando. 1940. *Contrapunteo cubano del tabaco y el azúcar*, edited by Jesús Montero. Havana, Cuba: Heraldo Christiano.
Otzoy C., Simón. 1999. *Memorial de Sololá*. Edición facsimilar del manuscrito original. Guatemala City: Comisión Interuniversitaria Guatemalteca de Conmemoración del Quinto Centenario del Descubrimiento de América.
Palsson, Gisli. 1996. "Human-Environmental Relations: Orientalism, Paternalism and Communalism." In *Nature and Culture: Anthropological Perspectives*, edited by Philippe Descola and Gisli Palsson. New York: Routledge.
Parajuli, Pramod. 2001. "Learning from Ecological Ethnicities: Towards a Plural Political Ecology of Knowledge." In *Indigenous Traditions and Ecology: The Interbeing of Cosmology and Community*. Cambridge, MA: Harvard University Press.
Perera, Victor, and Robert D. Bruce. 1982. *The Last Lords of Palenque: The Lacandon Mayas of the Mexican Rain Forest*. Boston, MA: Little Brown.
Peterson, Scott. 1990. *Native American Prophecies: Examining the History, Wisdom and Starling Predictions of Visionary Native Americans*. New York: Paragon House.

Poma de Ayala, Felipe Guamán. 1615. *The First Chronicle and Good Government: On the History of the World and the Incas up to 1615.* Translated by Roland Hamilton. Austin: University of Texas Press.

Pratt, Mary Louis. 1992. *Imperial Eyes: Travel Writing and Transculturation.* London: Routledge.

Pritchard, E. E. Evans. 1987. *Theories of Primitive Religion.* New York: Oxford University Press.

Quiroa, Nestor. 2011. "The Popol Vuh and the Dominican Religious Extirpation in Highlands Guatemala: Prologued and Annotations of Fr. Francisco Ximénez." *Americas* 67, no. 4, (April 2011):467–94.

Radcliffe-Brown. 1952. *Structure and Function in Primitive Society.* London: Cohen and West Publishers.

———. 1957. *A Natural Science of Society.* Glencoe, IL: Free Press.

Rappaport, Roy A. 1979. *Ecology, Meaning and Religion.* Richmond, CA: North Atlantic Books.

Recinos, Adrian. [1950] 1983. *Popol Vuh: The Sacred Book of the Ancient Quiche Maya.* Norman: University of Oklahoma Press.

———. 1980. *Memorial de Sololá, Anales de los Cakchiqueles y Título de los Señores de Totonicapán.* Mexico City: Fondo de Cultura Económica.

———. 1983. *Crónicas Indígenas de Guatemala.* 2nd ed. Guatemala City: Academia de Geografía e Historia.

Redfield, Robert, and Alfonso Villa Rojas. 1964. *Chan Kom: A Maya Village.* Chicago, IL: University of Chicago Press.

Reina, Ruben E. 1984. *Shadows: A Mayan Way of Knowing.* New York: New Horizon Press.

Richardson, Gill B. 2000. *The Great Maya Droughts: Water, Life and Death.* Albuquerque: University of New Mexico Press.

Rosembaum Brenda P. 1983. "El nahualismo y sus manifestaciones en el Popol Vuh," en *Nuevas perspectivas sobre el Popol Vuh*," edited by Robert M. Carmack and Francisco Morales Santos. Guatemala City: Editorial Piedra Santa.

Rubel, Arthur J., Carl W. O'Nell, and Rolando Collado-Ardón. 1984. *Susto: A Folk Illness.* Berkeley, University of California Press.

Ruiz de Alarcon, Hernando. [1629] 1984. *Treatise on the Heathen Superstitions that Today Live among the Indians Native to This New Spain.* Translated by Richard Andrews and Ross Hassig. Norman: University of Oklahoma Press.

Ruz, Mario Humberto, and Carlos Garma Navarro. 2005. *Protestantismo en el Mundo Maya Contemporáneo*, Centro de Estudios Mayas, Cuaderno No. 30. Mexico, D.F.: National Autonomous University of Mexico.

Saler, Benson. 1967. "Nagual, Witch, and Sorcerer in a Quiche Village." In *Magic, Witchcraft, and Curing*, edited by John Middleton. Garden City, NY: Natural History Press.
Said, Edward W. 1978. *Orientalism*, New York: Pantheon Books.
Sam Colop, Enrique. 2008. *Popol Wuj*. Guatemala City: editorial Cholsamaj.
Sittler, Robert. 2010. *The Living Maya: Ancient Wisdom in the Era of 2012*. Berkeley, CA: North Atlantic Books.
Smith, Carol A. 1990. *Guatemalan Indians and the State, 1540 to 1988*. Austin: University of Texas Press.
Smith, Linda Tuhiwai. 1999. *Decolonizing Methodologies: Research and Indigenous Peoples*. London and New York: Zed Books.
Sponsel, Leslie E. 1991. Spiritual Ecology: A Quiet Revolution. Santa Barbara, CA: An Imprint of ABC-CLIO, Greenwood, Praeger.
Stavenhagen, Rodolfo. 1996. *Ethnic Conflicts and the Nation State*. London: Macmillan.
———. 2001. *La Cuestión Étnica*. Mexico City: Publicación del Colegio de México.
———. 2008. *Los Pueblos indígenas y sus derechos: informes temáticos del Relator Especial sobre la Situación de los Derechos Humanos y las Libertades Fundamentales de los Pueblos Indígenas*. Mexico City: UNESCO.
Stephen, John L. 1841. *Incidents of Travel in Central America, Chiapas and Yucatan*. 2 vols. New York: Harper and Brothers.
Susuki, David, and Peter Knudson. 1992. *Wisdom of the Elders: Sacred Native Stories of Nature*. New York: Bantam Books.
Svalbard-Seed-Vault. 2012. Internet source: http://en.wikipedia.org/wiki/Svalbard-global-Seed-Vault.
Taussig, Michael. 1980. *The Devil and Commodity Fetishism in South America*. Chapel Hill: University of North Carolina Press.
Tedlock, Dennis, and Barbara Tedlock. 1975. *Teachings from the American Earth: Indian Religion and Philosophy*. New York: Liveright Publishing.
Tedlock, Dennis. 1987. Critiques and Responses on Dialogical Anthropology. *Journal of The Mayan Book of the Dawn of Life*. Rev. and expanded ed. New York: Simon & Schuster.
———. 2003. *Rabinal Achi: A Mayan Drama of War and Sacrifice*. New York: Oxford University Press.
The State of the Native Nations, 2007. Conditions under U.S. Policies of Self-Determination. The Harvard Project on American Indian Economic Development. London: Oxford University Press.
The World People's Conference on Climate Change and the Rights of Mother Earth. Bulletin. Cochabamba, Bolivia, April 19–22, 2010. https://www.therightsofnature.org/cochabama-rights/.

Thompson, J. Eric. 1956. *The Rise and Fall of Maya Civilization*. Norman: University of Oklahoma Press.

———. 1970. *Maya History and Religion*. Norman: University of Oklahoma Press.

Tozzer, Alfred M. 1941. *Landa's Relación de las Cosas de Yucatán*. A translation. Edited with notes by Alfred Tozzer. Cambridge, MA: Peabody Museum of American Archaeology and Ethnology, Harvard University.

Trosper L. Ronald. 1999. "Traditional American Indian Economic Policy." In *Contemporary Native American Political Issues*, edited by Troy R. Johnson. Lanham, MD: Altamira Press.

Turner, Victor. 1967. *The Forest of Symbols*. Ithaca, NY: Cornell University Press.

Tylor, Edward B. 1889. *Primitive Culture*, 2 vols. New York: Henry Holt.

United Nations. 2007. *Universal Declaration of the Rights of Indigenous People*. United Nations, September 13.

Varese, Stefano. 1996. "The New Environmentalist Movement of Latin American Indigenous People." In V*aluing Local Knowledge: Indigenous People and Intellectual Property Rights*, edited by Stephen B. Brush. Washington, DC: Island Press.

———. 2006a. *Witness to Sovereignty: Essays on the Indian Movement in Latin America*. Copenhagen, Denmark: International Work Group for Indigenous Affairs.

———. 2006. *La Sal de los Cerros: Resistencia y Utopía en la Amazonía Peruana*. Lima Perú: Fondo Editorial del Congreso del Perú.

Villa Rojas, Alfonso. 1945. *The Maya of East Central Quintana Roo*. Washington, DC: Carnegie Institution of Washington.

———. 1978. *Los Elegidos de Dios: Etnografía de los Mayas de Quintana Roo*. Mexico, D.F.: Editorial Libros de México, S.A.

Vogt, Evon Z. 1969. *Zinacantan: A Maya Community in the Highlands of Chiapas*. Cambridge, MA: Harvard University Press.

Von Daniken, Erich. 1968. *Chariots of the Gods? Unsolved Mysteries of the Past*, New York, Putnam.

Wagley, Charles. 1949. *The Social and Religious Life of a Guatemalan Village*. American Anthropologist 51, no. 4, part 2, Memoir Number 71.

Ward, Thomas. 2018. *The Formation of Latin American Nations: From Late Antiquity to Early Modernity*. Norman: University of Oklahoma Press.

Warren, Kay B. 1998. *Indigenous Movements and Their Critics: Pan-Maya Activism in Guatemala*. Princeton, NJ: Princeton University Press.

Watanabe, Hitoshi. 1973. *The Ainu Ecosystem: Environmental and Group Structure*. Seattle: University of Washington Press.

Wax, Murray. 1956. "The Limitations of Boas' Anthropology." *American Anthropologist* 58, no. 1: 63–74.

Weatherford, Jack. 1988. *Indian Givers: How the Indians of the Americas Transformed the World*. New York: Crown Publishers.

Wei-Ming, Tu. 1997. "Beyond the Enlightenment Mentality." In *Worldviews and Ecology: Religion, Philosophy, and the Environment*, edited by Mary Evelyn Tucker and John A. Grim. New York: Orbis Books.

Wilkins, David E., 2007. *American Indian Politics and the American Political System*. New York: Rowman & Littlefield Publishers.

Williams, Rowan. 2009. "Archbishop Warns of Ecological 'Doomsday.'" The Archbishop of Canterbury, lecture at York Minster, UK: Forum on Religion and Ecology. March 2009. news@religionandecology.org.

Wilson, Edward O. 1984. *Biophilia: The Human Bond with Other Species*. Cambridge, MA: Harvard University Press.

Wilson, Richard. 1995. *Maya Resurgence in Guatemala: Q'epchi' Experiences*. Norman: University of Oklahoma Press.

Whiteley, Peter M. 1998. *Rethinking Hopi Ethnography*. Washington, DC: Smithsonian Institution Press.

Wolf, Eric R. 1957. "Closed Corporate Communities in Mesoamerica and Central Java." *Southwestern Journal of Anthropology* 13:1–18.

———. 1982. *Europe and the People without History*. Berkeley: University of California Press.

Woodward, Ralph Lee. 1971. "Social Revolution in Guatemala: The Carrera Revolt." In *Applied Enlightenment: Nineteenth Century Liberalism, 1830–1839*, Middle American Research Institute Publication 23. New Orleans, LA: Tulane University.

Worley, Paul M. 2013. *Telling and Being Told: Storytelling and Cultural Control in Contemporary Yucatec Maya Literatures*. Tucson: University of Arizona Press.

Worley, Paul M., and Rita M. Palacios. 2019. *Unwriting Maya literature: ts'iib as recorded knowledge*. Tucson: University of Arizona Press.

Yojcom Roche, Domingo. 2013. *La Epistemologia de la Matematica Maya*. Guatemala City: Editorial Maya Wuj.

Young Bear, Severt. 1994. *Standing in the Light: A Lakota Way of Seeing*. Lincoln: University of Nebraska Press.

INDEX

Note: Italicized page numbers refer to figures and photographs.

academic traditions and Native knowledge, 2. *See also* anthropology and its theories; science and technology
activism, scholarly, 27
agricultural practices, 137, 211
Aguirre Beltrán, Gonzalo, 146
Ainu people, 190
Akatek Mayas, 168
allochronic distancing, 80
Alvarado, Pedro de, 87, 94
Andrews, Richard J., 34
animism, 5, 18, 46
Annals of the Kaqchikel, 87
anthropologists: call for more balanced research, 193; disciplinary pressures on, 46–47; focus of modern Mayanists, 66; Indigenous anthropologists, 98; and Native storytelling, 77; nonmutual methods used by, 60; oral traditions and fieldwork, 59–60; training of, 43

anthropology and its theories: aims of, 15, 17; and "backwardness" of Indigenous cultures, 10, 16, 17, 19, 30, 41; and a community's language, 98, 100; critiques of, 25–26; cultural materialism and idealism, 24–25; dialogical anthropology, 44–45; and dialogue with Indigenous cultures, 1; emic perspectives in, 96, 97–98, 99, 182; Eurocentric research practices, 42, 96, 100, 117, 193, 224; evolutionist theory, 15–20, 80; folk illnesses, 153–54; functionalism, 20–22, 180–81; historical particularism, 19–20; interpretive anthropology, 23–25, 43; postmodernist approach, 26–28; reliance on missionary accounts, 34; segmentation in, 184; structuralism, 21–22, 106; study of dichotomies, 152, 181; theories of bizarre religions, 136–37, 180. *See also* animism; ethnography

Antropología Comprometida, 25
Apocalypto (film), 206
Aq'oma' mountain, 166, 167
Arévalo, Juan José, 93, 175
Argüelles, José, 6
Arias, Jacinto, *The Numinous World of the Maya*, 98
Asad, Talal, *Anthropology & the Colonial Encounter*, 25
assimilation pressures, 10–11, 30, 66, 97, 134, 140, 176
Aztec philosophy, 124, 211

b'ak'tun cycles: 13 B'en, 83, 222; description of, 64, 79, 222, 225. *See also* 13 B'ak'tun
balance and harmony: as continual process, 157; and cosmic unity, 43–44; creation stories as daily teachings, 196; human responsibility for, 133, 189; and illness, 43–44; and meaningfulness of life, 62–63; oral tradition as method of, 78; reinforced veneration of, 206; through respect and reciprocity, 4, 5, 180–81; trialogical relationships in, 100; and true happiness, 213. *See also* cargo system; cosmic trilogy; respect and reciprocity; world maintenance
B'alunh Q'ana', 132–33, 164, 166, 167
Barrios, Justo Rufino, 93
Batalla, Guillermo Bonfil, 26, 27
Berger, Peter L., 198, 200
Berlin, Brent, 102
Berry, Thomas, 135–36
biophilia, 8, 135
The Bird Who Cleans the World and Other Maya Fables (Montejo), 68
Black Elk (Chief), 7, 192–93
Blue Cloud, Peter, 78
Boas, Franz, 19–20, 61
Bricker, Victoria, 81; *The Indian Christ, the Indian King*, 84
Brown, Radcliffe, 20, 21, 180
Buddhism, 135, 191, 213
Bunzel, Ruth, 43, 60, 65, 156; *Chichicastenango*, 146

capitalism: and assimilation, 180, 214; and clash of worldviews, 55; and cultural materialism, 24–25; disjunction from, 221; unnaturalness of, 185; and use of resources, 10, 214; view of nature under, 48, 182
cargo system: Catholic and political attacks on, 175; complexity of, 170; description of, 163–64, 174; disintegration of, 176–77; justice under, 173; to maintain balance and harmony, 12; prestige in, 169, 174, 175–76; sacred duty to serve in, 172–73, 203; transfer of power under, 169–70. *See also* diviners; prayer-makers; Principales
Carmack, Robert, 26
Carrera, Rafael, mythification of, 91–94
cataclysmic cycles, 121–22, 124. *See also* world destruction
Catherwood, Frederick, 61
Catholic Action, 175
Catholic church and Catholicism: accommodation of Indigenous worldviews in, 3; attacks on cargo system by, 175; integration with Maya religion, 65; Maya internalization of myths of, 94; and the natural world, 188–89; persecution of the Maya by, 192; and solutions to natural problems, 213–14
Cavender, Angela, 76
Chamula Mayas. *See* Tzotzil Mayas
Chan K'in of Naha', 57, 223
Chewong people, 126
Chilam Balam: on burning of books, 35; instructive stories of, 4; prophecies in, 81–83, 197, 210; stories of destruction in, 224–25
chimanes (mediators), 64–65
Christianity: conversion to, 141; criticism of, 188; and development of syncretic practices, 3; and the end of the world, 221; imposition of, 198–99
Chuj Mayas, 168
climate change, 30
colonialism: anthropology as enterprise of, 25, 42; effect on traditional belief

systems, 209; and forced labor, 37, 67, 71, 83, 98, 139; and Indigenous poverty, 176; need to control Indigenous People under, 16, 33; rejection of Native belief systems by, 1; resistance to, 212; view of Indigenous People as savages, 2, 16–17. *See also* Spanish invasion and colonialism
communalism, 125, 131–32, *201*. See also *komontat*
consumerism, 54–55
Cook-Lynn, Elizabeth, 182
corn: cosmic trilogy embodied in, 126; as sacred, 49, 120, 126; and world renewal, 217–20
cosmic trilogy (human-nature-supernatural): and belonging to totality of creation, 179–80; corn as embodiment of, 126; interactionist model as basis for, 43, 120, 121; maintaining balance and harmony in, 100, 180–81; in Maya belief systems, 43, 45–46; and Maya calendar, 64, 161; respect and reciprocity in, 45–46, 181–83; and time, 50, 80–81. *See also* human beings; natural world; respect and reciprocity; supernatural realm
cosmic unity: as basis for Native theory, 2, 209; creation myths in, 3; cyclical patterns of building and destruction in, 197; as holistic view of the world, 12; human behavior and, 152; Indigenous philosophy of, 3–5; Indigenous prophets and leaders on, 6–7; interrelatedness of everything in, 3–5, 58, 66, 196–97; maintenance of, 31; ritual language and, 101; union of earth with the cosmos, 67, 102, *104*, 123; Western attention to, 7–9, 192, 223. *See also* balance and harmony; cosmic trilogy; interactionist model; respect and reciprocity; spirit bearers
cosmocentric paradigm: architecture and cities under, 186–87; and collective consciousness, 179, 181, 182; and cosmic trilogy, 179–80; cycles of time in, 190–91, 225; houses as replica of the cosmos, 187; humans in the greater circle of life, 189–91; of Indigenous People, 189–93; spirituality as part of life under, 187–89; and Western capitalism, 184–85
Creationist (Christian) paradigm, 2, 17
creation stories. See *Popol Vuh*
Crowley, Ernest, 209
cultural idealism, 22–23
cultural materialism, 22, 24–25
cultural relativism, 19
culture: anthropologists' *versus* Natives' view of, 57–58; dynamism of, 44; functionalism's segmentation of, 20–21; innovative approaches to, 27; interactionism as key to understanding, 22–23; as web of relationships, 21, 23–24, 46. *See also* interactionist model

Dalai Lama, 213
Darío, Rubén, "Brother Wolf," 9–10
decolonization, 26, 77
Deganawidah, 7, 31, 213
de la Serna, Jacinto, 159
Deloria, Vine, 2, 13, 18–19
Descola, Philippe, 125
diviners *(ahb'eh)*: actions on the birth of a child, 148, 149, 168–69; and counting of the days, 63, 73; and illness, 160; as intermediaries with God, 129; interpretation of the calendar by, 63, 108, 112–13, 160, 177; as keepers of sacred knowledge, 3, 4; La Farge's deception as, 173–74; persecution of, 65; response to La Farge, 134; and spirit bearers, 147–48, 150
dreams, 69–71
Dresden Codex, 204
dualism, 119, 152, 181
Durán, Diego, 34
Durkheim, Emile, 98, 182; *Elementary Forms of Religious Life*, 179

ecological model of interconnection, 66–67

economy, Western worldviews of, 184–85. *See also* capitalism
Eliade, Mircea, 107, 191
environment: destruction of, 9; ecological renewal, 211–12; exploitation of, 15, 135. *See also* natural world
environmental policies, 8
epistemology, use of term, 95
ethnocide, 35
ethnography: dialogue across cultures in, 44–45; and improved training of anthropologists, 43; need for change in, 42–43; new ethnography, 96, 97–98; reporting 'the truth' in, 77; role of Natives in, 46; salvage ethnography, 19, 61; selection of informants, 60; Western biases in fieldwork, 59. *See also* Bunzel, Ruth; La Farge, Oliver; Wagley, Charles
ethnoscience, 22, 96
Evans-Pritchard, E. E., 209
evolutionist theory: animism in, 18; Boas's challenge to, 19–20; Indigenous People as "primitives" under, 15–16, 17–19, 80; premise and development of, 17; stages of religion under, 18

Fabian, Johannes, 80
Faris, James, 25
Farriss, Nancy, 67; *Maya Society under Colonial Rule,* 66
Fischer, Michael J., 99; *Anthropology as a Cultural Critique* (with Marcus), 26–27
Fisher, Ted, 6
Florentine Codex, 32, 35
Frazer, James, 18

Geertz, Clifford, 182; *The Interpretation of Cultures,* 23–24
gender complementarity, 63
Ghost Dance movement, 212
Ginés de Sepúlveda, Juan, 2
globalization as threat, 10–11, 192, 221
Gossen, Gary, 68, 88, 175, 202
Great Law of Peace and Unity, 7
Greek origins of knowledge, 95

Guamán Poma de Ayala, Felipe, *Nueva crónica y buen gobierno,* 37
Guatemala: conflict over Belize, 85–87; cultural revitalization in, 10; domination of the Mayas in, 83, 116; and forced labor, 71, 93; Germans in, 140; government structure in, 170; linguistic map of, 28; Natives' rights, 88; Truth Commission findings in, 116
Guiteras-Holmes, Calixta, 66
Guzmán, Jacobo Arbenz, 93

Harris, Marvin, *The Rise of Anthropological Theory,* 22
Harvard Project, 192
Haudenosaunee (Iroquois), 5, 7, 31, 78, 135, 213
Hellen, Roy F., 125
historical particularism, 19–20
history: cyclical nature of, 11, 12; and mythification, 83–84; Native methods for documenting important events in, 84–85
Hopi traditions, 72
Hueman the Elder, 31
Huichol Indians, 55
human beings, 131; destiny of, 147–48, 168–69, 172; gift of intelligence, 123; length of life, 147–48; mission of life of, 4–5, 11, 134, 136, 142–43, 195–96; practice of respect, 132–33; and recognition of interrelatedness, 131, 133, 212; relationship with natural and supernatural realms, 131, 138; religion and world building, 198; responsibility of, 189, 213–14; and theory of the self, 152–53. *See also* spirit bearers
Hunab' K'uh (Only One God), 3, 4, 33, 67, 172, 200

Inca culture, 211; documentation of, 37
indigenismo, 16
Indigenous cultural contributions: of Deganawidah, 7, 31, 213; denial theories about, 30, 38–39; documentation of, 31–33, 34–37, 36; Maya achievements, 38. *See also* Quetzalcoatl

Indigenous epistemologies: adoption of, 125; and the scientific community, 8, 27, 95, 96–97; stories as blueprints for, 77; weakening of, 192–93. *See also* Maya knowledge and epistemology

Indigenous languages and understanding cultures, 72, 98–99. *See also* Maya language

Indigenous People: activism in maintaining worldviews and practices, 11, 27; animistic views of, 5, 46; as anthropological informants, 46, 60; assimilation pressures on, 10–11, 30, 66, 97, 134, 140, 176; dehumanization of, 2; economies of, 25, 55, 180–81, 182; Eurocentric views of, 26, 42, 198; exploitation of, 83, 176; illness and disease, 43–46, 141, 153–56; *as indios*, 16, 80, 116; interrelatedness as truth for, 3–5, 58; marginalization of, 16–17, 38; and the natural world, 153; and perpetuation of stereotypes, 96–97, 119; religion and spirituality of, 18, 34, 152, 220; relocations of, 212; and revitalization of cultures of, 47. *See also* anthropology and its theories; colonialism; Maya people

Indigenous rights, 16–17, 18

Indigenous scholars: in anthropology, 46; auto-ethnographies, 77; limitations on, 224; and perception of Maya civilization, 68; and rectifying the scholarly record, 222; struggle to be heard, 8; training in anthropology, 98

Indigenous Traditions and Ecology (Montejo), 138

interactionist model: as basis for cosmic trilogy, 120, 121; to describe Indigenous cultures, 181; development of, 22–23; elements of, 12; humans in, 131–36; natural world in, 122–31; supernatural realm in, 136–43. *See also* cosmic unity; human beings; natural world; supernatural realm

Iroquois. *See* Haudenosaunee

Jacaltenango: communal fruit trees in, 167; La Farge and, 61, 173–74; location and name of, 164; protection for the people in, 168; sacred sites in and near, 166, 167, 169; sanctification of house sites in, 186

Jakaltek Maya calendar, 109

Jakaltek Mayas, 61–62, 65, 73, 76, 108; ancestors' protection of, 167–68; democratic participation, 52; and disease, 141; history and divine origin of, 164–66, *165*, 219; and language, 101–2; persecution of, 134; recitation of sacred prayers by, 4; testing of Carrera's leadership, 92; and Witz, 69, 138, 140, 156. *See also* cargo system; Carrera, Rafael; *komontat*; La Farge, Oliver; Maya calendar; Maya knowledge and epistemology; Mayalogue; oral traditions; Q'anil, Xuwan; respect and reciprocity; sacred ceremonies and rules; world renewal; Year Bearers

Kay, Paul, 102
K'iche Mayas, 65
Knudson, Peter, 8–9, 184
komontat (sacred land), 49, 166, 170
komontatism, 44, 45
Ko'w, Shas, 133
Kuhn, Thomas, *The Structure of Scientific Revolution*, 25
kusansum (mythical union), 67

Lacandon Mayas, 134
Ladino heroes. *See* Carrera, Rafael; Urbina, Erasto
La Farge, Oliver: burial of umbilical cord, 151; ceremonial participation of, 64; ethnography of the Maya, 43; on house building among the Maya, 186; Mayas' fear of, 134; method used to elicit information, 173; misuse of terms by, 146; on myths of world building, 199; prayer for protection of spirit bearers, 156–57; and Q'anil legend, 85, 87; on recitation of the omens, 73; and refusal to use one's gifts, 172; *Santa Eulalia*, 173–74; *The Year Bearer's People*, 61, 202; Yula' as place of origin, 168

Lakota people, 13, 181, 183
Landa, Diego de, 5–6, 34, 35, 108, 199; *Relación de las Cosas de Yucatán*, 36
Langness, Lewis, 21
las Casas, Bartolomé de, 2, 16–17
Leopold, Aldo, 8
Lévi-Strauss, Claude, 22, 106
lightning man, 86–88, 90, 111, 219
linguistics and culture, 100–102
Luk, Anton, 215
Lyons, Oren (Chief), 7, 127, 135

Madrid and Dresden Codex, 4
magpies and knowledge, 70
Malinowski, Bronislaw, 20, 21, 98; *Argonauts of the Western Pacific*, 180
Mam Mayas, 64, 168
Marcus, George E., 99; *Anthropology as a Cultural Critique* (with Fischer), 26–27
material objects, 54–55, 56
Maya belief systems and spirituality: and care of young children, 154–55; Christian attack on, 160; compared to Buddhism, 135; cosmic unity in, 6; death and the human spirit, 152; dogs in, 55–56; importance of Maya terminology for, 160–61; mission of humans under, 54; moral education, 189; myths communicating, 199; nature in, 107–8; non-Indigenous views of, 5–6; pervasiveness in daily life, 137; *pixan* (spirit of creation), 5; prayer-makers, diviners, and sacred speakers, 63–65; regions of sacredness on earth, 128; renewal of, 195; survival as collective enterprise, 66–67; syncretism in, 141–42; texts about disguised under Christianity, 73–75. *See also* cosmic trilogy; cosmic unity; diviners; Maya calendar; *Popol Vuh*; prayer-makers; sacred ceremonies and rules
Maya calendar: and the counting of the days, 32, 50, 63, 73; cycles established by, 79, 222; day names, 109–12, 147–48; denial theory and, 38; to ensure trialogical communication, 161; establishment of, 31; human activity and, 108, 116, 137; illustrations, *110, 207*; Ixh days, 65; modern views of, 51–52; Q'anil days, 65; sacred ceremonies and, 81; as source of all knowledge, 96, 108; understanding of, 215, 220; as unifying element, 12, 47, 50, 64, 122; Western attention to, 224; and world building, 195; Year Bearers in, 61–62, 87, 199. *See also b'ak'tun* cycles
Maya communities, establishment of, 164. *See also* Jacaltenango; Jakaltek Mayas
Maya education, 36, 68–71, 72, 77–78, 113, 114–15, 138
Maya knowledge and epistemology: and the ancient Maya, 117; classification and perception of colors, 102–6, *103*; complexity in, 106; and cosmic unity, 49, 107; day names in, 109–12; four corners and directions in, 48, 61–62, 102–4, 123, 137; holistic perspectives of, 189; hummingbirds and *txuyub'* in, 113–16; importance of Maya terms for, 12; loss of, 116–17; production of, 6; vision quests, 116
Maya language, 12, 36, 72, 76, 100–101, 160–61
Mayalogue: as an Indigenous theory, 46; as an interactionist model, 121–22; bases of, 12–13, 44–51; and emic approaches to culture, 99, 114; and ethnoscience, 22; example of, 57; motivation behind, 29–30; in reclaiming identity and traditions, 117. *See also* anthropology and its theories; balance and harmony; cargo system; cosmic trilogy; cosmic unity; interactionist model; Maya belief systems and spirituality; Maya calendar; Maya knowledge and epistemology; oral traditions; *Popol Vuh*; spirit bearers; world renewal
Maya New Year, 4, 63, 64, 73, 174
Maya people: burning of books of, 35; city organization for, 186; disappearance of Maya knowledge, 44, 47;

early ethnographies on, 61; efforts to liberate, 91–93; election of governing council, 170, 172; festivals and dances of, 55–56, 56, 128, 129, 202–3; as fossilized in the past, 80; history of Classic Maya, 80, 87, 116–17, 199, 206; homes for, 48, 69, 186–87; need for emic view of, 47–48, 96–97; pan-Mayanism, 28, 117, 220; regeneration of, 220; religious belief of, 3; respect and gratitude in economy of, 183–84; supposed harshness of, 17, 136, 199, 206. *See also* balance and harmony; cargo system; cosmic trilogy (human-nature-supernatural); Mayalogue; respect and reciprocity

Maybury-Lewis, David, 27
mechanical solidarity, 179–80
Memorial de Sololá, 50
Menchú, Rigoberta, 48, 78
Mesoamerican Natives: interaction of cultures among, 47; Western writers on, 38
Mexican Revolution of 1915, 88–89
Mignolo, Walter, 41
misrepresentation of Indigenous People and culture, 18, 20, 25, 26–27, 34, 96
missionaries: and eradication of Native culture, 33–34, 41; malicious actions of destruction by, 5–6; misinterpretation of Indigenous practices, 34; motivation of, 141; and *nawalism*, 159; persecution by, 36, 146; reports on Maya religion, 199
Mohawk, John, 133
moral economies, 190
Morgan, Lewis Henry, 31; *Ancient Society*, 17
Morley, Sylvanus G., 137
Mundo (Heart of Heaven; Heart of Earth), 65, 101, 136, 143
mythification process, 72, 83, 85, 89–94. *See also* Urbina, Erasto

Nabokov, Peter, 212
Nahua cosmology, 123, 142–43, 204, 219

Nahua culture, 34–35, 48
nahual, misuse of term, 145–47, 158
Native American and Indigenous studies, 37, 96
Native hermeneutics, 99
Native spirituality, 99
Native taxonomies, 68, 76
natural world: agricultural practices and, 108–9; and animals' rights, 126–28; catastrophes of, 129; as the center of spirituality, 3; and collective survival, 10; cosmocentric view of, 107, 183; creation of, 122; destruction of, 9, 56–57; earth as a living being, 5; give and take in, 78; humans' relationship with, 1, 7–8, 153; humans' stewardship of, 189–90, 211; and hunting, 126, 134–35, 138–39, 156; inner essence of, 125; interrelatedness and, 2, 135; maintaining balance and harmony with, 4–5; mastery over, 48; renewal of, 211–12; respect for animals in, 126; as sacred ecology, 187; as sanctuary, 137; wise use of resources of, 124
Navajo people, 3, 43–44, 190, 206
nawal (witch), 145, 149, 150, 157–60
New Age individuals, 6, 8, 56
Newberry Library of Chicago, 51
Niatum, Duane, 78

Oakes, Maud, 158
ohtajb'al, concept of, 12, 95–96
Oneida Indian Nations, 11
Only One God. *See* Hunab' Ku'h
oral traditions: author's personal experience with, 68–75; to communicate knowledge and information, 59; confusion with myths and legends, 60; documenting cyclical history in, 87; eloquence and poetic language in, 4, 57, 63–64, 74, 101, 133; importance of, 11; and Indigenous methodologies, 76–78; and modernity, 78; storytelling taxonomies in, 68; web of relationships in, 76
otherness and time, 80

Oxlanh B'ak'tun, 13, 83. *See also* 13 B'ak'tun
Oxlanh B'en, 79–80, 215

Palsson, Gisli, 125
People's Accord, 221
Pequot people, 11
Perera, Victor, 223
place, language of, 182
Plains Indians, 212
Popol Vuh: accounts of catastrophes in, 204, 216–17; on animals and pets, 55–56; as basis for Mayalogue, 12; classification of colors in, 102; creation stories in, 3, 52–54, 188, 217, 219; Creator in, 136; example of world building in, 199–200; four corners and directions in, 48, 102–3, 123, 148–49; four fathers in, 128, 148; as hidden text, 51–52, 216; and human responsibility, 120–21; immortalization of the ancestors in, 128; importance of, 49–50; on language, 100–101; major lessons in, 52–53, 56; Maya histories in, 168; and naming of individuals, 148–49; the natural world in, 9, 108; need for renewed attention to, 143; prototype of *nawal* in, 157–58; Q'anil in, 87; rules for hunting in, 126; sacredness of land in, 120; Sam Colop on transcription of, 36; scientific knowledge in, 123–24; struggle between good and evil in, 214–15; survival of, 50–51; world destruction and world building in, 30, 197
prayer-makers *(alkal-txah)*: election and role of, 63, 133, 166; La Farge on, 170; La Farge's deception as, 174–75; lead prayer-maker, 169; photograph of, *171*; practice of abstinence, 172–73; prayers of, 63–64, 149, 172–73, 186–87
priests *(ajq'ij,* Maya spiritual guides), 3, 147
Principales (council of elders), 63, 166, 173, 175, 177
prophetic cycles, 221–26. *See also* 13 B'ak'tun
Protestantism, 6
Pueblo Indians, 3

Q'anil, significance of name, 87, 89
Q'anil, Xuwan, legend about, 85, 86–87, 89–91, 128, 167, 215
El Q'anil (Montejo), 89–90
Q'anil mountain, 85, *86*, 128, 167
Q'anjobal Mayas, 65, 73
Q'anjob'al Mayas, 168, 170, 173
Q'eqchi' Mayas, 65, 139, 140, 174
q'inal (life): concept of, 1, 12–13; elements in, 46; relationship with the sun, 57; and time, 79
q'inh (sun), 57
Quechua people, 132
Quetzalcoatl (Q'uq'ul-kan), 6, 32, 35, 85, 199, 213

Rabinal Achí, 50
racism: and anthropological definitions of Indigenous People, 18–19; denial theorists and, 38–39; and white privilege, 26. *See also* evolutionist theory
Redfield, Robert, 43, 98, 108
religion: in Eurocentric worldviews, 198; legitimation by, 200, 202; separation of human from the world by, 188; and world building, 198. *See also* Catholic church and Catholicism; Maya belief systems and spirituality
respect and reciprocity: as center of ceremonies, 65; and collective labor, 131; environmental policies and, 8; as foundation of Indigenous culture, 27–28, 30, 131–33, 135; importance of compassion, 9–10; to maintain wellness of the universe, 4, 125; material objects and, 54; and the natural world, 120; as necessary to life, 106–7, 190, 213–14; in revitalizing Indigenous culture, 47; teaching through ceremony, 128, *129*; trialogical relationships in, 45–46
Rojas, Alfonso Villa, 67; *The Maya of East Central Quintana Roo,* 98
Ruíz de Alarcón, Hernando, 34; *Treatise,* 33

Sacred Book of the Mayas. See Popol Vuh

sacred ceremonies and rules: before building houses, 186; burial of the umbilical cord, 149, 151, 160; Catholic attacks on, 134; and ceremonial conflict, 173–74; in Christian *cofradías*, 174; cleansing ceremonies, 155; counting of the days, 32, 50, 63, 73; as forgotten, 176; interwoven with Christianity, 141–42; lighting of candles, 64; to maintain health and life, 108; and the Maya calendar, 81; for natural disasters, 129–31; women's participation in, 174; Year Bearer ceremonies, 166. *See also* Maya New Year

sacred houses *(popb'al nha)*, 49, 63, 174

sacred sites, 128, 166, 169, 197. See also *komontat*

sacred speakers *(ninq'omlom)*, 63–64

Sahagún, Bernardino de, 34–35; *Huehuetlatolli*, 31–32

Said, Edward, *Orientalism*, 25

Sam Colop, Luis Enrique, 36

Santiago the Apostle, 93, 94

Santu, Xap Pelnan, 132

Sapir-Whorf hypothesis, 102

science and technology: and cosmic unity, 5; and Indigenous epistemologies, 8, 96–97; and objectivity, 2; observations in the *Popol Vuh*, 123; scientific materialism, 1; and segmentation, 184

Seattle (Chief), 7, 58, 182, 196

self-determination, right of, 10, 11, 77

Sepúlveda, Juan Ginés de, 17

servant leadership, 170

seventh generation, concept of, 5, 135

Sindicato de Trabajadores Indígenas, 88

Sittler, Robert, 223–24

Smith, Carol, 26

Spanish encomenderos, 3, 37

Spanish invasion and colonialism, 16–17, 67, 81, 140, 146

spirit bearers *(yijomal spixan)*: concept of, 12, 145, 150–51, *151*; confusion with *nawal*, 158–59, 160; and destiny, 147, 149–50, 152; and giving of names, 148–49; illness and loss of, 153–56; and individuals' health, 149; misuse of terms for, 145–47

Stavenhagen, Rodolfo, 26, 27

Stephens, John L., 61

storytelling: to explain ecological problems, 211; on hunting birds, 113; and modernity, 72–73; myth of the bridles, 69; as source of knowledge and information, 71, 72, 76–77; Witz, 69, 138, 140

supernatural realm: colonialism's effect on Indigenous relationships with, 139; connection of capitalism to, 185, *185*; existence as linked to, 33; and giving thanks, 136; mediation with, 64–65; mythification of beings into, 11, 89; and world imbalance, 46; and the world's order, 34. *See also* spirit bearers

susto (fright), 153–54, 155

Suzuki, David, 184

Tausig, Michael, 185; *The Devil and Commodity Fetishism in South America*, 25

Taussig, Michael, 22–23, 55

Tecun Uman, 85, 94

Tedlock, Dennis, 44–45

temples, symbolism of, 186

13 B'ak'tun: and the end of the world, 193, 220, 221; the end of the world in, 83, 124; as mark of time of turbulence, 222; and the Maya calendar, 12, 79; and Oxlanh B'en, 215; significance of, 222; as turning point, 30, 38; violent changes after, 56; and wisdom of the ancestors, 223

Thompson, J. Eric, 126, 137

tihiloj (Indigenous interpretations and deconstruction), 99, 100

time: continual change in, 80; cyclical view of, 12, 79, 81; telescoping of time, 84–89, 94

Titles of the House of Nehaib, 87

Título de los Señores de Totonicapán, 50

Toltecs, ancient knowledge of, 31, 123, 124, 204, 219

tonalism. *See* spirit bearers *(yijomal spixan)*

Trosper, Ronald T., 183–84
Tupac Amaru, 85
Turner, Victor, 22–23, 98–99; *The Forest of Symbols*, 23
Tylor, Edward B., 18
Tzeltal Mayas, 87, 149, 175
Tzotzil Mayas, 66, 74, 88, 101, 149, 202

Ubico, Jorge, 83, 93
umbilical cord, myth and metaphor of, 67, 102, 186, 203. *See also* sacred ceremonies and rules
UN Assembly of the Indigenous Working Group, 127
Universal Declaration on the Rights of Indigenous People, 7
Urbina, Erasto, 88–89

Varese, Stefano, 26, 127, 182, 190
Vogt, Evon, 156, 170, 192
Voices from Exile (Montejo), 98

Wagley, Charles, 64
Ward, Thomas, 48
Warren, Kay, 26, 175
web of significance, concept of, 24
Western philosophy, 2, 41–42, 95–96, 107, 121. *See also* anthropology and its theories
Wilson, Richard, 139, 140, 174
Witz-ak'al, 65, 202
Wolf, Eric, 44, 61; *Europe and the People without History*, 25

wooden men, story of, 52–54, 55–56, 204
world building, 196, 198–200, 199
world destruction: belief in nearness of, 56, 83, 210, 221–22; and failure to maintain harmony, 197; flood stories about, 205, 216; Indigenous stories explaining ecological issues, 211; and preparation efforts, 217, 219–20; as warning, 223. *See also* 13 B'ak'tun
world dismantling, 204–8, 205
world maintenance, 200–204. *See also* cargo system
world renewal: Christian story of, 210–11; and cyclic processes, 208, 215, 221–22; ecological renewal, 211–12, 224; flood and regeneration, 216–18; and interconnected unity of life, 210; need for change in attitude, 213–14, 225–26; reenactments in rituals and ceremonies, 211; and use of resources, 214, 215; and veneration of supernatural realm, 214–15

Ximénez, Francisco, 51

Year Bearers, 61–62, 87, 108, 111, 163, 170, 199
Yucatec Mayas, 108
Yukatek Mayas, 102

Zapatista rebellion, 10
Zinacantec Maya, 113, 170

www.ingramcontent.com/pod-product-compliance
Lightning Source LLC
Chambersburg PA
CBHW030537230426
43665CB00010B/928